MICROENTERPRISES IN DEVELOPING COUNTRIES

MICROENTERPRISES
IN DEVELOPING COUNTRIES

Papers and proceedings of an International Conference held in Washington, D.C., USA, 6–9 June 1988, sponsored by the Committee of Donor Agencies for Small Enterprise Development

Edited by JACOB LEVITSKY

INTERMEDIATE TECHNOLOGY PUBLICATIONS   1989

Published by ITDG Publishing
103–105 Southampton Row, London WC1B 4HL, UK
www.itdgpublishing.org.uk

© Intermediate Technology Publications 1989

First published in 1989
Print on demand since 2003

ISBN 1 85339 016 X

All rights reserved. No part of this publication may be reprinted or reproduced or utilized in any form or by any electronic, mechanical, or other means, now known or hereafter invented, including photocopying and recording, or in any information storage or retrieval system, without the written permission of the publishers.

A catalogue record for this book is available from the British Library

ITDG Publishing is the publishing arm of the Intermediate Technology Development Group. Our mission is to build the skills and capacity of people in developing countries through the dissemination of information in all forms, enabling them to improve the quality of their lives and that of future generations.

Typeset by Inforum Typesetting, Portsmouth
Printed in Great Britain by Lightning Source, Milton Keynes

Contents

Introduction	ix
Summary Report of Conference JACOB LEVITSKY	xiii

Part I – The Microenterprise Sector and Policy Aspects

Structural Adjustment and the Informal Sector HERNANDO DE SOTO	3
Micro-Level Support for the Informal Sector VICTOR E. TOKMAN	13
Whatever happened to poverty alleviation? JUDITH TENDLER	26
The Role of Microenterprises in Rural Industrialization in Africa MARIA NOWAK	57

Part II – Informal Credit Markets

Informal Credit Markets in Support of Microbusiness ANAND G. CHANDAVARKAR	79
Linking Informal and Formal Financial Institutions in Africa and Asia HANS DIETER SEIBEL	97

Part III – Finance Assistance for Microenterprises

Financial Services for Microenterprises: Programmes or Markets? RICHARD L. MEYER	121
Banking on the Informal Sector HENRY L. JACKELEN	131
Grameen Bank: Organization and Operation MUHAMMAD YUNUS	144

Part IV – Technical Services for Microenterprises

Institutional Aspects of Microenterprise Promotion MARILYN CARR	165
Training and Technical Assistance for Microenterprises MALCOLM HARPER	177

The Role of Technology in Microenterprise Development 189
MATTHEW GAMSER and FRANK ALMOND

Microenterprise as a Social Investment 202
JAIME CARVAJAL

Part V – Review of Assistance Programmes

Benefits, Costs, and Sustainability of Microenterprise
Programmes 211
MARIA OTERO

Comparative Experience with Microenterprise Projects 224
THOMAS A. TIMBERG

Support for Women in Microenterprises in Africa 240
MARY E. OKELO

Appendix I: List of papers submitted 251
Appendix II: Agenda 256
Abbreviations 261
References 263
Bibliography 265

INTERNATIONAL CONFERENCE ON MICROENTERPRISES IN DEVELOPING COUNTRIES

HOSTING ORGANIZATIONS IN WASHINGTON, D.C.

United States Agency for International Development (USAID), Inter-American Development Bank (IDB), World Bank

DONOR AGENCIES CONTRIBUTING TO THE CONFERENCE

Canadian International Development Agency (CIDA), Canada; Finnish International Development Agency, Finland (FINNIDA); Caisse Centrale de Cooperation Economique, France; Ministry of Development Cooperation, The Netherlands; Norwegian Agency for International Development (NORAD), Norway; Swedish International Development Authority (SIDA), Sweden; Swiss Development Corporation, Switzerland; Overseas Development Administration (ODA), United Kingdom; German Agency for Technical Cooperation (GTZ), West Germany; Kreditanstalt fur Wiederaufbau (KfW), West Germany; Ford Foundation, United States; International Labor Office (ILO), Geneva; United Nations Development Fund for Women (UNIFEM), New York; United Nations Industrial Development Organization (UNIDO), Vienna

OTHER DONOR AGENCIES REPRESENTED AT THE CONFERENCE

International Development Research Center, Ottawa, Canada (IDRC); Danish International Development Agency (DANIDA), Denmark; Ministry for Economic Cooperation (BMZ), Bonn, West Germany; Asian Development Bank, Manila, Philippines (ADB); Commission of the European Communities, Brussels, Belgium; United Nations Secretariat, New York; United Nations Capital Development Fund (UNCDF), New York; United Nations High Commission for Refugees, Geneva (UNHCR); International Fund for Agricultural Development (IFAD), Rome, Italy

Introduction

The Committee of Donor Agencies for Small Enterprise Development which sponsored the International Conference on Microenterprise Development was established in October 1979 at a meeting in Berlin convened at the invitation of the World Bank, of representatives of bilateral and multilateral donor organizations from Europe, Japan and North America engaged in programmes of assistance in the development of small-scale enterprises in developing countries. At the meeting, the representatives welcomed the opportunity to exchange information on the programmes of their agencies in this field, on their experience in the implementation of the assistance projects, and on studies and research being undertaken on different aspects of the small enterprise sector. The different donor representatives agreed that supporting small enterprise development was a rapidly growing area of interest of all development assistance organizations and that closer contact in relation to programmes and projects would help harmonize thinking and prevent confusion arising from differing approaches.

It was decided therefore to set up a steering committee to plan for future contacts and activities. It was also agreed that it was desirable that subsequent meetings should include representatives from developing countries to facilitate a wider dialogue on the projects supported by the donors. The World Bank offered to act as the secretariat for the new committee.

The Committee of Donor Agencies for Small Enterprise Development set up after the Berlin meeting met subsequently in Paris, Washington, Geneva and Bonn, and agreed to convene a number of regional conferences. The first was the Asia Regional Conference held in Colombo in December 1981 hosted by the National Development Bank of Sri Lanka, followed by similar meetings in Africa in Abijan, Côte d'Ivoire, in June 1983 hosted by the African Development Bank, and in Latin America in Quito in April 1985 hosted by the Corporacion Financiera Nacional of Ecuador.

These regional meetings served to focus attention on a number of subjects of special interest and concern which included, among others, the role of commercial banks, special assistance for women entrepreneurs and expanding programmes of support for microenterprises. Meetings were sponsored by the Committee in London in June 1986 on the role of commercial banks, hosted by the Overseas Development Administration of the UK, and on women in small enterprise development in Ottawa, Canada, in October 1987, hosted by the Canadian International Development Agency.

At the Latin American meeting in Quito, a great deal of information was exchanged on programmes assisting microenterprises in that region. At later meetings of the Committee in Bonn and London, donor representatives reported that their organizations were now providing more and more assistance to microenterprises in a variety of projects in different countries. It was therefore decided to convene a special global conference to bring together all the available information on the special features and problems of these microenterprises, on the experience of working with this sector and the results so far achieved. As a change from the pattern of previous meetings, which had generally been confined to small groups of invited representatives from the donor community and from organizations working with the donors in the developing countries, the Committee decided that the conference on microenterprises would not only be global in character, but would also invite representatives of non-governmental organizations who had been actively involved in microenterprise support programmes.

The International Conference on Microenterprise Development took place in Washington, D.C., USA from 6–9 June 1988 in the Conference Hall of the Pan-American Health Organization. Twenty different donor agencies participated, including multilateral, bilateral and regional organizations.

The three Washington-based donor agencies which co-hosted the conference were the World Bank, the Inter-American Development Bank and the US Agency for International Development. The World Bank provided the secretariat for the conference and the three co-hosting agencies together provided 60 per cent of the finance needed together with administrative support. The remaining 40 per cent of the costs were covered by contributions from other sponsoring donor agencies.

The conference was divided into two parts. The first two days were opened to a wider participation, principally to representatives of invited non-governmental organizations and persons actively engaged in programmes assisting microenterprises, while the latter two days were restricted to invited participants from developing countries and representatives of donor agencies. The first part consisted mainly of presentations on different aspects related to microenterprise development with some limited discussion, while most of the second part was given over to an exchange of views, ideas and experience between developing country participants and donor agency representatives, mainly working in smaller groups.

Sessions were chaired by representatives from multilateral and bilateral agencies. In all, 232 persons, 70 from 33 developing countries, 90 from the USA, 42 from 14 other developed countries and 30 representing international organizations, participated in the first two days. From the developing countries, 14 were from Asia, 16 from Africa and 40 from Latin America. Around 100 also participated in the second two days of the conference. Conference participants were from government, public organizations and institutions, development, commercial and regional banks, international and national

NGOs, consultancy organizations, universities, private sector bodies, businesses, research and technology institutions, local and regional development corporations as well as from international, regional and bilateral donor agencies.

English-French-Spanish simultaneous interpretation was provided at all sessions. In all, 64 papers were prepared for the Conference: 34 in English, 14 in Spanish and 16 in French.

Unfortunately it has not been possible to reproduce in this publication of the proceedings all the many papers and presentations submitted to the Conference. A selection had to be made and 16 of the papers are published here together with a summary report of all the presentations and the discussion. The presentations chosen are considered to be representative of those dealing with the major issues, i.e. the structure of the microenterprise sector, government policies towards microenterprises, informal credit markets, financial and technical services, institutional aspects and a review of the experience of assistance projects. It is hoped that this publication will prove of interest and value to all concerned in increasing assistance to the development of the microenterprise sector in developing countries.

Finally, I would like to acknowledge the invaluable help in preparing the Summary Report of the excellent resumes of the discussions in the working groups in the second part of the conference of the rapporteurs Reinhard Schmidt, Professor of Finance at the University of Trier, West Germany; William Steel, Senior Industrial Economist at the World Bank; and Katharine McKee, formerly of the Ford Foundation.

Jacob Levitsky
February 1989

SUMMARY REPORT OF CONFERENCE
JACOB LEVITSKY

Opening session

The conference was opened at 9 am on Monday 6 June with a session chaired by Jacob Levitsky, Secretary of the Committee of Donor Agencies for Small Enterprise Development, and addressed by Enrique Iglesias, President of the Inter-American Development Bank, Alan Woods, the Administrator of the US Agency for International Development, David Hopper, Senior Vice-President of the World Bank, and Rep Benjamin Gilman of the US Congress.

Mr Enrique Iglesias, in his opening remarks, stated that the Inter-American Development Bank (IDB) 'aspires to be the Bank of Latin America's informal sector with a true appreciation of the important role the informal sector plays in the region'. The institution, he continued, would try to link its operations more closely with non-governmental institutions. It would also include the informal sector in the policy discussions of the Bank with governments.

According to Mr Iglesias, the role of the so-called 'informal sector' has increased greatly since the onset of the debt crisis. The sector presently makes up one-third of the economically active population in Latin America and the Caribbean, or some 30 m people. While the modern, formal sector of the region's economies grew a scant 2 per cent in the 1980–85 period, the urban informal sector showed an annual growth rate of 6.8 per cent during this same period.

Despite its undeniable importance, the informal sector has received relatively little support, but some pioneer efforts have been made — including the IDB programme which has shown how these small units can be helped with what they need most — credit and training.

The Small Projects Programme of IDB has, to date, financed over 170 projects in nearly all Latin American and Caribbean countries, providing training to some 200,000 persons and credits to an estimated 100,000 low-income beneficiaries. The programme began 10 years ago in August 1978 with a $500,000 financing for a cooperative of rural women in Uruguay, Manos del Uruguay, which has since become synonymous with handcrafted sweaters and other garments that find buyers from New York to Tokyo. Then,

---

JACOB LEVITSKY has been with the World Bank since 1976, as an advisor and consultant on Small Enterprise Development.

in Colombia, the IDB teamed up with private businessmen and provided the Fundacion Carvajal in Cali with $500,000 for training and credit programmes.

The IDB president made special mention of the key role non-governmental organizations have played in the Bank's Small Projects Programme. In all of its small-scale projects, the IDB directly lends up to $500,000 to an intermediary organization, generally a non-profit corporation, cooperative or agency set up by local business leaders, or by a church group. This intermediary organizes training courses and sometimes administers the credit programme, together with financial institutions.

In all cases, the credits finance productive enterprises and the projects receiving financing are viable and have good prospects for expansion.

In many respects, the IDB's Small Projects Programme has exceeded its objectives. Of 22 projects examined in a 1985 study, the total number of direct beneficiaries was 29 per cent more than anticipated.

Credits to individual producers are provided on terms similar to those offered by conventional lenders. They gain experience in using credit productively and hopefully go on to qualify for loans from conventional sources.

Arrears average 10 per cent or less in most programmes. The default rate is well below 5 per cent — a figure that compares favourably with the banking sector in general.

The experience gained with the Fundacion Carvajal project in Colombia showed the enormous potential for success of this type of project. The Bank subsequently approved $5.45 million to set up 14 similar microenterprise programmes in cities throughout Colombia.

The effort has been so successful that in 1986 the IDB approved its first major loan for microentrepreneurs — $7 m — to help finance the National Microenterprise Plan that has been designed by the National Government together with participating foundations and banking systems.

The Inter-American Development Bank is now considering a significant increase in its support to small-scale entrepreneurs in Latin America and the Caribbean, the IDB President concluded.

The second speaker was *Mr Alan Woods*, the Administrator of the US Agency for International Development (AID), who opened his remarks by pointing out that this was the first international conference on microenterprise development. In most developing countries, outside of agriculture, microenterprises employ more people than any other kind of business. Even among agricultural households, part-time and seasonal microenterprise activity often generate more family income than is earned through farming. In some countries where policies and regulations force businesses to remain small and underground, the value added in the informal sector can exceed that created in the larger, more visible formal sector. AID has long understood the employment generation potential of microenterprises. For more than 20 years it has encouraged the US private voluntary organizations, cooperatives and host country organizations to provide assistance to microentrepreneurs and has funded research on the nature of microenterprises and their relationship to financial markets.

Despite the record of achievement, AID is painfully aware that even the best-thought-out projects may be completely overwhelmed by a hostile policy environment. Where private enterprise, including microenterprises, cannot survive, help for microenterprises cannot substitute for a supportive business environment and a commitment to getting national economic policies right.

AID and the other donors present at the conference can help developing countries address the major challenge of stimulating the creation of microenterprises and jobs. In countries that are not committed to creating a policy environment that fosters economic growth, the donor community cannot make development occur just by pushing out financial resources.

Direct project inputs to help microenterprises will continue to make sense, as a complement to high level policy and structural reform initiatives. During the last year, AID, together with the US Congress has made an explicit commitment to expanding work on microenterprise development. During the fiscal year 1988 more than $50 m will be made available for this purpose. Within this programme, technical assistance will be channelled to developing country institutions that are aiming at income enhancement and employment generation through microenterprise development. Credit will be made available to financial institutions to help demonstrate the financial and economic worth of lending to microenterprises.

AID's work in this area will include efforts to broaden access to financial resources through cooperatives and credit unions. Through organizations like Appropriate Technology International, and VITA, USAID will be making information on new productive technologies available to expand the potential of small private enterprises.

AID maintains an active research programme to review the effectiveness of financial, as against non-financial, assistance in promoting microenterprise growth. In addition, AID is looking carefully at the question of institutional sustainability, at the financial performance of microenterprise assistance institutions and the extent to which these institutions that have been supported prospered.

This is a very ambitious programme, one which it is intended will grow larger and more effective over the next few years. Meetings such as this conference can be watersheds. Mr Woods looked forward to receiving the report on the conclusions and achievements of the conference.

The third speaker was *Mr David Hopper*, Senior Vice President of the World Bank for Policy, Planning and Research. Mr Hopper opened by welcoming the participants on behalf of the World Bank, referring to the conference as representing an excellent example of cooperation between donor agencies, the developing countries and the NGOs.

Microenterprises have only been recognized in the last few years as an important subclass of the enterprise sector. But the evidence is that as much as a third of the population in developing countries derive their income from the microenterprise sector; the very small, non-farming income generating units, including artisanal operations, family businesses, cottage industries and other enterprises in the informal sector. These small microbusinesses include a wide spectrum of activities from rural traditional crafts handed down through the generations, to the first steps in entrepreneurship taken by the impoverished unemployed for whom the formal sector has been unable to provide gainful employment. Microenterprises embody an impressive array of initiatives, skills and talents which, if effective forms of assistance can be developed, have the potential to make an enormous contribution to economic growth.

The World Bank has been aware for some years of the tremendous latent resources that exist in the microenterprise sector. The Bank has set poverty alleviation as a major goal of its lending activities and has tried to help the poor through comprehensive projects in rural and urban development, through loans to assist small enterprises and through other projects. It is estimated that around $500 m of the $3 bn or so lent for more than 60 small enterprise projects since 1975 have benefited the microenterprise sector.

In the last period, efforts have been made by the World Bank to add microenterprise components to loans for Latin America and Africa projects. Also a number of urban development projects have in the past included components for microenterprises. Nevertheless, even though the World Bank has made significant efforts to help microenterprises, he was aware that so far the Bank had not developed programmes comparable to those implemented by the two cohosting agencies, both of which he commended for the special programmes they have initiated in this field.

There are, however, other ways in which the World Bank may provide significant help to this sector. An important part of World Bank finance is now linked to major policy reform and structural adjustment programmes. As the Bank conducts its discussions with developing country governments it will attempt to reduce the onerous policy and regulatory framework imposed on the microenterprise sector. The World Bank already has recorded some successes, he said, giving new impetus to entrepreneurial initiatives in the microenterprise sector.

Hopper also stressed the role of non-governmental organizations (NGOs) in assisting microenterprise efforts. The World Bank believes that the energy, talent and dedication of the NGOs must be harnessed in this endeavour. NGOs operate at the grass-roots level, with low costs, high motivation and a comprehensive knowledge of the local scene. They also have played an important role in mobilizing the resources, both financial and political, of the business community to help microenterprise development. Support for microenterprises is also a way of providing greater help for women who play an important role in setting up and operating microbusinesses.

The concluding speaker at the opening session was *Rep Benjamin Gilman*, a Representative from New York State in the US Congress, a member of the House Committee on Foreign Affairs and of the House Select Committee on Hunger. Mr Gilman also was coauthor and sponsor of the microenterprise legislation recently passed by US Congress.

Microenterprise is not just the latest 'buzzword' in development assistance. It is a massive endeavour that now embraces hundreds of private development institutions throughout the world. This international conference is itself testimony to its rapidly growing importance.

Mr Gilman stressed the need to encourage the involvement of domestic banks in financing microenterprises. When the banks are involved as lenders, the number of beneficiaries is in the millions. Non-governmental and private voluntary organizations cannot fill the bill alone. Organizations such as the World Bank, the IDB and USAID must work with central banks to institute policies that will make it attractive for domestic banks to lend to the indigent.

For example, a central bank can keep its deposits with banks that lend to microenterprises, provide domestic banks with guarantees for any losses incurred and give domestic banks preferential interest rates if they engage in microenterprise lending.

Bilateral and multilateral agencies can induce the central banks and financial regulators to implement these types of incentives by making such policies the condition of their larger loans to those governments.

Mr Gilman believes one of development's best kept secrets will soon be public knowledge, namely, investing in poor people is good business. Not only are the poor bankable, they may be one of the most productive and safest investments today. He concluded by urging conference participants to believe in the indigent, because with that belief, it is possible to work wonders throughout the world.

Report of presentations and discussions

Following the Opening Session, the conference proceeded to hear presentations on a number of subjects and issues related to promoting microenterprise development in developing countries.

The following represents a summary of the information and points of view presented on the subjects and issues covered in the sessions and of the discussion in groups. Where appropriate, the report refers to consensus as indicated from the presentations and the discussions, although it was not intended that the conference would approve formal resolutions or take decisions. The objective was to facilitate an exchange of experience and this was largely achieved. The summary covers both parts of the conference including both plenary and working group sessions.

Microenterprises and the informal sector: the target group

In general the conference regarded the microenterprise sector as identical to the informal sector, but some participants did consider the term microenterprises as comprising a broader target group. Most speakers did not see great purpose or benefit in a prolonged discussion as to a suitable size definition to define a microenterprise. They did agree that the term referred to very small income generating units, owned and managed by entrepreneurs who worked in it themselves, from which they derived most of their livelihood, which employ very few people, if any, mainly relying on family members, and using very little capital. In most countries this was largely synonymous with the informal sector but in some cases could include traditional family, cottage industries or artisanal units and the self-employed.

Some participants at the conference did try to define microenterprises in size terms. Maria Nowak (36) attempted a broader definition of a microenterprise as an entity employing less than five persons, generating income from non-farm production, services and trade. She went on to break down the type of activities that this might comprise in rural areas.

Hernando de Soto (64), in one of the leading presentations of the conference, stressed strongly his view that the microenterprises that needed help were within the informal sector. This paper is printed in Part 1.

Another speaker, Victor Tokman (63), while recognizing that the informal sector historically played an important role in Latin America, suggested that the sector's total employment was more in the nature of 20 per cent of the labour force. He saw the development of microenterprises and the informal sector as partly illustrating the failure of the 'trickle-down' strategy in aid programmes when it was thought that larger projects would create sufficient jobs through rapid growth. (See Part 1)

The surplus labour force that cannot obtain gainful employment is forced to create its own employment opportunities in order to survive. Henry Jackelen (18) pointed out that the growth of the informal sector is affected by different factors in different countries. (Part 3)

The informal sector is not protected by any laws concerning contracts, minimum wages, social security or safety. Because entry to the informal sector is easy, life for the microenterprises is very competitive and actual incomes are low. Philippe Hugon (54) pointed out in his presentation that ease of entry of the sector also increased competition *within* the sector because apprentices and other very low paid employees of microenterprises develop informal activities of their own. In most cases the income obtained through these informal microenterprise activities is no more than the return the entrepreneur receives for his own work and very little for his managerial activity and the activities of his family. In most cases the capital involves no more than the household premises, and perhaps a vehicle, or a few tools. The

Numbers in the text refer to the list of papers submitted to the Conference in the Appendix.

informal sector microenterprises are often family activities, and the relevant income has to be considered as the total received by the family. Economic and social factors usually determine that the income per person in the informal sector is below the comparable income in more modern, larger scale activities.

One economic view of the informal sector was that it was subordinated to the formal sector and therefore had little possibility of expansion. However, according to another economic point of view, the formal and informal sector were complementary, and the informal sector could increase through autonomous growth induced by growth in the whole economy. In general, manufacturing accounts for about 20 per cent of informal employment and, in this sector, cost differentials between the formal and informal sector can be significant. However, the other sub-groups in the informal sector which are closely linked to location and which provide services of a specialized and formal type such as in retail commerce, repair shops, restaurants, laundries, hair dressing, etc may amount to 30 per cent of informal sector employment. In the long run, the share of the informal sector in gross national output is on a diminishing trend, but there can be fluctuations based on political and technological changes which can promote temporary growth in the informal sector.

De Soto and Tokman both based their presentations on the problems faced by the informal sector on Latin American experience, and stressed these as very much bound up with legality. Muhammad Yunus of the Grameen Bank, Bangladesh (14), saw the major issue not as one of the legality of an enterprise but rather as to how to generate employment which could reduce poverty. When wage employment was not available, the only alternative was self-employment. He thought there was little point in discussing the character of a microenterprise, its size, its nature, or its characteristics, but rather to see the whole objective of assistance as reducing poverty. This he considered should be the main aim of all assistance toward development. Income generation was, therefore, the most important way of reducing poverty and this could best be done through providing opportunities for self-employment. (Part 3)

Other speakers, mainly from Asian countries, saw little purpose in prolonged discussion on the characteristic of the 'microenterprise sector' and the problems of legality. They thought that the focus in assistance programmes should be on assisting those below the poverty level, helping them to take the first steps in creating micro-businesses and in generating income for themselves and their families.

While most participants identified microenterprises closely with the informal sector, it was recognized that there were in many countries other types of very small productive units that could be considered as microenterprises. Some countries have long traditions of artisanal activities and cottage industries, most of which operated in a way which made them fit into the category of microenterprises. They operated as family units from which the entrepreneur or owner derived his livelihood and provided for his family directly from this activity, where the capital employed was very low and generally only family members worked in the enterprises.

Some participants discussed the relationship of microenterprises and larger enterprises. They stressed that in many countries government support was available for the larger enterprises through investment codes, government loans, industrial zones, and subsidized loans. Little account was taken of the effect of these policies on existing microenterprises which rarely received similar preferential treatment. Governments sometimes subsidized the development of larger enterprises which preempted opportunities for some informal activities. Van Dijk (17) gave examples from West Africa where activities such as the fabrication of agricultural implements, metal beds, and some food items had been for years the output of small informal sector microenterprises. The development of state-owned and poorly conceived large industrial enterprises led to the closing down of many of these microenterprises as they were unable to compete because the large enterprises, both public and private, were heavily subsidized.

In general, the participants felt that there could not be a clear global definition of a microenterprise. Such a definition, if required to determine eligibility for an assistance programme, will have to vary from country to country. Defining a microenterprise loan programme based on loan size — such as up to $300 per loan — might fit a particular credit oriented programme aimed at increasing incomes for microbusiness, but would not help in a wider definition of the target group that needed assistance. However, there was general agreement at the conference that this target group comprised very small income generating units, possibly of one person or members of a family or a few employees, that might or might not be of a semi-legal or informal character, depending on the legal structure of the country concerned. It could in some cases include family businesses, cottage industries and other traditional forms of business activity provided the capital used was minimal and the business was the main source of income of the entrepreneur. A number of participants felt also that a microenterprise should be considered such only if it was an operation run by the poor — as poverty was defined in that country — and for whom assistance represented an act of 'poverty alleviation.'

Government policies

There was no clear consensus as to what positive government policies might be recommended. Rather, speakers considered the government role should be to avoid imposing stringent regulations and bureaucratic burdens that impeded development of microenterprises. Most participants felt that microenterprises developed and grew better without government interference and even in opposition to government regulations. In no way could it be considered that this sector depended on assistance from the goverment. Some speakers such as Maria Nowak thought that the variety of policies that had been followed by governments, such as over-valued exchange rates and subsidized interest rates, encouraged investment in machinery and worked against labour intensive production systems of microenterprises. While it was accepted that microenterprises would thrive, and even prosper, without direct government help, it was nevertheless important that the government, in its policies and in its attitudes, encourage the microenterprise sector and not impede its growth by its actions. This involved the attitude and behaviour of all the bureaucrats and technicians that implemented the law. Furthermore, the government was a major buyer of goods and services, and it was important that some access to government purchases was available for microenterprise producers as well. In some countries, governments control raw materials and small microenterprises could encounter difficulties in obtaining the raw materials they need unless the government took positive action to ensure that this was made available for them.

There was some lively debate on whether the government should take positive and affirmative steps to subsidize and protect microenterprises, or whether the appropriate approach was simply to be neutral and to eliminate biases against the sector. The prevailing opinion seemed to depend on whether microenterprise development was viewed from a social aspect and not only as a contribution to economic growth. When the social aspects were considered of primary importance, help for these enterprises was used first and foremost as an action to alleviate poverty and then subsidies and direct affirmative action was more acceptable. Even reserving the manufacture of certain products for the small and microenterprise sector — as in India — or protecting uncompetitive cottage industries, was acceptable. However, those who were more concerned with the economic impact would emphasize the cost to the taxpayer or to consumers of such government subsidies to any category of enterprise, and they argued that the government role should be one of facilitating the activity of the sector, rather than direct intervention. The government, some thought, could perhaps play a positive role in coordinating the activities of organizations helping microenterprises and refrain from putting difficulties in their way.

Most participants supported the views of de Soto, Tokman, Yunus and others that the government should follow policies of deregulation. In fact, several participants thought that registration of microenterprises was not really necessary, while others felt that ways should be found to simplify legal requirements reducing bureaucracy and providing a one stop facility where microenterprise could register and become legal without too much difficulty. Others thought the government should introduce laws that automatically made all 'self-employment' legal.

Even participants who did not support outright subsidies thought that ways should be found to exempt microenterprises from certain types of taxes. However, a number of participants did feel that this might, in the end, impose even further problems on the very smallest and poorest income generating units. Just as small businesses often have difficulty in competing with large firms, because the latter were subsidized in material supply, energy, credit, exemptions from imports duty etc, the very smallest might not be able to compete with the small if the latter were exempt from taxes. Perhaps the answer may lie more in less subsidies for *all* firms, large or small, creating a situation of equal opportunity for all enterprises regardless of size.

Several speakers supported the contention made by de Soto and others, that in developing countries smaller firms often pay, in one form or the other, a higher share of taxes than large firms. Moreover, taxation of the microenterprise business involves heavy administrative costs in dealing with the tax authority.

Some participants, particularly those from Asian countries, repeated that the focus should be on the poor and government regulations and policies had little impact since the action of the government was so far out of the range of the poor who engaged in microenterprises. Microenterprise development was viewed by these participants as a major tool in generating self-employment and addressing problems of poverty, and this took place independent of government policy or action. A point referred to by some participants was that the government existed not only in capital cities but also in the form of local authorities at the district or village level. The people who have to give out licences wanted to tax the micro-businesses and wanted to be sure that they received their share of bribes. You could have changes in national policy but if the attitude at the local level did not change, the result might still not really benefit the microenterprises.

Judith Tendler (4) stressed in her presentation that she had found that in some successful programmes of assistance for microenterprises those in control of the project seem to be well connected politically. This fitted into the view expressed by several participants that what was needed was to give more political voice to the poor and those engaged in the microenterprise and informal sector.

The prevailing view on the government role seemed to be that less government intervention and regulations was needed, that ways should be found to facilitate access to credit and to markets, but there was no need for special subsidies but rather for equality and neutrality. Despite the strong feelings against government interference, Judith Tendler and some others thought there was a role for government in helping fund NGOs and that breaking down distrust between public agencies and NGOs and replacing it with cooperation might be of value in strengthening help for the microenterprise sector.

Structural adjustment programmes
One aspect of government policies addressed was the effect of the structural adjustment programmes and policy reforms that had taken place in many countries (often on World Bank or IMF recommendation) on the microenterprise sector. Philippe Hugon (54) dealt specifically with this aspect,

noting that adjustment programmes can, in the short term, have a regressive effect on microenterprises, by reducing demand for its products or making it more difficult for these informal sector enterprises to have access to materials or any equipment they may need. An illustration of this was given to the conference by the complaint of an African participant that adjustment policies had produced sharp devaluations and introduced foreign exchange auctions, making it almost impossible for the very small enterprises to obtain the imported items needed. The liberalization of imports, the lifting of price controls and the raising of interest rates, while all possibly desirable from a long term macroeconomic point of view, could cause hardships to the microenterprise sector. On the other hand, the increase in rural incomes which might be brought about by higher prices paid for farm products, might sometimes benefit the informal sector enterprises if they were in a position to satisfy quickly increased demand for products.

Even though improved rural incomes might cut migration to urban cities and so relieve pressure on the informal sector, structural adjustment would generally increase competition and might work against microenterprise development, at least in the short term. In the long term, if carried through successfully by governments, it might make it easier for microenterprises to grow and to have better access to credit and markets. It was felt, however, that governments should consider the short term effect of such reforms on the microenterprise sector and, if necessary, take active steps to ease the hardships on the sector in making the required adjustments.

Financial assistance
Many speakers repeatedly referred to the lack of access to credit for microenterprises. Inadequate collateral, the illegal or semi-legal status, the high transaction costs and the inability of the microenterprises to cope with the time consuming complexities of dealing with formal financial institutions were all presented as reasons for the failure of microenterprises to benefit from institutional finance. The conference reviewed the different sources of finance for microenterprises, the various models for providing financial assistance, and the different approaches to the subject.

Informal credit markets
Several speakers pointed out that the first step towards self employment or starting microenterprises rarely called for borrowing from institutions. Anand Chandavarkar (1) showed that overwhelmingly these microenterprises rely on own or family savings which overall may add up to 90–95 per cent of the total of small investments involved in any country. Both Hans Seibel (5) (Part 2) and Chandavarkar stressed the significant role played by informal credit sources (including money lenders, pawnbrokers, rotating savings and credit associations — ROSCAs — wholesalers and shopkeepers, etc.) in micro-business 'start-ups' and in providing working capital. Maria Nowak gave an illustration of 'tontine money' of $300 or more being 'snapped

up' at double the asking prices in Cameroon and of informal credit interest rates of 25 per cent per month in the Ivory Coast and at 500 per cent per annum in Burkina Faso.

Both Chandavarkar and Seibel stressed the need to forge links between informal and formal lenders. Some informal lenders might be helped to formalize their activities and this could help expand available credit sources. Appropriate policies and procedures would need to be worked out.

Considerable discussion took place on the most appropriate credit delivery system to provide financial assistance to microenterprises when needed.

Specialized institutions

Several speakers focused on the success of the Grameen Bank in Bangladesh (14) and whether such a specialized institution was always needed and could be replicated in other countries. It was stressed several times that perhaps the greatest success of the Grameen Bank was that it showed that the poor could be commercially viable clients of a banking institution. This challenged the conventional wisdom that microenterprises could not be reliable banking clients. (See Tendler (4) (Part 1) Timberg (2) (Part 5), Yunus (14) (Part 3)).

Other credit delivery systems

Several participants referred to other ways of delivering credit to microenterprises, apart from Grameen-like specialized institutions and the informal credit markets. NGOs had developed successful programmes but these were usually limited to localities, cities or regions and generally did not reach large numbers of borrowers. Several of the earlier NGOs' credit programmes had had very poor repayment records but, under pressure of donors and with improved management, some had now improved recovery rates although this still remained a problem in many cases. Opinions were given that some of the NGO credit programmes had the character of welfare activities and the organizations were neither willing nor able to undertake vigorous collection measures. Many NGOs had the support of religious institutions and were less inclined to emphasize the business and profit-making character of the microbusinesses supported although this too was undergoing changes in some cases.

Apart from NGO credit programmes, reference was also made to the success of saving and credit cooporatives, credit unions and cooperative and savings banks in providing credit to microenterprises. Some participants strongly supported using these institutions.

Interest rate

There was a virtual consensus (there were a few dissensions) that microenterprises did not need credits at a subsidized level lower than the prevailing commercial interest rate. What they needed, it was stressed, was greater access to institutional finance. Grameen Bank has effective rates of 25 per cent (high by Bangladesh standards). Other programmes in Bangladesh have annual rates of up to 30 per cent while the BKK, a successful programme in Indonesia, lends to poor people at a rate of 5 per cent to 10 per cent *per month* — close to levels of the informal credit market. Richard Meyer (11) points out that in all these cases the relatively high interest rate has not adversely affected demand nor repayment records, while there are many cases of subsidized rates with poorer performance on both accounts. (Part 3)

Although there seemed to be something approaching unanimity, at least among the speakers, that microenterprises did not need loans at lower than prevailing commercial interest rates, there was less than consensus that programmes did not need any subsidy. Some thought that lending institutions might need access to low cost funds. There might also be need sometimes for indirect subsidies to intermediaries to cover higher transaction costs; for help by NGOs in promoting programmes and in screening and appraising borrowers; for assistance in training staff; for tax concessions and credit guarantees.

Volume of credits

This was considered by a number of speakers to be an important issue for several reasons. Only a certain level of credits and borrowers could hope to achieve any degree of economic or social impact. The volume of an operation as set by number of borrowers and amounts lent could also determine the viability of the operation by having the potential to reduce transaction and administrative costs. Maria Otero (3) pointed out that the question of the sustainability of a lending programme, namely its ability to continue operating without continuous recourse to outside funding, is very much affected by the volume of operations. Only when a programme reaches a minimum volume can it hope to achieve sustainability. (Part 5)

Some microenterprise lending programmes have reached impressive numbers of borrowers. Papers presented (Timberg, Meyer, Jackelen) refer to the IRDP (Interest Rate Differential Programme) in India which benefited 15 m families in the period 1980–85, to the BKK programme in Indonesia which provided 2.7 m loans totalling over $55 m in the period 1972–83 and the Grameen Bank in Bangladesh which is currently reported to have 70,000 groups and to have reached 400,000 borrowers. Grameen has also mobilized US $7 m in savings (averaging more than one month's wages per rural borrower).

According to information given to the conference, no programme in Latin America, nor in Africa, has approached the volume of lending achieved by the programmes in Asia. Most Latin American programmes have been localized, have been developed by local NGOs with expatriate assistance in most cases, have done better in obtaining funding from the local business community but generally have reached only a few thousand recipients. The highest volume Latin American programmes, UNO in NE Brazil, INDESI in

Peru, claim to have reached up to 40,000 borrowers. All the foundations in Colombia together (at last count over 20 in number) may also have benefited similar or even a higher number of borrowers.

Meyer refers to programmes that reach very few beneficiaries (one NGO programme in the Philippines had only 8 loans). Many non-bank NGO type programmes operate only in very limited geographic areas and cannot hope to reach more than a few hundred participants at most. Significantly, as Timberg pointed out, most Latin American programmes are of integrated character laying great emphasis on combining credit with training and technical assistance as exemplified in the programme of the Carvajal Foundation in Cali, Colombia. Evidence seems to show that to reach a really high volume of borrowers the lending has to be operated and managed as a bank, or at least with a large regional branch network covering a wide geographical area and population. It has to have access to considerable funds and resources and concentrate more on giving out credits and less on other forms of assistance, such as training and technical assistance.

Involvement of banks

All participants stressed the indifference, unwillingness and inability of most formal banks to become involved in providing credits to microenterprises for reasons already mentioned (transactional costs, risk, lack of collateral, etc). However, the view was expressed that if a way could be found, it would be desirable in the interest of volume, impact and sustainability, to involve commercial banks more. One method mentioned by Meyer is the action of a few governments (India for example) of imposing portfolio quotas or mandated targets for the banks to lend a minimum percentage of its loans portfolio to the poorest elements, including the microenterprise sector. This is a requirement of the commercial banks quite apart from the setting up of specialized institutions or programmes for lending only to this sector (Grameen Bank in Bangladesh, Kupedes/BRI in Indonesia, etc.) Meyer's findings are that lending quotas and targets are largely ignored or evaded by lenders through 'creative loan documentation'. Some participants from India maintained that the mandated quota and targets have had a beneficial effect in increasing lending to microenterprises.

De Soto stated that when informal sector enterprises were legalized in some form and had titles to property on which they could obtain mortgages or could use as collateral, some commercial bank lending to microenterprises did take place, but a better solution was to use insurance companies to give mortgages against such property titles.

Several speakers thought that ways should be found to establish links between the informal sector and formal financial institutions. Jackelen proposed that such links can be developed through 'specialized intermediaries'. (Part 3)

Some commercial banks have carried out limited lending programmes of their own for microenterprises (Banco de Pacifico in Ecuador, Syndicate Bank and Bank of Baroda in India, BRI and other regional banks in Indonesia, etc). In some Latin American and Asian countries some banks have played roles in managing NGO lending programmes. In this arrangement, the NGO takes all relevant decisions in approving credits, bears most of the administrative costs in promoting the scheme, identifying, screening, appraising, and supervising the borrowers and bears the risk of non-payment. The bank is paid a fixed fee for disbursing, drawing up the formal loan contract and collecting the payments. This arrangement is followed by most of the foundations in Colombia. In some cases, the NGO deposits funds in the bank which are used for making the loans. The system has the merit, it was pointed out, of involving the banks who may later make direct loans from their own resources to borrowers with good payment records and growth records. In fact it was stated that in some programmes in Asia some banks gradually developed from the role of managing loan programmes to integrating the lending later into their own operations (India).

While some participants claimed the banks, both development and commercial banks, were only interested in assisting large enterprises and maximizing profits and that there was little point in expecting a change in their attitude, others thought that involvement of the banks in some form or other was almost indispensable to expanding credits to microenterprises to large numbers of borrowers. There were also some who claimed NGOs had failed to make efforts to involve the banks in their lending programmes, not only because of indifference and resistance from the banks, but also because in some cases the NGO was reluctant to give up control of the programme or to let go of their clients.

Savings
Although the conference did not specifically address in detail the question of mobilization of savings, several speakers expressed themselves strongly that linking savings mobilization and credit delivery was desirable from many points of view. Through savings, resources are built up to expand the volume of credit and to achieve sustainability of a lending programme without resource to continuous inflow of funds from outside. Through savings, microenterprises are encouraged to build modest capital reserves toward growth or as a buffer against downturns in income. Linking savings and credits could encourage participation of borrowers in the management of a lending programme and in ensuring adequate repayment levels.

Seibel in his presentation (5) stressed the need for linkage between savings and credit, pointing out that institutions that had these linkages could generate collateral for bank refinancing through the savings deposited. He gave several examples of ROSCAs and other informal groups in Africa and Asia that had successfully linked savings and credits in the form of self help organizations.

In supporting the idea of linking savings and credits, some participants saw an important role for saving and credit cooperatives, also for credit-unions and for savings banks that had successfully supported microbusinesses in European countries and elsewhere. Maria Nowak referred to a large scale savings movement in Zimbabwe, mostly of women, of the credit unions in Ghana and Cameroon and of savings and loan associations assisted in Central Africa by savings institutions in France, Germany and Canada. (Part 1)

While supporting the idea of linking savings and credit, Chandavarkar observed that informal credit markets are better geared to the retailing of credit than the collection of savings which is better left to formal financial institutions of one type or another that are more adequately supervised by the central bank. Judith Tendler also thought that when clients have to save in order to borrow, the credit organization will have to prove first that it is a trustworthy place to put one's savings. Saving, it was agreed, gave depositors, and therefore borrowers, a financial stake in the organization and this could be important.

Minimalist or integrated approach
The term 'minimalist approach' was used in the conference to categorize programmes which operated in a narrow focus supplying *only* credit and no other form of assistance as in the cases mentioned by Judith Tendler. In describing programmes as minimalist credit, she also sees the objective as lending money to microenterprises and being repaid, without becoming too involved in how the money was used. A successful project, according to the minimalist approach, would be judged solely by the repayment records. To others, minimalist credit would mean providing credit without providing additional assistance in the form of training, technical assistance, marketing help, etc.

Many participants, particularly those from Latin America and some other NGOs, argued strongly that credit alone without training and technical assistance was of limited value. In fact, the Carvajal Foundation of Cali, Colombia (56), holds that training and technical assistance are the main services needed and credit should be available only to those who have passed through training programmes on how to manage their enterprises. They contend that there is evidence the credit is then better used. While many participants supported the need for training and technical and management assistance programmes, they pointed to the high costs of such activities and to their limited effectiveness. Malcolm Harper (8) in his presentation thought that technical assistance has a limited role to play, as opposed to credit, in the microenterprise sector. (Part 4)

Others, who disagreed with this view, argued that credit given without adequate training and advice would be misused and achieve poor results in improving and expanding microenterprise operations. Some, like Marilyn Carr (13), thought that technical assistance agencies were needed to help with technical appraisal of loan applications and to make sure the most appropriate technologies were used.

The evidence seems to show that programmes that reached large numbers of small borrowers have diversified least into non-credit activities. Inevitably, programmes that have concentrated heavily on training and technical assistance together with credit have served much smaller numbers of microenterprises, have usually been limited to a locality or a sector and have required large inputs of funds from outside. No general hard evidence has emerged that beneficiaries of such programme perform better.[1] If the training and technical assistance costs are included, the expenditures may run in the range of 30 per cent to 50 per cent of the amount lent. The situation is exemplified in the figures presented by one of the programmes regarded as one of the most successful, the Carvajal Foundation of Cali, Colombia, which states (56) that during the last 11 years the Foundations through the country have trained over 30,000 microenterprises of whom 8,542 obtained credits from a total $10 m in loan funds. Although tuition fees were collected, a sizeable part of the training costs were covered from a 12 per cent interest charge earmarked for training in IDB small project loans.

Whether the minimalist (credit only) approach or integrated programme (credit with other forms of assistance) is preferable, the integrated approach was certainly followed and advocated for many years. Van Dijk (17) points out that in the earlier pronouncements on small enterprise assistance (from ILO, UNIDO, World Bank, Staley and Morse, Ford Foundation, USAID, and others) the importance of providing technical assistance and training together with credit was always advocated. Only in recent years has more focus been placed on the high cost and limited impact of such programmes.

Still, out of 42 microenterprises assistance programmes reviewed by Timberg in his paper (2) only five could be classified as minimalist, ie financial assistance only, five were training programmes only and the remaining 32 (76 per cent were integrated programmes combining financial assistance with some other form of help. This leads to the conclusion that most donor agencies, particularly NGOs, favour the integrated model. Mainly programmes operated through banks or financial institutions seem to favour credit-only programmes.

Technical assistance

Several participants stressed the importance of non-financial aid, despite reference to the benefits of the 'minimalist' approach, namely credit only without integration with programmes of technical assistance and training. Harper, while casting doubt on the cost-benefit and effectiveness of technical assistance and training for microenterprises, suggested that training might be given to government officials to change their attitude to microenterprise development. (Part 4).

Several participants did not agree with Harper's views. Matthew Gamser in his presentation (10) considered that some specialist institutions have succeeded in generating numerous micro-production innovations quoting the work of the Technology Consultancy Centre in Kumasi, Ghana, as an example. He admitted, however, that many institutions have failed to establish strong relationships with micro-producers. Gamser favoured the establishment of small enterprise technology support units within financial institutions or within development agencies. He stressed the need for an understanding of the practical needs and constraints of small production operations. Donor agencies and governments could play a key role in ensuring that institutions established to promote microenterprises can provide practical help to very small production-based, as well as service, enterprises. Small-scale production units needed help in introducing new appropriate technologies as well as in obtaining access to capital.

Several of the Latin American representatives strongly supported technical assistance and training programmes which they believed could be made meaningful for the needs of microenterprises. Training could be practical and technical assistance could be sector-based, namely to groups of microenterprises of the same subsector, eg textiles, leather, woodworking etc. Linking credit to training had resulted in better use of the finance provided. Programmes of technical assistance had helped microenterprises to produce new products. Improved product quality and design and lower costs were also some of the results achieved in some training and technical assistance programmes. It was agreed that technical assistance was costly, but ways could be developed to reduce costs through the group approach, help from private companies, from equipment or material suppliers, using volunteers or students, etc. NGOs had succeeded in many places in developing low-cost training courses which had raised the standard of microenterprise operations.

Despite strong doubts expressed by some on the effectiveness of non-financial support — training and technical assistance — many participants still favoured such programmes.

Graduation
There was some discussion on the question of graduation, namely the movement and growth of microenterprises out of the informal into the formal sector and into the small enterprise category. Meyer (11) points out that data on this subject is sparse. (Part 3)

Some aspects of the graduation issue were discussed. Lending agencies may actually discourage graduation because while such enterprise development can be considered as a success, the credit programme loses a good participant and has always to face high costs in handling new clients with all the risks involved. It is argued by some, that if lending programmes are run by banks, possibly with NGO assistance, then good performers and successful microenterprises will more automatically graduate to larger loans and growth. It was also noted that when the upper loan limits on microenterprise programmes are set low, the gap is too great for borrowers to 'graduate' to borrow from formal institutions. The regulatory framework governing formal enterprises tended also to be a deterrant to graduation. The number of microenterprises graduating was generally quite low.

Success
On various occasions participants discussed the criteria used for deciding whether a microenterprise aid programme was considered successful or not. Judith Tendler quotes Hirschman[2] on this point that 'there are no successful projects, only those that have less problems than others.' She prefers to refer to better performing programmes rather than to successes believing that even these programmes are riddled with problems, mistakes and false starts.

Discussion revealed that the notion of success was more controversial than might be considered at first glance. An observer's role in a programme seemed to influence the assessment of a programme as successful or not. Some programmes could be regarded as successful at the level of the target group, namely the impact on the microenterprises who were the beneficiaries or participants (as some preferred to call them). Success, it was pointed out, can however also be measured at the level of the entity which carried out the programme. If the entity or agency carrying out the programme could be considered viable and displayed sound institutional development, even if it failed to reach the target group on a large scale, it could be considered from one point of view, a success. As impact is difficult to assess, there was a tendency generally to judge success at the level of the delivery agency or institution. Some thought that the target group reached and the effect on it were the criteria for success, not the efficiency of an agency's operations. In the view of these participants, mostly from Asia, a programme was only successful if it reached the poorest strata of the population and not just by supporting dynamic entrepreneurs who by local standards were not really poor. Others, mainly from Latin America, but not exclusively so, thought that the best contribution to economic and social development (employment, income distribution etc) was achieved by helping more middle class microentrepreneurs who could ultimately provide employment for the poor.

From the donor agency or external evaluation viewpoint, success or failure tended to be judged by such elements as the extent and speed at which funds were disbursed, expansion in number of borrowers and, more often than not, by the repayment record, if a credit programme. In the light of the very poor repayment performance in early microenterprise credit programmes, there was now a tendency to regard all programmes with a relatively high repayment of credit — possibly 80 per cent or 90 per cent or higher — as successful, irrespective of who got the loans and how they were used. Everyone agreed that repayment was important (for many reasons already mentioned), but some wondered if the pendulum had not now swung too far to the other side, when programmes with good repayment records were automatically judged as successful without considering other factors.

The issue of criteria for assessing success was linked by some to that of replicability. A successful programme, some thought, will be replicated except if it has features which are country-specific or if it depends too much on one strong charismatic leading personality. Interestingly enough, it was pointed out that even programmes classified as successful, or better performing, had weaker and stronger features while programmes dismissed as failures might also have some limited successful aspects. It was agreed that the criteria for evaluating programme success or failure were important, since a great deal could be learnt by examining why a specific programme was more or less successful and for this one had to agree what this meant.

In general, it was agreed that while this may differ from country to country, the economic and social impact, the number of beneficiaries, the financial and economic viability of the institution and its ability to reach self sufficiency and sustainability, were all important elements in determining success. The latter element would reflect the level of loan repayment. Because of the many factors to be considered, the evaluation of programmes was a complex business and might prove costly, especially if carried out by foreign consultants. Nevertheless, most participants thought evaluation of programmes was important but ways should be found to reduce costs, possibly by using local personnel as much as feasible, and providing for information systems and monitoring, as programmes were being implemented.

Non-governmental organizations (NGOs)

There was general consensus at the conference that there was an important role to be played by NGOs in assistance to microenterprises. These organizations are much more cost effective in their activities than public agencies, are more highly motivated and generally had greater understanding of the cultural and social environment in which they operated.

Bertrand Schneider (49) stressed the important role for NGOs, after criticizing the failure of aid programmes that had invested in large scale projects based on western models but which were inconsistent with the needs of the target groups in the developing countries. Most of these projects had benefited only a few, and in many cases clashed with local structures and cultures. A study that he had undertaken for the Club of Rome in 19 countries in Africa, Asia and Latin America had shown that voluntary and non-governmental organizations were much more able to carry out aid programmes and to deliver assistance to small scale projects. There were thousands of these NGOs in developing countries throughout India, and in other Asian countries and hundreds more in Africa and Latin America. The Club of Rome report says there are more than 7,000 NGOs in India, 3,000 in the Philippines, 1,600 in Brazil, 1,000 in Thailand, 650 in Nigeria, 370 in Kenya, 380 in Peru, 300 in Ecuador, 270 in Indonesia, 200 in Botswana and 110 in Cameroon. They were rooted in the society in which they operated and they were able to use efficiently the scarce resources at their disposal if they could also get some support from NGOs in the developed countries.

In Schneider's view, NGOs in the developing countries were grass roots organizations which understood that project success depended on community involvement. These NGOs in the developing countries are now taking the leading initiative in improving the living conditions of the poor in their countries. He stressed that NGOs had to broaden their role to make them able to be fully recognized as equal partners by governments and national organizations. They needed to be consulted regularly on the design of strategy and projects. Schneider thought that NGOs in the developed countries had not fully recognized the growing force of these southern NGOs and were still not providing them with the resources they needed.

The largest and best organized NGOs are finding it increasingly difficult to avoid institutionalization. There is now a second generation of NGOs which were based on interdependence between the developed and the developing countries' organizations.

Participants agreed that NGOs had already been active in this field for some time and constituted an important delivery system in helping microenterprises, but some questions were raised about these organizations, their manner of operations as well as their relationship to governments and international donor agencies. It was recognized that the term 'NGO' applied to a wide variety of institutions, only linked together by the fact that they are not part of government. Some thought one could break up NGOs into two distinct types. There were the membership or participating organizations, voluntary associations of self-employed, women's associations (SEWA, Annapurna in India), and there were also NGOs that are more technical and/or financial intermediaries. The membership organizations have more legitimacy because they have a constituency, usually of the poor, but the second type of organization can also play an important role and, for the donors, it will be easier to support the second or technical type of organization.

There were participants who stressed that while some NGOs were able and willing to provide technical assistance to help microenterprises, some of them were hesitant in supporting business operations because they didn't always feel at ease with profit-making activities. There was no doubt that NGOs have performed better when they were involved clearly in working towards social objectives such as helping poverty alleviation. Several participants stressed the fact that the NGOs were often based in rural districts or in urban slum areas where most microenterprises are located, and that they usually had a dedicated staff who were living with people, as distinct from expatriate consultants and experts who rarely did this. Because they live among the people they are trying to help, they develop a capacity to understand the needs of these microenterprises and to gain their trust and cooperation. They tended to be flexible and willing to take risks and in most cases less subject to political control, at least in comparison with public agencies.

Marilyn Carr (13) saw some problems in NGOs generally lacking the staff needed to understand technology and business management in order to give advice in this field to microentrepreneurs and she also thought the influence and impact of most NGOs was limited because they were too small to reach large numbers through direct intervention. There was also a desire, it was pointed out by some participants, for some NGOs to remain low key or 'invisible' so as to avoid government interference, but this also meant that they developed little interest or ability to influence the policy environment.

Reviewing the experience of the Ford Foundation, Judith Tendler thought that concentration on supporting NGOs was based on sound reasons. The NGO was a place where everyone was committed to alleviate poverty and where there was now substantial programme experience in the subject. If the aim was to increase the income of the poor then there was no doubt that NGOs were the best organizations to help to do this. Nevertheless, she thought that NGO programmes in this area did not make serious inroads in attacking poverty in a country, both because they reached insufficient numbers and also because they were unable to affect policy or influence the programmes of larger organizations. Tendler saw the main success of NGOs as when working with ethnic, religious or socially homogeneous groups and when these organizations expanded they lost some of the comparative advantages in working with these groups. They did sometimes compete with each other, and with the public sector, for funds from foreign donors and this at times made them tailor their product to obtain financial support, compromising on occasion some of their basic principles. She pointed out that in some cases NGOs preferred funding from foreign donors because they were far away and this generally resulted in less interference than from local government.

Tendler thought donors should place priority on the potential for achieving large scale impact rather than building NGO institutions for their own sake. There was a distinct problem in trying to scale up the small scale experimental activities operated by NGOs which had been reasonably successful on a small scale, but which required different approaches and structures when they grew larger.

It was pointed out by some that even though NGOs tried to keep a distance from government and made a great effort to prevent interference, evidence does show that a substantial part of all NGOs' budgets come from governments.

Women and microenterprises
Although the conference was not planned to focus specifically on the subject of women in microbusinesses the subject was raised on several occasions. A separate meeting on the subject of 'Women and Micro and Small Enterprises' was sponsored by the Committee of Donor Agencies on Small Enterprise Development in Ottawa, Canada, in October 1987 hosted by CIDA (Canadian International Development Agency). A number of participants represented organizations engaged in promoting women in business (SEWA and

Annapurna in India, Women's World Banking, Philippine Business of Social Progress, SUWATA in Tanzania, Manos del Uruguay etc) and it was pointed out by a number of speakers that women played a major role in most developing countries in operating successful microbusinesses. Some participants observed that in many countries the participation of women varied inversely with the size of enterprises. It was agreed that whether through promoting special programmes or through ensuring that women benefit fully from general programmes, it was important to recognize that microenterprise development had to provide for assisting women to become involved in business.

Ms. Veronica Nyamodi of Kenya discussed the special problems of women in microbusinesses in Africa and described a number of programmes in her country, including the work of a branch of Women's World Banking, which helped women entrepreneurs. Mary Okelo of the African Development Bank (although unable to attend) presented a paper (61) on the subject for distribution at the conference. (Part 5)

Role of donor agencies
As was intended, a considerable amount of discussion was devoted to the role and the potential contribution of donor agencies in microenterprise development. It was recognized that donors differed in their objectives and approaches and sometimes these were not stated openly. Some donors were concerned almost exclusively with social goals — alleviating poverty, improving the quality of life and enhancing incomes of the poor through self employment. Other donors were more concerned with enterprise development and overall national economic goals. These different concerns often resulted in aiming at differing target groups. Some aimed at the bottom 20 or 30 per cent of income levels and others targeted small enterprises already operating in the belief that the prospects for growth and economic impact were greater through assisting this group. The goals of a donor might also be reflected in the choice of institution with which to work.

The view was repeated several times that political considerations entered into donor agencies' actions and choices. Those who believed that the target group should be the poor, and the principal goal income generation and self employment, did not have much confidence in those mainstream institutions (which were often the main recipients of donor aid) in serving this constituency. Some donor agencies believed strongly in the mechanism of the market and were averse to publicly supported institutions. Some participants went even further and addressed the core issue of whether external donors and their funds were really needed. They argued that there were sufficient resources within their countries if these could be mobilized, but most seemed to believe that there was still need for external funding. The role of donor agencies it was argued, however, should go beyond funding assistance projects. Many thought they should finance institutional development so as to build up the capacity of these organizations. Institutional capacity was identified by Maria Otero as one of the major constraints in reaching sustainability. A third role was identified for donor agencies not involved in direct funding but mainly in exerting influence on a government to follow policies that were conducive to microenterprise development.

On the role of donor agencies in directly financing projects, many participants thought it was important that it allowed for experimentation with different approaches. Marilyn Carr referred to the first and second generation of projects, the first being mainly experimental and the second involving more complex relationships, possibly bringing in public agencies, banks, private sector organizations and NGOs. Donors were also needed to help with these second generation projects. In the matter of working with NOGs, most donors seemed to encounter more difficulty in working with the larger membership organization type of NGO which was more constituency based. It was suggested that this was possibly because these operated more within the political environment.

Funding projects directly would always have its limitations in the numbers that could benefit so that some participants believed that, ultimately, donor agency support for institutional capacity building would be the way to achieve long term impact. The institutional infrastructure was still weak and fragmented in most countries and there was a distinct danger that if a major flood of funding should be directed by donor agencies in the near future for microenterprise development, the institutions were not in a place, nor in a position, to ensure that the money will be well spent. Some donor agency representatives admitted that they sometimes agonized on the dilemma, when pressed to increase the volume of activities, of whether an expansion of funding would be effective because of the doubts about institutional capacity to handle a major increment in external resources.

Even though some, if not all, donor agencies, recognize the above dilemma they find it more difficult to provide institutional rather than project support. Many reasons were given or speculated upon for this. It is more difficult to assess and display the impact and results of institutional support. It was also often problematic for donors to choose which organizations should be given large scale support. There were also administrative problems of accountability and control. Despite recognition of these real problems, the consensus (with some dissenters who still favoured financing projects directly) seemed to be that donor agencies, after an experimental stage, should be prepared to provide more long term support in the development of those institutions that had proven an ability to carry out microenterprise assistance activities in an effective manner.

A recurring theme in this discussion was the unrealistic expectations of donors. Possibly because of their need to reassure constituents and supporters back home that funds were used effectively, international donors seemed to want recipient organizations, usually local NGOs, to accomplish the ambitious task of having a major impact in providing assistance to a large number of poor micro-business beneficiaries in three or four years and then become self sufficient while remaining small and beautiful. Some of these organizations — such as SEWA in India, BRAC and Grameen in Bangladesh, Sarvodaya in Sri Lanka, Solidarios in Latin America — wanted to grow, become larger and more significant, so that they can do more to address the poverty issues in their country and reach large numbers of the poor. Donors were criticized by some, who argued that they did not really want recipient organizations to grow but rather wanted to work with a lot of smaller organizations. This might not apply to all cases, nor to all donors, but representatives of some recipient organizations in developing countries stressed that coming back for more funding from donors did not mean failure to achieve sustainability — now a much sought goal — but rather a desire to expand, face new challenges and to help more people. This was the challenge of meeting the needs of the second generation of broader microenterprise assistance programmes. Some warned that expansion of programmes through increased funding from donors could present problems for some organizations as this might open the gates for government interference.

On the other hand, it was mentioned that some donor agencies preferred to help the well performing successful institutions and programmes that have all passed through the experimental stages, rather than help smaller more risky newer programmes. Many participants thought that there was need for more collaboration between donor agency and local recipient organizations in designing projects. There was a general consensus that there was need to minimize, or even avoid completely, the use of outside experts and consultants who were both costly and less familiar with the local culture and government. It was stressed that more use must be made of local experienced persons, before donor agencies send in consultants on short missions to decide what should be done. Donor agencies could give advice and help but it was felt that donors should not *dictate* what sort of programmes should be developed.

Donor agencies were asked to recognize the need for funds to pay for staff development and training in institutions, for monitoring and evaluating the costs, expenses and benefits (often specifically demanded by donors) and for instituting and developing an internal management information system. In assessing impact some, like Maria Otero, thought this should be done at all three levels: on the beneficiaries, on the community and the policy environment and on the implementing organization.

There was a strong call for the donor agencies themselves to coordinate their programmes better, especially when funding a single organization. There was need to coordinate not just the flow of funds but also the administrative and reporting requirements. The problem of over-dependence of some recipient organizations on continuous donor agency support was also raised. A long-term realistic programme for building up a self-sufficient organization, whose development could be sustained from national and domestic resources, needed to be discussed with the donor early on in the relationship, especially if the donor insisted on supporting relatively short-term projects. Sometimes, stumbling from project to project, donors failed to ask the tough questions as to what was the long-term plan and strategy of the organization. Withdrawal of donor support, if and when it comes, is bound to be difficult and to come as a shock. There will be greater problems and the withdrawal symptoms will be worse if there has not been adequate preparation for this moment.

Apart from providing funds donor agencies could establish a dialogue with governments for policy changes. This was more likely to be the role of the large multilateral and regional donors (World Bank, regional development banks). Some smaller donors, it was stated, had made some contribution in this field by pointing to successful model projects and to the policy constraints that have impeded the success of assistance projects. Seibel gave an interesting example of a consortium (APRACA-Asian and Pacific Regional Agricultural Credit Association) involving an international network in Asia of multilateral and regional banks and other such agencies, with national development and commercial banks who conducted a dialogue on how a new kind of delivery mechanism could be developed to bring more assistance to the microenterprise sector in rural areas. Initiating policy dialogues to effect changes to benefit the microenterprise sector may be the most effective way in which a larger multilateral organization, such as the World Bank, can help microenterprise development, but to do this most effectively it must inform itself fully on project experience in this field.

Other fields in which it was felt donor agencies could help was in promoting research, in studying the sector and its problems and in supporting networks of NGOs to promote exchange of experience and learning from each other's successes and failures. Donors could also help governments to open special 'windows' in banks, and in introducing and supporting guarantee mechanisms to expand access to credit for microenterprises. The large donors could also introduce experimental microenterprise support components when carrying out larger urban or rural development projects. For bilateral donors, the consensus of participants was that they should work more in supporting selected proven local NGOs supplementing assistance given by the government and business community.

There was, however, a strong feeling that all donors should play a role in strengthening institutional capacity. Small private NGOs' donors could best use their resources to support experimentations and self-help organizations of the poor. In this way the larger donor agencies would put pressure on the government, on the banking system and on the business community to create an environment more helpful to microenterprise development, while smaller agencies worked more at the grass-roots levels.

PART I

The Microenterprise Sector and Policy Aspects

Structural Adjustment and the Informal Sector

HERNANDO DE SOTO

I will be addressing the subject of structural adjustment and the informal sector. My institute in Peru has done a lot of research on the legal constraints that refer to what we call informality, ie the operation of basically illegal enterprises which have legal objectives. The informal sector is a euphemism for the illegal sector. We should point out, however, that their objectives are clear and honest as opposed to, say, those of the drug trade.

In the past structural adjustment has been contrasted with the microenterprise or the informal sector. This view used the idea that structural adjustment, which essentially involves dismantling market distortions, would permit growth in a developing country. It means replacing pervasive government regulations and laws and, in this sense, too much attention given to the microenterprise or informal sector can drive attention away from good structural adjustment. Helping the informal sector meant concentrating resources on precisely those sectors of the economy that were the most unproductive — the small enterprises which have no economies of scale and pay low wages. Small firms are simply programmed to survive and stay small.

You won't be hearing much about that in a conference like this.

It has already been stated that more attention is being paid to microenterprise and the informal sector. In fact, if you look at the budgets of the different intergovernment organizations and the budgets of national governments, the microenterprise sector is still a poor relative. At the point where you have to take hard decisions, it is generally labelled as glorified charity work. In Peru, the total amount of credit that goes to the informal sector of total national credit is only about 0.3 per cent, so, although a lot of lip service is paid to it, micro-credit, which everybody applauds, is really the poor relation.

I would like to argue that there is a political case to be made for helping microenterprises. It's not only that microenterprises should be taken into consideration by those people that make structural adjustment, who approve of structural transformation, who are the advocates of policy reform, but that in fact the informal sector is the solution, the missing link that will help policy adjustment to take place. If you actually think about policy adjustment or

---

HERNANDO DE SOTO (Peru) is the President of the Instituto Libertad y Democracia (Institute for Liberty and Democracy) in Lima and author of the book *El Otro Sendero* (The Other Path) dealing with the informal sector in Peru.

structural transformation — at least in a country like Peru — it has not had much success. I think that the informal sector is crucial not only to understanding why structural transformation proposals that come from the West are not successful in developing countries, but also to making sure that structural transformation is politically viable. To do this I have to bore those of you who have already read or heard on other occasions these basic statistics but this is unavoidable. Also, I would tell you of a project that we have recently promoted in Peru which is really structural transformation and that is based on the informal sector there.

The first thing that we found out, and I think this is especially true in Peru, is that the informal sector is very large comprising at least 50–60 per cent of the man-hours worked in the country. The informal sector covers 47 per cent of the population on a permanent basis and, taking man-hours, it accounts for 61 per cent. Moreover, it amounts to 38 per cent of gross domestic product. In housing, we found by counting the homes in Lima that those that had been built informally, ie outside existing regulations and the law, had a value of $9bn and constituted 47 per cent of the total in the city. In fact today, of every 10 homes being built in Peru, seven are being built informally and only three formally. So it's a growing phenomenon. We also found by looking at the public transport system that if we include taxis, 95 per cent of Peru's public transport system is informal. If we don't include taxis and vans, 87 per cent of the buses are informal. They operate at no deficit, of course, while the state corporation, which only manages 5 per cent of public transport, operates at a yearly deficit of about $12 m.

The street vendors, who compose a rather large proportion of the sales force of Peru — 60 per cent of all sales take place through street vendors — continually informed us that they would like to move into regular market places. So we spent a year counting the markets in Lima, combing the streets one by one and we found that there were 331 markets, with stalls, running water and electricity and a sewage system and it turned out that of the markets built since the time of the Spanish conquest, 57 had been built by the states and 274 by the informal sector. So, we see the importance of the informal sector is a component once you start counting it and viewing it as a sector which operates outside the law, mainly through microenterprises. It's a very large part of the economy and must be taken into account. You cannot do structural adjustment, you cannot do policy transformation, without taking into consideration that part of the economy.

Then we asked ourselves: 'Why does the informal sector work outside the law? Why doesn't it do all these marvellous things that it's doing within the law and take advantage, for example, of formal credit, of property rights, or of any of those facility elements of the law which are crucial to the growth of business?' The reply, we found, was that it was because of the structures themselves, because of the legal system itself. To find this out, we didn't read a textbook, we went out and simulated the incorporation of a small enterprise. One of the first trials we did, which most of you I'm sure are familiar with, was to set up a small workshop in a district of Lima with two sewing machines and asked a lawyer and his four assistants to actually go through all the red tape that was necessary to make those two sewing machines operate legally. Working 8 hours a day, with four assistants and a stopwatch, it took them 289 days to register the firm. We did the same experiment in Tampa, Florida, it took us 3.5 hours and we've just completed it in New York, when it took 4 hours, which means that a Peruvian entrepreneur, to start off a small clothing workshop, has to work 700 times more than a US entrepreneur just to get started — provided, of course, he's read our study report which he probably hasn't!

In terms of housing, in most Latin American countries at least half of the buildings are the squatter dwellings that surround the cities. In Peru we call them — whether legal or informal — *Pueblos Jovenes* or young towns. They have different names in other countries. I believe they are called *favellas* in Brazil and *ranchos* in Venezuela. Well, we asked ourselves why these people that could not live — given the property values — in the centre of town, did not simply have sand dunes allotted them. After all, the state has procedures for handing over government land to people who need it. Again we found by simulating in part and by putting together 'red-tape' histories that it takes the head of a housing association with about 100 people, on average, 6 years and 11 months working 8 hours a day to complete 207 bureaucratic steps and visit 52 government offices. This explains why, in 1985, in Lima alone, there were 282 illegal occupations of land and only three legal cases of land requisitions. It wasn't that Peruvians or Latin Americans favour doing things illegally, it was that the law had enormous costs, especially for poor people. In terms of actually helping to build markets, for produce, we found that between the time a group of street vendors in the streets of Lima decided on building a market and the when they are actually allowed to build it by law takes 12 years of 'red tape'.

For all of those who say that the reason people are informals is that they don't like to pay taxes, I would simply like to point out that in fact Peruvian informals pay more taxes than Peruvian formals. Only 120,000 Peruvians pay income tax, so the majority of government income does not come from it, but from such things as the gasoline tax which is 40–45 per cent of its income. The gasoline, as you know, is mainly used by the public transport system and that is mainly informal. Another part of Peruvian government income as a source is inflation. In other words, as the government produces excess currency, the people who pay for it are those who have to maintain large cash balances — the informals. We have even found that there are very quaint taxes in Peru, like a tax that the street vendors pay in the cities to municipal police for using the sidewalks, plazas or roads. In Lima alone, Peruvian municipalities collect from this tax twice as much as from legal formal property taxes throughout the country. If you add to that the fact informals have to pay 15 per cent of net income, or 50 per cent of gross income, to authorities in bribes to appear on the market, it ends up that the Peruvian informal sector gives more to the state than in fact the formal sector does. So there's a lot of room for structural adjustment in the informal sector.

Now, structural adjustment doesn't only mean getting rid of those laws the previous list would incline one to do, it also means putting in good law. It means, for example, putting in the right kind of property law. In Peru, we found that legal property rights are most important for development. A specific case where all this started was in an area just outside Lima. There were two young towns — Pueblos Jovenes. One of the towns was rather developed with three-storey homes with curtains. You could see Toyotas and Volkswagens downstairs and television antennas on the roofs. There were neatly trimmed lawns outside the houses as opposed to the other town which was a real dump made of cardboard and corrugated iron. We told ourselves that obviously here you have people from two different cultures. The people in the first town are clearly more developed working people and those in the other are not. We were told afterwards, in fact, that the people in both of these places originated from the same Andean village. We studied both communities and were able to confirm that both came from the same area.

The difference between them, we were able to confirm, was that the leaders of the first town had dedicated most of their time to obtaining property titles. In the second town people had devoted most of their time to organizing themselves internally. The result was that the people of the first town succeeded in obtaining property titles. To achieve these, they even named their place after the wife of the President of the Republic to gain political favour. The value of their homes after 10 years increased 41 times more than the value of homes in the second town. The study has been extended through 38 young towns to make sure that the conclusions were correct, and the finding was that the difference between having a property title and not having one was a difference of 9:1 in the value of homes. We noticed that with property titles you get an access to credit, even if it is informal credit, on better conditions, you get some stability regarding the future, you lose your fear of detection and expropriation and therefore you invest and work, you convert human capital into real material capital. We found that without contracts it was very hard to develop an informal business. There was no way of making long-term arrangements, of achieving economies of scale. Moreover, we also found that if it takes 289 days to register a business, it also is very difficult to operate on an informal basis. It means an incredible amount of hardship to get businesses together when you have none of the facility aspects of the law.

I always give an example here which I think will be familiar to all of you, because it actually refers to something we've seen continuously in the young towns of Peru which is when people wish to associate together to form a business. After all, entrepreneurship is all about pooling resources together and combining them in the best way possible. These don't have to be natural resources as the Japanese have proven, Asian countries and Western countries who don't have natural resources have proved. They can just be human capital. So, we are in a situation where there are two Peruvians in a young town, Michael and myself. I'm a button manufacturer and I'm the best button manufacturer in Lima. It's logical that I should want to be associated with Michael, because, it is known, he is one of the best button sellers in town. Now, logically, we should want to get together. The trouble, of course, is that Michael's wife is going to tell him, 'Now, you've got a problem in associating with de Soto. After one year, he's going to know who your clients are and then he won't need you any longer. It's a big mistake to associate with him.' On the other hand, my wife would probably say something similar, 'Watch out, he might learn more about the business.' Now, if we were both legal, of course, if it didn't take 289 days to register, we could form a partnership of one sort or another, he could take 30 or 40 per cent of the shares in terms of compensating his ability and I could take the remaining 60 or 70 per cent. Whatever would happen in the future, we know that in fact he will always get 30 or 40 per cent no matter if I become intimate with the customers and no matter if he actually gets to know the business of manufacturing better than I do. Instead Michael will have to associate with someone he trusts and therefore he will associate probably with a family member, either from his wife's family or his own, whom he can control through family or tribal mechanisms, and I will do the same. Then some development expert from the US will come and visit us. 'Look,' they will report, 'Peruvians like to work in small family units'!

The law is very important and the law is precisely what keeps microenterprises micro and the fact that people involved in politics and policy adjustments do not study the informal sector very much leads, of course, to this lack of facility law.

Though they are the majority of the country, the informal sector is very unpopular in Peru and in most of Latin America. They're not only called disloyal competition, they are regarded as dirty. They produce a lot of negative external opinion. Operating private businesses outside the law makes absolutely no sense. I would like simply to point out the following:

1 the study of the informal sector leads us to confirm that it can be an important source of growth;
2 it should be an important part of structural adjustment — structural adjustment is not only policy reform but should try and benefit the informal sector as well.

Structural adjustment will probably only work in democratic developing countries with a large informal sector when you actually get the support of the informal sector and get those in it to identify their interests with structural adjustment. I would even go as far to say that the reason structural adjustment programmes of international organizations have not been successful in countries like Peru is precisely because structural adjustment is not popular with the large number of people in the informal sector. This need not be so. As a matter of fact, within the structural adjustment programmes, there was a proposal to deregulate the 289 days needed to make a firm legal and at the same time to convert assets into collateral. I'm sure that this action would have the majority of the votes of Peruvians and that politicians would find it easy to carry out structural adjustments in this way; but the fact is that structural adjustment does not address the informal sector and generally treats it as the informal sector — the sector that deals with charity which the President's wife takes care of. This means, of course, that these inputs are not politically viable. I will give you one example of something that recently occurred in Peru.

We have been trying to promote a change of structure as a matter of the law relating to credit for small enterprises. We developed this project over the last 30 months. I would like to say that we published it on 21 January 1988 in the Peruvian official gazette and by 7 April it had been picked up by representatives of 98 per cent of Peru's political parties and introduced into parliament. Moreover, on 10 April, President Garcia converted it into law through a decree because he found it rather popular. The reason he has found it popular, of course, is because we canvassed the informals to support this law.

The informal sector is a class and can be identified as such. We hold hearings, we know their leaders — whether they happen to be of the transport sector, or the housing sector, or the industrial sector, or the street vendors — and we get signatures from them and present these signatures together with proposals. In the case of credit, we obtained 580,000 representative signatures and therefore the government paid attention, because it realized that the informal sector were not only marginal businessmen, they were also the majority of voters inside the country. Also, this proposal that we put through was based not on a lot of studies of what structural adjustment means from the ivory towers of an Ivy League university but on the results of observing both foreign Western institutions and our own institutions and how they work.

As you will remember, we saw that the informals have property or have possession of property that in Lima alone has a value of $9 bn. In Peru in total it has a value of $18 bn and if all those $18 bn exist, why can they not be used as collateral for financial organizations? The reply is, of course, that they are informal, that they are illegal, so the question is, 'How can we collateralize them?'

Our first inclination was to title them as quickly as possible because, as we will recall as well, we had found out that once there is title to land, the value of land itself and of homes goes up nine times in 10 years as opposed to when you don't have title, so we thought titling was the solution. Now we found out that on average, the Peruvian system of titling for people of the informal sector takes 20 years between the time that you obtain a squat on land and you actually obtain title. So, we said, 'Well, probably we will find something better in Western countries. They must have a better way of doing this' and we travelled around the US and found out that the only massive titling venture that was identifiable was the one in Alaska. Because of the pipeline, there were hundreds of thousands of claims from Eskimos wanting their land titled, and we also found out that the solution they gave to that land was to form into corporations because the titling itself was a 16-year process in Alaska. We decided therefore we have very little to learn from the US. We studied homesteading and found out that it was a more gradual process and also left room for a lot of shooting which we, of course, need less and less in Peru.

Then in California we came across a very interesting institution which nobody had suggested to us. We visited an American company called the First American Titling Insurance Company and found out that they hand out insurance for titles, so you do not need to research your own title. When you buy a home and you obtain title, you get some insurance and you know that any risks that you run are actually borne by the company. Well, in Peru, the problem is, of course, not having titles and so we have a conceptual challenge: 'How about possession insurance?' The reply was 'Well, why not' and that's what we've been working on for the last 30 months and that is what today is law in Peru, and it is a system that we hope to put into effect. It consists of three essential elements: firstly it sets up a possession register for informals, secondly possession mortgage for informals and thirdly credit insurance for informals.

1 The first thing you need to know if you are going to be able to use the possession of informals, is that it really belongs to him or her and that requires a registry, a registry that says who owns what. The problems of the normal registry in Peru, of course, is that all the requirements to obtain the title, as I've said before, take 20 years.

The first thing that an informal does to assert his property right over the land is build on it. So, we ask ourselves why don't we reverse the process. Instead of finding out who the land belongs to, let's find out who the building belongs to: that's much easier to prove. Because there's no effective police force to provide protection, the Peruvians in the informal sector always first build a wall around the property. As the buildings themselves touch wall to wall, we told ourselves that the proof of the title is in a photograph showing up to where each person has allowed his neighbour to build and we will assume that whoever has built on the land owns it. Let's give most of the people the credit required. So, in fact, today, the new registry that will be held by insurance companies and municipalities — jointly or separately — will receive as proof, first of all, the registers of the informal sector, because there's no such thing as a land invasion in Peru without a previously drawn map of the area to be invaded, as we found out from the informals themselves from their own (informal) register. From now on that can be legal tender in Peru.

If you happen to be one of the few people that have not massively invaded land with previous organization, which is rare indeed, you can use the photographs we talked about and the building will certify that you in fact own the property as well. If you happen to be semi-formal and have the receipts of electricity, water and sewage payments, or you have in fact already paid a tax or you have obtained a loan from a micro-credit organization, that also is good evidence to make sure that you are included in the register. As a result, we expect that in Peru, 4 years from now, the value of informals' homes in Peru will have risen by $3 billion, simply through registration.

2   What do we do for credit? Well, the idea is to make the possession that is registered for all practical effects a property that can be handed over to an insurance company or a credit institution in the form of a mortgage. The way we actually stimulated the informals to obtain mortgages is that we said that in countries like the US, 80 per cent of small businesses started up through home mortgages and how was it possible in Peru that this is so ignored. What informals did in Peru was to let government know that they, too, had the right to a mortgage. We have therefore established by law a system through which the established possession is actually registered. This can be handed over to the majority of the Peruvians which today have property of sorts. This allows them to obtain credit if they are adequately registered.

There cannot be a country that has 50 or 60 per cent of its population that is informal without some kind of law or common law actually guiding or ruling their transactions. So, we have adjusted these laws to fit the case of the informal sector. One of the main problems is to make sure that nobody speculates with their land. If there are foreclosures on the mortgages, if somebody who obtained a credit using the mortgage cannot pay that credit, the property is auctioned off, but only to people who also live in these 'young towns', only to people who one way or another are people who do not already have a home. Moreover, the mortgage can be deposited as a trustee in the hands of the 'informal' authorities who are the elected authorities of the 'young town' and they can decide whether they're going to support the cause of the person who has defaulted on his payment or whether they are going to act so as not to lose credit for the whole neighbourhood. We have placed these decisions in the hands of the informal authorities themselves.

3   In terms of the credit industry, which is the third pillar of the system, we have also simplified things. One of the reasons banks do not serve the informals is because the informals don't have collateral. With the registration system and the mortgage, they now have collateral, but it's still too complicated for banks. As you know better than I do, it is much easier to develop 100 loans of $500,000 than 500,000 loans of $100. Some banks just don't want to be bothered with property that, on average, as in case of the informal property in Peru, has a value of $9,600 per unit. However, we found out that insurance companies in Peru were very interested in looking at that kind of property. They insure bicycles and motorcycles and they would be willing to

give out credit insurance. In other words, they would be willng to accept the mortgage and on the basis of the mortgage extend a letter of credit of sorts to the informal who would then go to the bank and solicit credit on the basis that his guarantor was a triple AAA insurance company.

So far, the government, the private sector, the informals and all the political parties of Peru, from the extreme left to the extreme right, have accepted the project. We expect that will allow us to raise, without using foreign resources from international organizations, credit to the informal sector from 0.5 per cent of the total credit market to 5 per cent of the total credit market in the next 4 years. In other words, we expect that about $200 m of Peruvian savings will be able to go to the informal sector. Moreover, we expect that only the installation of the system will increase GNP per capita by 1.2 per cent pa.

Now, let's look at what that particular measure, which is one of the many we have suggested on how to relate structural adjustment to the informals, will do. By addressing the needs of the informals, we have been able to obtain 98 per cent political support for structural adjustment. It has given the dispossessed majority a stake in the private sector economy. It has ensured that every person, each of whom is a potential member of a terrorist movement in Peru, becomes part of the system. We have begun to deregulate the banking system by simply creating a parallel to work with which even people with titles will want to use because credit insurance is an additional security. We have been able to give the formal private sector an interest in the informal sector which previously they thought was only disloyal competition. We are reducing the scope for corruption and we are reducing the dependency on foreign sources of support. We are decentralizing by using more informal mechanisms and the elected political authorities of the informal sector and we are recognizing the registers as sources of formal law. Also, of course, by not limiting these loans to small enterprises, we are allowing the quick graduation without anybody having to make a political decision and we are bringing in something that Anglo-Saxons thought was their privilege — the common law into the statutory legal system.

We did this by making the project popular with the informal sector who are the majority of the voters that politicians listen to in developing countries. In other words, structural adjustment needs the informal sector as much as the informal sector needs to be considered by structural adjustment. Essentially the message behind this is the following.

The informal sector is not a marginal sector. It is the majority of the people in many developing countries. It is important if you want to transform your countries democratically to use their will. People from the microenterprise sector must actually be heard. The informal sector, as Marxists would like to hear, is in fact a social class, it is a group of pepole who have entrepreneurial abilities, but who are also dispossessed and poor and who are also being fought over by people who believe that they are nothing more than a proletariat. If you want structural adjustment to make sure that certain values are kept, or certain values are introduced in developing countries, like markets, like private entrepreneurship, like democracy, it is important that the informal sector stop being the poor cousin of financial organizations and actually become the focus and not the enemy of structural adjustment.

Micro-Level Support for the Informal Sector

VICTOR E. TOKMAN

Introduction

The informal sector has, historically, played an important role in the process of labour absorption in Latin America. In spite of rapid growth and employment creation in modern sectors, the share of employment in the informal sector in total employment expanded from 16.9 to 19.3 per cent between 1950 and 1980, while its share in the non-agricultural labour force remained constant at around 30 per cent. To this long-term role an additional buffer function developed in the 1980s, during the international crisis which affected the region. The economic recession affected the capacity of modern enterprises to create jobs, and in some cases adjustment meant a reduction in the absolute number of jobs available while the labour force continued to grow. The result was an accelerated growth of informal employment between 1980 and 1985. The number of persons expanded by 39 per cent and its share in the non-agricultural labour force increased by 4.6 percentage points.

The outlook for the future is not good. Most of the forecasts available conclude that the international economy will be less dynamic in the 1990s than in the 1970s, while in Latin America the still unresolved problem of the heavy foreign debt gives little expectation for rapid economic growth which is needed to increase employment creation. Reducing the informal sector will be therefore a slow process, both because the transfer of labour to the rest of the economy will be less dynamic, but also because of the enlarged size of this sector following the crisis. The main result will be that any policy for growth and equity cannot avoid the issue of how to increase employment and how to raise the productivity of informal jobs. There will then be a need for supporting informal activities.

It is more feasible today to design a national policy, more than it has ever been in the past. After 15 years of continuous research on the employment characteristics of a significant and growing number of people who, because of the lack of better job opportunities, had to perform low-productivity and badly remunerated activities and of pilot supporting programmes implemented by some non-governmental organizations (NGOs), there are signs

---

VICTOR E. TOKMAN since September 1988 has been Director, World Employment Program at the International Labor Office, Geneva, Switzerland. Formerly he was Director of PREALC, the ILO employment programme for Latin America in Santiago, Chile.

the situation is changing. Governments and the private sector are showing increasing interest in, and political will towards, this issue. This is reinforced by more clear support by international organizations, by financial institutions and by private foundations.

There are many reasons for this change. On the economic side, the crisis of the 1980s brought forward an explosive expansion of the informal sector, particularly on its most visible segments, illustrating the long-run failure of the trickle-down strategy to create sufficient jobs in spite of rapid growth. There is also today, as a result of the crisis, growing concern about poverty in developing countries and the need for targeting the persons most affected. It is recognized that the poor are not only those unemployed but mainly also those working in informal activities. In 1980, between 75 and 80 per cent of those employed in the informal sector received incomes lower than the minimum. Practical pilot experiences and studies available have also shown that these policies do not need large amounts of resources to be implemented, a finding which in times of acute scarcity of resources is very appealing. Capital:labour ratios in these activities are low and the financial support required usually involves very small amounts which, even if the programmes reach a large number of units, will involve less resources than alternative financial support for the modern sector. Other policies, such as the revision of legal regulations, training and technical assistance, can also be undertaken with a reduced financial outlay.

There are also non-economic causes. The emergent unregulated economy in the developed countries, although different from the informal sector on the periphery, gives universal acceptance to the discussion of this issue. The increasing violence in big cities associated with poverty conditions and informal employment, adds another reason of concern. Also the return to democratic regimes in the majority of the Latin American countries allows for more open pressure of these groups and a control of the repressive action of public authorities because of the need to enlarge the political constituency and because they have to assume the responsibility for the results of their policy decisions. There is, finally, an increased awareness that in developing countries the mass of people employed in the informal sector constitutes a social factor that cannot be ignored. By some, they are seen as potential entrepreneurs whose expansion should be promoted by avoiding excessive and inadequate state intervention.[1] According to others, they constitute a natural enlargement of the organized workers movement.[2] In any of the interpretations, the result is an increased awareness of traditional social factors (ie employers and workers organizations) about this issue.

There is need to support the informal sector. Hopes should not however, be raised unduly. The development of Latin American countries is and will continue to be, determined outside the informal sector where most of the accumulation takes place. Support for the informal sector could contribute to better efficiency in allocation and distribution, but growth will mostly depend on adequate development and macro-economic policies. In addition, not all informal activities are productive. Some of them are only a refuge for the unemployed in countries without social protection. Hence, support for productive activities can only benefit a part of those employed in the sector.

In this paper we will explore two issues. The first will be the conceptual base for policy design which requires some clarification of the characteristics, the role and the heterogeneity of the informal sector. The second will refer to policy guidelines for a selective policy.

Conceptual basis for policy design

Nature and genesis of the informal sector

The genesis of the informal sector in Latin America is linked to the development process of a peripheral region which, unlike the developed countries, incorporates imported technology which does not take into account their factor endowments. Indeed, on the contrary, they reflect relative factor scarcities of developed countries and changes in goods consumed whose demand is transferred through imitative consumption. In addition, incorporation of technology takes place in a different structural setting. Capital is scarce and more concentrated, while labour is not only abundant but also growing at a fast rate. The result is that consumption is highly concentrated in those groups with higher incomes due to their privileged access to capital resources, who closely follow the consumption patterns originated in the developed countries. On the production side, this results in a diversification and differences in productivity between sectors and size of establishments. Employment generation is insufficient to absorb the rapidly increasing labour force and the benefits of economic progress cannot reach a large part of the population because market imperfections do not allow for price competition and well-remunerated opportunities are scarce.

The surplus labour which cannot find well-remunerated employment has to create its own employment opportunities given their desperate need to obtain income for survival. These are partly determined by the existent scarcity of financial and human capital of this section of the population, which leads to activities where there are few restrictions to entry, and results in production units characterized by low levels of technology, small size, low capital requirements and limited social division of labour. The informal organization of production and of the labour process is also reflected in its institutional characteristics. The majority of the activities take place beyond the limits of the present institutional framework, since these are unable to fulfil the established requirements, while in most cases, the government cannot enforce them even if there is a will to do so. Labour relations are not protected because laws concerning contracts, social security and minimum wages cannot be applied and the productive unit does not meet the existing legal registration and tax requirements.

Easy entry also means more competitive markets, and average incomes become the variable of adjustment to changes in the employment level. Informal employment will increase until the income per person approaches the opportunity cost of labour which will be close to subsistence level. The situation is still more complex, since not all markets register equal access nor are they related to the rest of the economy in a similar manner. In addition, not all the surplus labour is uniformly without capital. The growth process of the informal sector will imply increased differentiation among subsectors with different roles in the economic system and among units within the sector, since the initial capital endowment differences are increased by the differing capacity to accumulate resources, although generally at low levels, of small firms organized on a quasi-capitalistic or family basis. The adjustment process will not be restricted to variations in labour incomes but will also include differing returns on capital. The income obtained will be in many cases the return to an indivisible package which characterizes small firms, where the entrepreneur supports its management and capacity, the labour of his family and some limited capital. Capital is, in many instances, partly non-transferable since it serves a dual purpose of being a household and a productive asset, as is the case of shops installed in the household or vehicles serving both family and business. Nor is labour easily available full-time, since families share their work in the firm with occupations outside the labour market (house care and school). In these cases, the relevant income will be the total received by the family and mobility of both labour and capital will be restricted.

The income per person in the informal sector will be generally below the comparable income in modern activities. Given the size of the labour surplus and the limited job opportunities outside the sector, average income will be determined by the share of the sector in total incomes and this is linked to the interrelationships which prevail within the rest of the economy.

Informal-formal interrelationship

Discussion about the kinds of inter-sectoral links presents a diversity of approaches in the literature.[3] They vary from assuming dependency and exploitation to the assumption of the existence of benign relationships. The former approach sees the informal sector as the result of subordination prevailing both at international and national levels. In this approach the market for informal sector activities is subordinated, residual and without the possibility to expand. Given this conceptual framework, informal employment expansion results in decreasing income per person since the market share cannot expand because of its dependent relationship. Informal sector growth can then only be involuntary.

The second approach assumes that informal activities are complementary to those of the modern sectors and that they will benefit from output expansion. Complementarity is derived from the sector's efficient use of the resources available and by playing an important role in different aspects of the economic process. According to this approach, the informal sector can increase its size by autonomous growth or by expansion induced by growth in the whole economy. Evolutionary growth is then possible.

Subordination is the characteristic of underdevelopment; the informal sector analysis is one way of looking at a more comprehensive phenomenon. The problem is to determine how strong is the subordination and whether there is room left for evolutionary growth. The subordination of the sector as a whole is the result of different processes occurring within it. It should distinguish those informal activities operating in sectors where modern activities have an oligopolistic structure from those where that is not the case. This division will generally, though not always, coincide with the breakdown of activities according to type of product (manufacturing goods, personal services and services linked to distribution and finance).

The different types of interrelationships that a group of activities within the informal sector has with the rest of the economy will determine its share in total income and its evolution. The analysis suggests three main subgroups of informal activities. The first operates at the base of concentrated markets where cost differentials can be significant. This is the case of manufacturing industries which account for around 20 per cent of informal employment. A second subgroup operates in markets where product differentiation and location are important, but operative costs are similar (mostly retail commerce, repair shops and semi-skilled services, accounting for around 30 per cent of informal employment). The rest of informal activities, mostly constituted by personal and domestic services, operate in competitive markets. In all these cases only normal profits can be expected in most informal activities, while a diminishing trend of the share of the informal sector's output in the total can be envisaged in the long run. Such a trend may not be stable and its rhythm is difficult to forecast given the mechanisms of resistance which exist, the cyclical fluctuations of economic activity, and the unpredictable technological changes, as for instance the present decentralization of production which is being registered in some leading manufacturing sectors.

Heterogeneity within the informal sector

A third important aspect for policy formulation concerns the degree of heterogeneity within the informal sector. Contrary to the prevailing image of a decade and a half ago to the effect that the informal sector was of a homogeneous nature, it is clear today that there are different segments within this sector. If the form of organization is taken as the main variable to define an informal activity, a difference should be established between those units using additional labour (whether paid or unpaid) and those representing activities performed by only one person. In addition, although on the average capital is scarce, it is not evenly distributed among all informal activities. In some, like domestic services or street-vendors, little or no capital is required.

In others, like taxi-drivers or small shops, more capital is involved in the operation. Hence, income resulting from informal activities is in some cases restricted to labour remuneration while in others it also includes earnings on capital.

Most of the surveys available show that the lowest income is received by domestic servants.[4] The next occupation is that of waged workers in informal firms, who obtain two times or three times the pay for domestic services. The self-employed receive around 50 per cent more than wage-earning workers in informal activities, while the owners of the informal shops make more than double the level of the workers employed in their own firms. When compared with the wages in the formal sector, it is clear that the self-employed receive incomes that are similar to or even slightly above the wages of workers in small establishments of the modern sector, while definitely below those received by workers in larger establishments. The owners of small etablishments, however, gain larger incomes than all of the workers except those employed in the public sector, but they earn less than the average income of owners of larger establishments and self-employed professionals with university degrees.

Income differences, when adjusted by problems of estimation, seem to suggest that, in spite of heterogeneity, incomes tend to be determined within a limited range. However, differences in forms of organization as well as in income determination rules also give support to the idea of dividing segments within the sector. The discussion on this topic has advanced less than in the other fields, particularly because there seems to be a mixture of analytical categories with regard to markets of products and factors.

The analysis has been concentrated on the unit of production, while labour market aspects received less attention in spite of their relevance for a significant part of the informal sector. An important issue to consider in this perspective is the pattern of mobility, since policy design should take into account the individual's behaviour. A study for Costa Rica[4] suggests that the mobility patterns differ according to each occupational position. The self-employed and the owners of small shops register little mobility, but their pattern of development is tied to the growth possibilities of their unit of production. They are entrepreneurs. At the other extreme, workers in domestic services perform in the labour market, moving from domestic services to waged work in formal establishments. Workers in larger modern establishments do not become informal owners, save for a small proportion. However, the pattern of mobility of workers in informal shops or in small establishments of the formal sector is mixed. Some of them become self-employed or owners of informal shops, thus being retained within the informal sector. Others move through the labour market to be hired as workers in larger establishments.

Specific actions in a comprehensive policy framework

The above analysis shows that setting policies for the informal sector is not a simple task. The structural nature of the interrelationships and the heterogeneity prevailing in the sector requires a comprehensive policy framework. There are no easy answers to such complex development problems but there are possibilities for action.

There is always the attraction of searching for what has been called 'the missing piece strategy',[5] that is, to identify a single constraint which, when removed, will allow more productive and profitable livelihoods for the beneficiaries. At macro level the most popular missing piece is excessive or inadequate state regulation and bureaucratic intervention. Removal of this constraint would allow for diminishing transaction costs and would improve access to the economy. At micro level the most common missing piece identified for direct assistance programmes is credit. While this is not assumed as the only constraint, it is considered to be a significant one in that making capital available would allow for the creation and expansion of small enterprises.

The missing piece strategy, both at macro and micro level, is also attractive because its effects are expected to be automatic. Both policy interventions are necessary components of a more comprehensive package, but isolation will only produce partial and, in many instances, marginal results. Inadequate regulation is only one characteristic of informal production, the main underlying constraints being structural. Access to capital is also a key factor affecting the low incomes of the informal producer, but other significant economic constraints must be recognized, such as access to skills and more dynamic markets. In addition, policy interventions cannot be limited to the informal sector since the most important determining factors are really in the rest of the economy. Policies followed for the economy as a whole will also affect the outcome of micro level interventions.

Because of this, what is required is a series of measures that may be mutually reinforced. In this section we shall explore four ways of supporting the evolutionary growth of the informal sector, three of them directly targeted at the informal units and the other on development policies.

Direct policies for the informal sector

The productive assistance package

One of the main constraints of the informal sector is its restricted access to productive resources (capital and skills) and to more dynamic markets. Because of this, the first priority is to set up mechanisms to permit access to these markets and to eliminate the discrimination which this sector suffers in practice by being excluded. This implies the design of at least three types of measures. The first is to improve access to product markets. This can be done by overhauling the systems whereby the state invites bids from suppliers and by eliminating the restrictions that prevent informal enterprises from participation. Subcontracting arrangements could also be promoted to ensure expanded markets as well as technological upgrading of informal activities. In addition, their competitive capability will be reinforced by measures, which may also result in an increased share in both public and private markets. The second is to facilitate access to both investment and working capital in order to reduce the high interest rates facing the informal producers when, because of their exclusion, they have to resort to parallel credit channels. This necessarily leads to the conception of collateral mechanisms not linked to individual assets, for example by the introduction of insurance schemes or trusts to serve this purpose. A third measure would be to train the informal producers in the use of accounting and managerial procedures. They and their dependants would benefit from improved expertise in production matters, which at the same time could become suitable vehicles for the introduction of new technologies.

The welfare package
Given the heterogeneous nature of the informal sector, productive assistance action has some limitations in terms of potential effects. The two main ones are that productive assistance may only be directed to the more organized productive units that constitute the central nucleus (mainly in industry and some non-personal services), and that within them the benefits derived from this assistance may involve a larger income for the entrepreneur, which may not necessarily be transferred to the informal workers. What conspires against improving wages is the large existing labour supply and the scant or non-existent negotiation capacity of this sector of workers. However, its productive reinforcement may imply an increase in the hours worked per week or the creation of new jobs and in this more indirect way the benefits would be transferred to the informal workers.

This leads to three conclusions. First, if the policy for supporting the informal sector is limited to this instrument, it should not be justified in terms of the full size informal employment, since it will overestimate the scope of these policies. Second, the policy will be more efficient in terms of its productive results rather than its impact on extreme poverty in the short term. Informal entrepreneurs, particularly those in the core activities which will be the direct beneficiaries, receive the higher incomes, while wages will probably not be affected and the employment effects will require time to mature. Third, a significant proportion of the informal sector will be excluded from the benefits of productive support, since to a large extent it depends on its own work force and falls into sectors, such as services in particular, which are unlikely to be offered support anyway. For this reason, measures tending to improve the welfare levels of the population are also required, in order to ensure that basic nutrition, education, health and housing conditions may be improved. It is obvious that such an assistance policy will have to tackle the constraints imposed by the availability of resources in almost all developing countries, but this situation makes it imperative, on the one hand, to focus the present social spending on these target-groups and, on the other, to study the possibility of increasing it by cutting down on other spending which may be socially inefficient.

The improvement in the welfare levels of the poorer groups, a vast majority of which can be found in the informal sector, will also have productive effects. It will permit them to reinforce their capacity to compete for better jobs by preventing the minimum requirements which are more frequently demanded (mainly in health and education) from becoming barriers excluding those employed in the informal sector. There is also an additional dimension that may make the combination of the welfare package and the productive assistance package more effective. The informal units are characterized by their dual home-enterprise nature and the resources available are allocated to both uses. The reinforcement given to the needs of the home will free resources for productive purposes and in this way a 'virtuous circle' of expansion will be generated.

The legal-institutional package
The illegality of informal activities is the result and not the cause of the way it operates. Owing to this, the actions adopted in this field do not solve the deeper problems that determine the low incomes prevailing in the sector. However, there are measures that can be adopted and that in conjunction with the use of the former packages should contribute to the desired target.

There are three aspects of legality: legally recognized existence, legality in respect of tax liability and employment regulations. These should be analysed in a separate way since they pose different problems and options. They are, however, interrelated since, for example, legal recognition is a prerequisite to regularize both the tax and labour status and is also important for the application of the productive assistance package.

We shall deal first with the aspects related to the attainment of legal status, and here we must distinguish between two situations. The first occurs when illegality has been the result of a prolonged bureaucratic process to meet the multiple legal requirements. This involves such high costs in terms of resources and time that, in fact, it constitutes what has been called the paper wall,[1] which is equivalent to a prohibition to operate legally. There is a need to revise and simplify both norms and procedures in order to facilitate and not impede the progress of informal activities towards legality. The second occurs in cases where there is state regulation protecting the general interests of the community. The municipality must, among other things, watch the flow of traffic in the city, over the environment and over the population's access to a safe and efficient transport system. Because of this, the municipality regulates building permits, trading licences, transport licences for public transport (taxis etc, which is jointly done with the national transport bodies).

Regulation generates benefits that favour some protected groups, or alters the rules of competition with respect to a situation in which there is no intervention. However, economic calculations should also incorporate protecting the common good which can be affected with deregulation. Neither is regulation effective if not observed or if, on the contrary, reality outgrows it as is the case of pedlars, unlicensed taxis or buildings with no permits. The answer is not increased coercion, by for example use of the police force to deal with street vendors. However, the effectiveness of control is variable and the causes of non-compliance are different. In cases such as public transport, control is feasible and desirable. In others, such as housing, it will be necessary to differentiate between housing that does not comply with current legislation for real reasons, as happens in shanty towns, or because of reasons of convenience, as happens with zoning laws in medium- and high-income areas. The latter must most certainly be controlled; the former calls for a revision of the regulations and procedures to prevent unrealistic institutionality from being detrimental to people who are not able to comply. Finally, there is little or nothing to be done with such clearly overflowing sectors as street peddling. It is always feasible to apply transitory measures that alter the situation in a temporary way. However, sooner or later it reverts to its former state because, in fact, its permanent nature is determined by the existence of a structural labour surplus that will only decrease when sufficient productive employment is generated. Until this happens, and since due to the crisis rock-bottom has been reached, the tension produced as a consequence of the action generated when an increased degree of coercion is seen as necessary will be inevitable.

The second aspect of legality has to do with taxes. It is necessary to differentiate between direct taxes which, given the income and profit levels at which the informal sector operates, are not important, and indirect taxes. In particular, among this group we shall refer to value added tax (VAT), of almost universal application in Latin America and whose rates assign greater importance to this than to direct taxes. We shall restrict ourselves to pointing out three aspects that should be taken into account on designing the fiscal policy. The first refers to the need to incorporate VAT exemptions for small commercial transactions. The second has to do with the need for increased control at all levels, not restricting it only to the last links of the chain, but incorporating the intermediate producers. Finally, in connection with the nature of this tax, it will be necessary to advise the informal producers on the mechanics of this type of taxation, in which payments made in previous stages are deductible. If this tax is duly worked out, the net amount to be paid is considerably reduced.

The third aspect has to do with features of the labour regulations. The cost of complying with labour regulations could absorb all the small profit margin generated by the informal activities. It is necessary, therefore, to reconcile the objective of protecting the workers and their families with the need to preserve this source of employment which, precarious as it may be, is preferable to full unemployment.

The answer may be sought in several ways. One part of labour protection is to cover illness or accidents that the worker or family may have, which should be directly dealt with by the welfare system. Another part of the legalization cost goes towards financing a series of national activities which, in the long run, derive in benefits for the workers and which, therefore, are partly financed with the workers' contributions deducted from the payroll. This is the case of, among others, training and housing contributions. Given their incapacity to pay, it seems advisable that the informal enterprises should be exempted from this type of tax.

The problem is therefore restricted to social security and family allowances. Within the former, if we exclude such aspects as labour accidents and health, what remains is job security and pensions. The usual conception of these systems assumes an employment relationship whose nature is that of permanence. The regulation only tries to ensure that this should be so by reducing the chances of insecurity and safeguarding the interests of the workers in case of changes in activity. The informal sector jobs lack these characteristics. On the contrary, insecurity is one of their main features and for this reason, it is necessary to adapt the regulation either to make an exception in such units or part of them (as occurs in practice in several countries) or to introduce special features that may take into account their operational characteristics. Another possibility is to revise the form in which the social security system is funded and that instead of making a contribution on the payroll, such funding should come from another type of taxation, be it production, sales or capital. The effect of this may imply a growth of employment in general, and releasing or, at least, reducing the number of informal sector enterprises from this obligation which may make it possible for them to protect their workers.

Development policies

The previous measures would create necessary conditions for an increase of average income in the informal sector. The final result will depend on the evolution of structural factors which are related to the overall development. There are three main areas which can illustrate the importance of this issue. The first is to increase job opportunities in modern sectors, a key component of a comprehensive strategy, since if employment creation outside the informal sector is not sufficient, there will be an increased surplus labour entering into the informal sector compensating any benefits that might be obtained by better supporting policies. The second factor is the degree of capital concentration, since capital scarcity in the informal sector is not a marginal problem but if massively confronted, would involve a better allocation of capital in the whole economy. The third is income distribution since equity, apart from being an end in itself, could generate more employment given the changes that would imply in the structure of consumption and in foreign exchange requirements. In particular, an increased demand for wage goods would enlarge market possibilities for informal sector production.

Policies in areas like these relate to development and macro economic management and hence open a wide field of discussion which goes beyond the scope of this paper. It would be however sufficient to note that the effects of micro-level interventions in the informal sector will depend on the overall policy framework and a policy for supporting it should, from its own perspective, examine the implications of the different policies set.

A final comment on complexity and intervention

The policy outlined could convey the impression of being a proposal for a multiple programme of state intervention. The issue of intervention is usually discussed with a highly ideological content, where biases of different kinds impede a pragmatic approach to this important question. Our objective in this paper is to search for ways to improve the efficiency of the state's intervention without getting mixed up with the ideological aspects. In the present context, this could imply rationalization of public intervention in some cases, reduce or eliminate it in others, and increase it in a few cases.

It is a multiple programme since there is no single factor which can explain by itself the low income generated in the informal sector. There are several constraints which not only exist at micro level but refer to the overall policy framework. This should not deter those advocating policy support for the informal sector from suggesting better macro policies, since experience has shown that wrong macro economic management cannot be compensated by a successful micro intervention.

The degree of state intervention cannot be determined *a priori*, since it could be discussed at different levels. When state intervention, such as inadequate regulation or heavy bureaucracy, hinders possibilities of expansion procedures might be revised and simplified. This does not ensure that the objectives will be automatically reached and could well require more intervention, not necessarily by the government. A case which clearly illustrates this aspect is credit for the poor producers. Successful ventures in this field have created a new institutionality, since access to the conventional financial outlets is restricted by many constraints. Indeed, an important one is the need for collateral which can be solved by solid guarantees or other means; there are more affecting the whole procedure. Only when the new way has been successfully implemented can it be transferred to other conventional institutions. The several cases available of this kind of intervention are mostly operated on private basis.

Another level of intervention can be found in credit allocation. One criterion generally followed in massive programmes is to avoid getting involved in picking up the winners, while in other, more restricted, programmes a feasibility analysis of potential borrowers is undertaken. There are arguments for and against any of these strategies, simplicity and lower cost being one of the more outstanding pros of the former. Whatever the procedure selected, there will still be need for a clear diagnosis of sectoral interrelationship and macro policies more conducive to informal sector evolutionary growth. This of course, could be located at a different level, since a successful NGO intervening at micro level cannot become responsible for national policies which constitute government's obligation. This role of government cannot be delegated, because a comprehensive approach requires the design and implementation of macro policies which orient sectoral and micro initiatives as well as the decrease of tensions arising from the action that the different social actors take in pursuing their own objectives. In a democratic society this is, perhaps, the main challenge which any government confronts.

Whatever happened to poverty alleviation?

JUDITH TENDLER

Executive summary

Of the Ford Foundation's programmes in Livelihood, Employment, and Income Generation (LEIG), six stand out: their beneficiaries number in the thousands, they have grown into competent organizations, and they have had an influence on policies that affect large numbers of poor people. Though five of the six programmes are carried out by non-government organizations (NGOs), one is part of a public-sector enterprise. The NGOs, moreover, are quite different from the typical NGO in this field: three are trade unions, one is registered as a bank and the other is a private consulting firm. Despite the difference between these programmes and their environments, they share a surprisingly consistent set of traits — traits that are absent from a large number of the LEIG programmes funded by the Foundation and other donors. While the six programmes do not represent the full breadth of the Foundation's grantees, the findings about the traits they share help us to gain a better understanding of programming in the LEIG field.

The common traits are:

1 a narrow focus on a particular trade or sector, at least at the beginning,
2 or a narrow focus on one activity, particularly credit, in an unusually 'minimalist' form,
3 organizational leadership well linked to powerful institutions, and
4 an urban setting, or at least an urban beginning with its economies of agglomeration and the closeness it allows to important centres of power.

The economic activities of the clients supported by the better-performing organizations also shared common traits which, in turn, were different from the activities often promoted under LEIG programmes:

1 clients were already producing what they were receiving assistance for or, if new activities were introduced, these new activities were well known in the region and easily mastered;

JUDITH TENDLER is Professor of Political Economy at the Massachusetts Institute of Technology, Cambridge, Massachusetts, USA. This paper was prepared in March 1987 as a report reviewing the Ford Foundation's programmes on livelihood, employment and income generation. We are indebted to the Ford Foundation for permission to distribute this paper at the Conference and to publish it.

2   the grouping of clients for purposes of assistance did not require collective production or, if it did, managerial and work requirements of the ongoing collective operation were minimal;
3   assisted activities did not face competition from large-scale capital-intensive industries;
4   the assisting organizations did not need to support marketing activities because sales markets were securely in place;
5   supplies of basic inputs were assured;
6   many of the supported products or services had high social value in economic and distributional terms, such as garbage-collection services and the provision of irrigation water; and
7   powerful consumers often played an important role in bringing about support for the assisted producers.

These findings should be of use to the Foundation in designing future LEIG programmes and advising grantee organizations. At the same time, however, the fact that so few of the LEIG grantees reached a significant number of the poor, and that the better-performing NGOs were so different from most, suggests that the search for effective LEIG programmes must be more selective, on the one hand, and be broadened beyond the NGO sector, on the other.

The non-government sector, where much of the Foundation's LEIG programme is concentrated, has a certain structural inability to expand or to have its experiments replicated. This is why the impact of NGO projects is usually quite limited, a disturbing finding for donors interested in having an impact on poverty. The constraints on NGO expansion and replication by others have to do with the fact that:

1   NGO strength and effectiveness often derive from smallness and social homogeneity, which get lost when NGOs try to expand;
2   NGOs see each other and the public sector as competitors for scarce donor funding, rather than as cooperators in a quest to alleviate poverty, which makes it inherently difficult for them to cooperate with each other or imitate each other's successes;
3   foreign funding accounts for a large share of NGO funding in some countries, which places the NGO sector somewhat at odds with the state, thereby blocking the path to replication of NGO experiments by the public sector;
4   though NGO projects may have small budgets in comparison to the public sector, their costs per beneficiary are often high, which means that even their successful projects are not necessarily feasible as models for serving larger populations; and
5   NGOs themselves often do not strive to serve large numbers of clients, nor are they under pressure to do so, which means they are often content to accomplish programmes that work well in a handful of communities.

For various reasons, our better-performing NGOs were free of the above-listed constraints, or they operated in an environment that forced them to be different from the pattern traced above. Part of the task of choosing effective LEIG programmes, then, involves watching for NGOs that have the traits that facilitated expansion, one of which is the ability and willingness to link up to the public sector. The Foundation's efforts to improve its LEIG programming might therefore focus on those NGOs with links to the public sector, or with the capacity and the will to develop them.

Though narrowing the Foundation's requirements for supporting NGOs might increase the probability of greater impacts, it would also make the Foundation's task more difficult by limiting the already scarce supply of NGO programmes from which to choose. A complementary strategy is to broaden the supply of opportunities by opening up the search to include the public sector, whose policies and programmes have major impacts on employment and poverty. The Foundation itself is accustomed to working more with the public sector in its programmes in agriculture, water, and forestry; the Delhi office has in particular tried to broaden its LEIG programming to the public sector. If experiments carried out in the public sector work well, then the institutional infrastructure to expand them is already in place, as well as the political pressure to do so.

Opportunities for experimentation with LEIG programmes in the public sector are greater today than one might think, and are in some ways greater than they were in the 1970s when, ironically, poverty alleviation was in style. This is because;

1 the harsh austerity programmes of the 1980s have made third-world leaders more politically vulnerable than usual, creating a more receptive political environment for targeted programmes, or at least for political gestures toward the poor;
2 the current economic conservatism of economists and policy advisors, with its emphasis on 'getting the prices right', is sympathetic to policy reforms favouring informal-sector producers;
3 the current balance-of-payments and debt problems of third-world countries, leading to restraints on imports, have made it possible for some informal-sector producers to flourish;
4 the current sympathy for decentralization has created a more enabling environment for local-level experimentation in the public sector; and
5 public-sector actors, humbled by the disappointing experience with state-sponsored poverty-alleviating initiatives of the 1970s, have become more receptive to modest approaches, and to learning from the NGO experience.

Finally, government policy and programmes have had major impacts on employment over the last forty years of development assistance — not only through policies on exchange rates, credit subsidies, and agricultural development, but through the ways that powerful ministries spend funds and set standards for the construction of buildings, roads, and waterworks. We know a lot about the adverse effects of government action on the poor, which means that we also have learned a lot about what it takes to turn some of these programmes to their advantage. But the rush of academic and policy interest to issues of debt and macroeconomic policy has left a vacuum in this area, and a dearth of support for public-sector actors who want to do something, have an idea of how to do it, and can mobilize considerable resources. This kind of experimentation is difficult for governments to undertake, even when funding is not a problem, because of the political problems involved in favouring certain geographic areas over others.

LEIG programmes have difficulty achieving impact partly because they are plagued, more than others, with the syndrome of 'reinventing the wheel'. NGOs claim they are pioneering with a new approach when, indeed, they are not; project proposers allege that past efforts have not worked when, indeed, there is not enough of a record to know whether or not this is true; NGOs claim they 'do better than the public sector' at poverty alleviation when, indeed, there is little evidence to support this claim. The LEIG sector, in other words, suffers from a lack of comparative knowledge about what has worked and what has not, in the public as well as the nongovernment domain.

The reasons for the lack of a comparative record on LEIG initiatives have to do with:

1 the 'premature' abandonment by the development field of the state-sponsored poverty alleviation programmes of the 1970s — much like what occurred in the US with respect to the 1960s War on Poverty — and hence of the efforts to evaluate these programmes and modify them accordingly;
2 the change in focus of the field of development economics from institutions to prices and markets, resulting in a decline of interest in, and funding for, comparative evaluation studies of poverty-alleviating initiatives in both the government and nongovernment spheres;
3 the increased macroeconomic problems of third-world countries, starting in the mid-1970s, which replaced the research interest in poverty alleviation with issues of debt, austerity, and macroeconomic policy;
4 a mood of disappointment and disparagement about poverty alleviation among the researchers who did carry out evaluation studies, which resulted in an abundant chronicling of failures and what caused them, but very little understanding of the more successful efforts and their ingredients. If the Foundation's programmes are to strive toward impact, then they will also have to create a record of what has worked and what has not. To do this involves not only the funding of comparative evaluation studies, but also restoring academic prestige, and therefore power, to this particular subject matter.

If the Foundation were to broaden its LEIG initiatives to include the public sector, it could distinguish its programming from that of other donors and move closer to its comparative advantage:

1   though the need for experimentation with programmes capable of reaching large numbers of the poor is recognized by large donors, they cannot support it themselves because of the pressure on them to transfer large amounts of resources in relatively short periods of time;
2   most small donors in the LEIG area, unlike the Foundation, work only in the nongovernment sector and do not have the public-sector contacts that the Foundation has;
3   few donors who work in the public sector are well connected as the Foundation to the non-government sector as well, which puts the Foundation in the unique position of linking the NGO experience to the public sector;
4   among donors, the Foundation is unusual in spanning the research sector as well as that of government and nongovernment, which means that it can play an important role in funding the badly needed comparative studies on LEIG initiatives and, just as important, in making sure the results of these studies are used to guide programming by governments and NGOs.

The good performers

Out of the various organizations I reviewed, six stand out: the Grameen Bank of Bangladesh, the Self-Employed Women's Association (SEWA) of Ahmedabad, the Working Women's Forum (WWF) of Madras, the Annapurna Caterers of Bombay, the women's dairying project of the Dairy Development Federation of the Indian state of Andhra Pradesh (APDDCFL), and Environmental Quality International (EQI) working in conjunction with the association of Zabaleen garbage collectors in Cairo. In addition, I was impressed with three of the economic activities assisted by two other organizations — the landless pump groups of Proshika in Bangladesh, and the collectively-owned rental houses and standpipes of the Undugu Society's women's groups in Nairobi. When I refer to 'programmes', I am including these last three activities; 'organizations' refer to the six I name above.

Four of the organizations I discuss are in India, one in Bangladesh, and one in Egypt. They stand out because they are reaching an unusually large number of poor people (Grameen Bank 160,000 borrowers, WWF 38,000 members, SEWA 15,000 members, Annapurna 8,000 members, APDDCFL women dairying project 5,000 women members) or are indirectly affecting large numbers through their impacts on policy and institutions. Or they stand out as 'successful' organizations in that the Foundation and other donors have found them to be honest, strong, self-criticizing and highly capable.

The six organizations differ markedly from each other, as well as being different in form and origin from most nongovernmental organizations working in the LEIG area. One is in the public sector (APDDCFL), while the rest are in the nongovernmental sector. Two arose out of the women's wings of Indian trade union organizations (SEWA, Annapurna) and another out of political-party organizing in India (WWF). These latter three are organized as trade unions, while Grameen Bank is registered as a financial institution and EQI is a private consulting firm. Four of the six programmes work only with women (SEWA, APDDCFL, WWF, Annapurna. The majority of APDDCFL members are men, but the Foundation-funded programme works only with women). Four work mainly in cities or started out there, while only two work predominantly in rural areas (Grameen Bank, APDDCFL). Though all of these programmes provide credit, each has a quite different mix of credit, business and technical assistance, organizing for group production or marketing or input-supply, social services like death-benefit and pension funds, or strong advocacy for clients vis-a-vis public institutions, political authorities and monopolistic buyers and sellers.

What is remarkable about this set of cases is that, despite their diversity and their location in very different countries, they share a common set of characteristics or traits. To many readers, this list of traits and their association with good performance may seem obvious. But many LEIG programmes and organizations, including those supported by the Foundation, have exactly the opposite traits. In addition, we tend not to notice these traits when looking at any of these organizations in particular, because their rhetoric obscures the traits, because some of the traits go back to times when these organizations were quite different than they are today, and because we usually do case studies of individual organizations rather than comparative studies across them.

For reasons akin to Hirschman's statement[1] that there are no successful projects, only those that have less problems than others, I purposely do not refer to this set of better-performing programmes as 'successes.' They are also riddled with problems, mistakes, and false starts. Some of them are having a difficult time expanding beyond their first victories (Annapurna, in moving from individual credit to collective food catering). Some of them seem to be diversifying too fast and into more difficult activities (Grameen Bank into duck-raising and venture capital, EQI and the Zabaleen into collectively-owned garbage-collection services, Proshika into fish ponds). Only time will tell whether they will do well or poorly at these more difficult tasks. Some of these organizations, finally, seem to be expanding into new activities before they have exhausted the potential for reaching larger numbers of people by continuing to do what they are good at. This premature diversification is a common pattern, caused by the greater lure to expanding organizations of complex programmes over simpler ones and by the very success of the initial programme, which attracts swarms of donors, each with its own project agenda.

At least one of our organizations seems stuck at the level of serving a limited number of beneficiaries with an increasing array of services, some of which it will do better at than others — the EQI in Cairo, and its work with the Zabaleen Association in a garbage-collecting settlement of 1,000 households. (There are actually six garbage-collecting Zabaleen communities in Cairo. EQI says it plans to move into these other communities, but its hands already seem quite full with the array of services it has been setting up for the one community.) Because of its single-community focus, EQI may end up standing out more as an impressive organization than as an instrument for alleviating poverty in Cairo. In fact, the significance of the Zabaleen programme as a model of LEIG activity may have been somewhat exaggerated because of the fascinating quality of the Zabaleen microeconomy and because of the winning nature of the EQI staff—urban, Western-educated, English-speaking, skilled, and committed. I nevertheless included the Zabaleen project, albeit with some ambivalence, because EQI possessed many of the same traits as the other better-performing organizations.

The organizations or programmes left out of this list should not be considered failures. They were just reaching far fewer persons and having much less of an impact on thinking in professional circles and the public sector (Tototo, Partnership for Productivity, Undugu, Manipal Industrial Trust). In other cases, the programmes were too new to allow definitive comment (KWFT, ISSC, PRADAN, Euro Action Acord, MYRADA, the Indian sericulture projects, the new Foundation-funded womens' programmes of PfP and Undugu). I nevertheless had misgivings about these latter programmes; they seemed to be doing too much too soon, taking on too difficult tasks, spreading themselves too thinly, or expanding large amounts per beneficiary.

Bound by the trade

All the better-performing organizations started out with a narrow focus and some continue that way to this day. They concentrated on a particular task (credit), to be discussed in the next section, or on a particular trade, sector, or income-earning activity (eg garbage collectors, food preparers, dairy producers, vegetable vendors, landless groups owning tubewells). An evaluation of the Foundation's minority business programmes in the US found that one of the most successful programmes was sector-specific, focused on cable radio and television.[2]

The narrow sectoral focus of these organizations forced them to tailor their interventions to the needs of that particular sector or trade. This meant that they proceeded by doing careful studies of a sector, after which they would identify possible points of intervention. In this process, they gained a highly grounded understanding of one sector—production processes, sources of supply, product markets, industry structure. The meticulous sectoral studies of these organizations, which informed so much of their thinking, were carried out by bright young generalist staffs. Though they were usually untrained in social science research, their previous work experience in the field combined with strong intelligence, passionate dedication and street 'smarts', helped them to produce remarkably complete pictures of the trades they were studying. Because of the high 'labour-intensity' of the work required to map the structure of these trades, a more sophisticated research effort would probably have been much more costly.

The trade-by-trade way of proceeding contrasts sharply with the many LEIG programmes that work across various trades and even try to introduce new ones. These 'generalist' organizations get less involved in the details of a particular trade, trying as they do to provide nonspecific income-earning assistance. The trade-specific programmes were no less concerned about the broader issues of poverty than were the generalist ones — namely, denial of access to public services, lack of information, discrimination, exploitation and poor health. Indeed, many of the trade organizations were passionately driven by these larger social issues and added programmes that dealt with them later on, but they anchored their work around the economics of a trade, or a succession of trades.

In contrast to our set of better-performing organizations, many LEIG programmes take a multi-task approach to their work. This broader approach is based on widely held notions of what is 'needed' for development to take place, or of how services are 'supposed' to be supplied. Though the broader vision has substantial truth — communities *do* lack various services — it often does not work well in practice, because it is too demanding on the organization. The importance ascribed here to learning about a trade, then, does not reflect a judgement that economics is more important than social, political, and service issues, but rather that many LEIG interventions fail because they are too ambitious. They represent unrealistic assessments of what organizations can do and of how people can improve their incomes. Out of a deep concern about poverty, they cast their nets too widely. Organizations and leaders with social welfare and service backgrounds, in particular, need a way of proceeding that teaches them about economic reality, and forces them to be guided by it.

Learning about a trade is a process that leads organizations to propose small changes in the way existing things work — institutions, market structures, production processes. One tries to identify bottlenecks, and then work on them one at a time. With women vegetable vendors, for example, SEWA learned that police harassment was a major problem, leading to frequent losses in income. It therefore negotiated for the vendors with municipal authorities, and only after some results were achieved, did it move on to the next problem. Similar processes of inquiry led to EQI's decision to provide credit to garbage collectors for simple re-cycling equipment, to Annapurna's decision to provide working-capital credit to women providers of meals to textile workers, and to the Delhi office's decision to support the organization of women-only dairy coops within an already functioning system of federated dairy coops. All these actions were carried out by organizations in a continual process of study, identification, and intervention. Their way of thinking was iterative and incremental.

Many LEIG organizations do not see their actions as so constrained by existing economic systems. Indeed, they see existing ways of doing things as keeping their clients down and they want to help liberate them from these structures — introducing new economic activities into communities, having people produce goods collectively who previously worked individually, providing new sources of credit independently of existing financial institutions. Though these attempts are admirable, they usually do not produce the same quality of results as the less ambitious way of proceeding.

This emphasis on the 'marginal' qualities of the interventions carried out by the trade-bound organizations is consistent with the findings of two other comparative studies of projects — one of a set of technical assistance projects in sub-Saharan Africa,[3] and another of a set of community-development projects in East Africa.[4] The most successful projects, according to these studies, were those that supplied a 'missing component' to a set of activities that was already in place. Though the projects studied were not all trade-specific, what they shared with our set of programmes was the incremental nature of their interventions. The trade orientation, then, is not the only way to come up with powerful incremental interventions. The narrow focus on credit, in the 'minimalist' form discussed below, also represents a incremental approach: credit without any complementary services was the missing ingredient provided in support of a system of economic activities and financial institutions that was already in place.

The trade-bound organizations bargain with authorities for their clients as a class, whereas the generalist organizations negotiate on behalf of individual clients or small groups of them (eg SEWA *vs* Kenya Women's Finance Trust). These struggles for trade-wide concessions and the victories they sometimes lead to constitute one of the important potential impacts of such programmes, particularly when they are carried out by small organizations that may not be able to directly serve a large number of clients. Just as important, trade-wide bargaining raises these matters to powerful authorities in the form of social *issues*, whereas individual cases brought by NGOs to the authorities are seen by the latter as the granting of favours in particular cases. Given the strength of the trade orientation, it is not surprising that three out of our five better-performing NGOs were trade unions (SEWA, WWF, Annapurna), almost the only trade-union grantees in the Foundation's entire LEIG programme. Trade unions actually define their principal task in terms of the struggle to obtain concessions from powerful institutions, whereas most other NGOs define their task as providing a service, in the course of which they may or may not need to take on the authorities for the cause of their clients.

Trade-based struggle, of course, is not limited to trade unions. EQI of Cairo, a private consulting firm, engaged in an ongoing struggle with the governorate of Cairo for concessions to garbage collectors. The Foundation's Delhi office struggled with the Indian dairy parastatal for a long period of time to gain recognition for women producers. The Delhi office, in fact, proceeded in a manner quite similar to SEWA: it identified eight production systems in which women were important, commissioned studies on how these systems worked, and then struggled with the authorities who held power over each of these systems for concessions and action programmes.

The trade-bound approach defines LEIG problems in a way that attracts powerful technocrats and government agencies. That the Zabaleen microeconomy was built on garbage collection and disposal made its problems interesting to a small engineering elite in a prestigious consulting firm, specialized in solid-waste and other urban infrastructure projects. The Delhi office defined its LEIG women's programme in terms of eight production systems all of which were located in 'ministries of importance' and had 'significant Seventh Plan outlays.' That the Grameen Bank defined its task in terms similar to commercial banking practice, as explained below, attracted professionals from the country's Central Bank, who took leave from their jobs to work with Grameen.

Getting prestigious professionals to see LEIG programmes as professionally challenging is one way to get around the much-bemoaned problem of technocrats and their institutions showing little professional interest in the poor. Attracting skilled persons by defining a project in trade-bound terms also bears on a staffing problem discussed perennially in the LEIG sector — that of insufficient salaries to attract skilled professionals, coupled with the problem of training committed generalists in 'hard' skills, a problem to which the Foundation and other LEIG donors have devoted considerable attention. Attracting technocrats with trade-based tasks, in other words, is a way of getting around the 'skills *vs* commitment' formulation of the LEIG staffing problem: the technocrats in our cases turned out to have more commitment than anyone thought, when presented with the problem in professionally interesting terms and, of course, they already had the right skills.

The trade-bound view of LEIG problems has its limitations. An organization may end up serving virtually the whole trade and still be working with only a small number of people — the case of the EQI and the Zabaleen garbage collectors being the most obvious one. EQI's work with the Zabaleen Association involves only 1,000 garbage-collecting households in one settlement, which does not even represent all the Zabaleen garbage collectors, who live in six different settlements of Cairo. The trade orientation may also leave an organization 'stuck,' once it reaches every member of the trade. The Annapurna caterers is a case in point: after providing credit to 8,000 members of this trade in Bombay, Annapurna had a difficult time figuring out what to do next that would be as easy and as effective. SEWA, in contrast, escaped the limiting problem of the trade approach by taking on one trade after another — from vegetable vendors to foodhawkers to quilt makers to fish marketwomen. It could therefore benefit from the discipline and power of the trade orientation, while at the same time not being confined by the number of persons in any particular trade.

Minimalism in credit

Credit turned out to be another way by which the better-performing organizations were able to approach their task narrowly. Four of our programmes started out by providing *only* credit. Even though they later moved into other activities, credit continues to be a central part of their programme. (Two of these credit organizations, SEWA and Annapurna, also followed the trade approach.) Though other LEIG programmes customarily provide credit — in Kenya, for example, Tototo Industries, Kenya Women's Finance Trust, and Partnership for Productivity — the approach of our four organizations to credit was quite different.

First, all four organizations started out only as credit brokers, providing their clients with access to existing financial institutions, rather than lending from their own funds.

Second, they all required savings as a prerequisite to borrowing.

Third, these organizations financed activities mainly in the trade and commerce sector, as opposed to manufacturing and services, sectors in which economic and employment payoffs may promise to be higher but where risks to lenders are also higher.

Fourth, these organizations all provided a kind of stripped-down or 'minimalist' credit, which entailed little or no evaluation of the merits of investments for which applicants wished to borrow and no technical or business extension. The burden of the selection process was shifted from the credit entity to peer groups of borrowers themselves. Though groups might give opinions on a member's purpose for borrowing, their ultimate acceptance of the member was based on an assessment of that person's likelihood of repaying, regardless of the viability of the proposed project. Though group members were not necessarily jointly liable for each other's loans, the group could not receive subsequent loans until all were paid up. This process of decisionmaking about credit, though decentralized, was not 'participatory': borrowers were not included in decisionmaking councils of the credit-proving organizations, they had no say in setting credit policy or in declaring and prosecuting delinquency, and the credit agency itself made the ultimate decision as to who could borrow.

Fifth, though our four credit organizations now provide some social and other services in addition to plain credit, they started first with credit. This is in distinct contrast to many LEIG grantees, who are trying with difficulty to make the opposite transition — from social and welfare services to the income-generating ones. Although our four organizations shared this common set of credit characteristics, they were quite different in other ways — one a bank (Grameen), the second a women's trade union working with various trades (SEWA), the third a women's trade union working with only one trade (Annapurna), and the fourth a trade union working on a neighbourhood rather than a trade basis (WWF).

Many LEIG credit programmes, unlike our four, do not start out by trying to link their clients up with existing banks. Typically, they get funding from donors to start their own credit operation (eg Tototo, Undugu, Partnership for Productivity). This gives them little chance to learn the business through a division of labour between themselves and the established banks — the banks taking care of the money, and the NGOs the processing of applications. Though three of our four organizations ultimately did create their own banks (SEWA, WWF, and Grameen), this occurred only after a long tutelage of doing no more than working as brokers between their clients and an established bank.

Many credit-providing NGOs would view the minimalist credit provided by our four organizations as 'insufficient'. Businesses, they say, need to learn how to keep books, improve their production techniques, learn about inventory, and find better markets. Credit, according to this assessment of need, must therefore be accompanied by assistance with these other matters, and credit applicants should be helped to evaluate the financial viability of their proposed use of loan funds. Though this view seems perfectly reasonable, it also leads to higher unit costs of lending and greater demands for organizational sophistication. Evaluation studies, moreover, have cast doubt on how much this assistance actually leads to increased incomes.[5,6,7,8] Because of the higher costs and greater encumbrances, 'complete' credit is almost never found in programmes that have succeeded in reaching large numbers of small borrowers. Thus it is no surprise to learn that the Grameen Bank, with many more clients than any of the Foundation's LEIG grantees, insisted most on the minimalist form of credit, and diversified least into noncredit activities.

The link to performance
Why was this particular approach to credit, and the way in which it evolved, so central to the better performance of these four organizations? That these organizations spent a long apprenticeship providing access to existing credit, rather than lending their own funds, made the task easier. It divided credit into loan processing and banking, allowing the new organizations to take on and master the task of processing first, before having to go into the more difficult task of banking. That a banking infrastructure already existed was crucial to this sequence, an advantage of credit that we tend to forget because of our ire at banks for the way they exclude the poor. Other LEIG activities, like business and technical extension or the formation of group production or marketing ventures, do not have such well established institutions to which they can turn for structure, advice, and sharing of the task.

Minimalist credit was also easy because clients borrowed more for trade than manufacturing. As indicated by bank practice all over the world, lending to trade and retail establishments is less risky than to manufacturers, partly because repayments can be made with greater frequency and within a shorter time period. Though some researchers believe that lending to manufacturers will have greater employment and income impacts than to traders, trade credit may nevertheless be easier on fledgling banking operations.

Minimalist credit was also easy because the repayment rate constitutes a clear and concise measure of good performance. With such an indicator, performance can be ascertained by any good evaluator who spends a few hours at a bank office, and the credit agencies themselves can keep close tabs on how they are doing. Performance in other LEIG activities, including credit with business and technical extension, is more difficult to measure and can be verified only over a longer term. That minimalist credit provides such a conspicuous performance measure means that organizations working this way are quite exposed to outside scrutiny; in this sense, credit is a hard taskmaster, as well as being 'easy'. Given that other LEIG activities lack this clear and accessible indicator of performance, mediocre performance will elicit less censure from the outside, as well as less concern within the organization itself. In lieu of clear performance indicators, organizations tend to look at commitment, honesty, and hard work as proxies for performance. Mediocrity gets tolerated more, simply because the results of what these organizations do are more difficult to see.

Small-loan programmes usually run high costs per dollar spent because of the time and skills required to evaluate numerous small applications Banks resist small loans because of these high unit costs, and because of the impossibility of making character judgements about applicants with whom they are not familiar. Minimalist credit reduces these problems by shifting much of the cost of processing loan applications from the bank to borrower groups, an important advantage of the group mechanism used by all four organizations. Groups base their decisions as to who gets loans on character judgements about the borrowers, rather than on an evaluation of their finances and business proposals. Surprisingly enough, this system of judging credit applications seems to work well, as attested to not only by repayment rates in these four cases but by studies of other programmes of this nature.[6,7] By reducing markedly the credit agency's need for staff trained in financial analysis, the group selection mechanism also reduces the problem of finding skilled professionals to do such work and of paying them adequately.

Credit institutions that require savings prior to borrowing, like our four, usually point to the wholesome impact on the borrower who, it is said, needs to learn the discipline of giving in order to receive, and of repaying regularly. More generally, LEIG donors have been increasingly asking their grantees to require some payment from clients in exchange for the services they receive — credit, technical assistance, or other services meant to increase income. Requiring savings or charges for services, the argument goes, not only helps the client to learn the behaviour required in a modern economy, but also helps to set the service-providing organization on the path towards financial self-sufficiency.

Less commented on is the fact that when clients have to save in order to borrow, the credit organization will have to first prove that it is a trustworthy place to put one's savings. And if the organization performs poorly once it possesses the savings, clients can withdraw their deposits overnight and bring the organization to ruin. Even if depositors are not allowed to withdraw savings, as is often the case with savings required for borrowing, their financial stake in the organization gives them the right to make trouble if they are concerned; and organizing them into groups gives them a social form in which to make more effective trouble. Charges for services make an organization even more vulnerable to outside pressure to perform: if clients are dissatisfied, they need not even protest and can simply refrain from buying the service.

Though LEIG organizations often argue against charging for services on the grounds that the poor cannot afford to pay, they also fear that they will lose their clientele if they start charging. The organization that agrees to charge for services or require prior savings, then, has considerable confidence in the quality and worth of what it provides. Put in another way, charges and savings requirements can force an organization to be more responsive to the poor and their definition of their needs, than a situation of no charges, justified out of sympathy for the plight of the poor. Again, this is a somewhat different approach to the issue of finding committed staffs: in this case, the structure of the situation helps make the organization responsive, rather than just the hiring of committed staff.

Required saving, in sum, introduces external pressures to perform into the worlds of fledgling credit organizations. Donors usually deal with the matter of organizational performance by a combination of helping (funds for training, budgets for hiring capable staff) and monitoring (by donors themselves, by requiring and funding audits, by funding monitoring and evaluation operations). All of these approaches, though standard good practice, are costly and timeconsuming, and often do not yield the desired results. Some of this concern might be invested, instead, in finding tasks and structures that produce these pressures themselves, without the expenditure of time and funds. Forced savings and charges are one way of providing that external pressure. The easily measurable repayment rate of minimalist credit is another.

Leaders, links, and upscaling
All the leaders of our five nongovernmental organizations were strong and driven individuals who, through class or previous work experience, had links to important political figures and powerful institutions in the public and private sector. All five, moreover, had founded their organizations. Though donors look up to these strong and charismatic leaders, they perpetually worry about whether the organization could survive their loss. Will the leaders learn to delegate? Can they build strength in their managerial staff?

In a study of successful development programmes in the public sector, Paul also found the same dynamic person who had led the programme from the organization's founding to the present moment.[9] Paul's reason for emphasizing this continuity was to say that the person who initiated the project as an experiment was the same one who carried out the transition to a nation-wide programme. It was the energy of the single founding leader that drove the successful expansion of the programme, in other words, and not just the force of a particular organizational model.

A common argument for funding small NGO projects is that they are experiments which, once the bugs are worked out, will be replicated. But Paul's findings, along with mine, suggest that unless the experiment is replicated by the original experimentor, it may not grow beyond its original size, no matter how well it works. And if replication actually takes place, the leader of the pilot project is likely to have had large ambitions, along with the status and connections to carry them out.

These are the kinds of visions, status, and connections that our set of NGO leaders had. Two of the leaders were technocrats with PhD degrees from the US — a sanitary engineer (EQI) and an economist (Grameen Bank). By virtue of their class, foreign educations, and professional specializations, they were members of a small elite class. Two more of our leaders came out of a long-established trade-union movement (SEWA, Annapurna). Another, also well-connected, came from a long experience with political organizing in the neighbourhoods of Madras for India's dominant Congress (I) party (WWF). The trade-union and party-organizing backgrounds accustomed these leaders to thinking in terms of reaching large numbers of persons, and familiarized them with powerful institutions — big management, and state government officials who mediated labour-management disputes.

That our leaders had these particular backgrounds should come as no surprise, given the success of their ventures. But many NGO leaders do not fit this image, and we ourselves usually do not think of LEIG leadership as coming from the ranks of technocrats or social elites. Many NGO leaders shy away from people in power. They may prefer to work in remote areas, where their programmes can operate undisturbed by powerful institutions. And they often wear their distance from the holders of power with pride, as a kind of badge of commitment to their clients. They tend to describe themselves as 'against' the system, not part of it. This kind of remoteness is not necessarily bad. Indeed a few studies have pointed to geographical remoteness from powerful institutions as an element of success.[3,9] But our leaders were anything but distant from power, even though they may have liked to portray themselves that way.

The urban edge

Closeness to power among our set of organizations was spatial as well as social. Four of our nongovernmental organizations got their start in cities, and most continue to have their greatest number of clients there. (I explain the exception, Grameen Bank, below.) This is a somewhat surprising finding, given that the Foundation emphasizes rural rather than urban poverty in its LEIG programming. The Foundation's rural emphasis is consistent with that of many researchers and donors, who believe that rural poverty is a more serious and widespread problem than urban poverty and that the agricultural aeconomies of rural areas provide more possibilities for off-farm employment than do urban economies. Nevertheless, there is something about the dynamics of LEIG organizations in the urban setting that sets them apart from the rural programmes. I suggest four explanations for this difference.

First, the four cities where these organizations work are large and important. Bombay, Ahmedabad, and Madras are capitals of their respective states, as well as thriving economic centres; Cairo, aside from being the national capital, is a city of 13 m people. Powerful elites live and work in these cities, and powerful institutions are seated there — bank headquarters, municipal authorities, politicians, and government parastatals, ministries, and departments. The impact achieved by our organizations resulted, in part, from the influence they had with these holders of power and the concessions won from them. Rural-based programmes provide much less of a chance to have an influence on power.

Second, and related, programmes for the poor usually have to win over local elites in each community where they work — or, at least, gain their acquiescence. Since elite opposition often undermines LEIG projects at the community level, the investment in gaining elite tolerance or support is crucial to the success of these programmes. Having influence with elites arises, in part, from a lifetime of living with them. This kind of familiarity is difficult for the leaders of organizations operating in rural areas, because there is no one geographically concentrated set of elites or powerful institutions that controls decisions affecting thousands of people. As one of our leaders said, in commenting on the difficulty of expanding her urban programme into rural areas, 'I couldn't just call up somebody powerful and say he should help out. There were so many of them! I didn't know them and they didn't know me'.

Third, the trade- or sector-bound approach discussed above works better in urban areas. Because the rural poor live more dispersed and change from one income-earning activity to another with changes in the agricultural cycle, it is more difficult to find large numbers in one place who work at a single trade, let alone at the same trade throughout the year. (This point has also been made by Chen [10]). LEIG organizations in rural areas, then, find fewer opportunities to work with only one trade or sector.

Fourth, and implicit in these last three points, there are agglomeration economies in serving dense populations. In cities, one can see more clients per staff trip away from the office, one can use public transport instead of having to invest in vehicles, one can spend less on the operation of one's own vehicle, and one's service is less vulnerable to problems of vehicle breakdown, shortage of spare parts, and lack of budget monies for fuel and maintenance. All of the latter are central problems in rural service programmes.

The lesson of our finding that urban programmes have a certain edge over rural programmes is not that we should fund more urban projects, though that might be a perfectly logical conclusion. Rather, the urban stories help us to see that the path to impact in the LEIG area often lies in the influence wielded over powerful persons and institutions. The experience should encourage us to search for rural programme strategies that imitate these urban configurations, or compensate for the lack of them. Though the suggestion may seem fanciful, the Grameen Bank provides us with a quite realistic illustration. Grameen Bank was the only rural exception to the urban siting of our better-performing programmes. And Grameen had by far the largest number of beneficiaries of them all, so its status as an exception requires explanation.

The Grameen exception

Grameen Bank operates in a country with one of the highest rural population densities in the world, thus making it possible to reach a larger number of clients per unit space than is typical for a rural programme. The minimalist credit practised by Grameen, moreover, requires less understanding of the economy and social structure of each particular locality where the bank has a branch, and less adaptation to local forms of production — in contrast to more complete credit services and other LEIG activities. Grameen's leader felt strongly about providing a 'franchisable' service that, once perfected, could be applied anywhere throughout the nation, regardless of local conditions. Minimalist credit can accommodate this kind of vision. Just as important, it took a leader who wanted to make his mark in large numbers to be attracted to this particular form of the credit task, and to resist the blandishments to embellish it. This vision contrasts sharply with that of many other NGO leaders, who see their task as doing a good job at providing various services to ten, twenty, or thirty communities.

Grameen Bank provided a service to landless labourers that, in contrast to our experience with many other such programmes, pleased local elites. Local landowners did not mind that Grameen organized their labour force into credit groups, thereby freeing the labourers from dependence on landowners for credit. Indeed, some landowners even said they *preferred* being relieved of these credit obligations to their labourers, and that this new and independent source of credit made for a more 'stable' work force in the region. This reaction, by the way, is just the opposite of that predicted by the economic literature on interlinked contracts for labour, land and credit.

We tend to notice the importance of elites only when they oppose projects, because so many LEIG projects have been undone by such opposition. But we can see from the Grameen case that it is also important to understand the circumstances under which elites are not opposed. One of the lessons of the Grameen exception to our urban cases, then, is that the rural handicap can be reduced if activities are supported that are to the liking of elites. We may not know in advance, of course, how elites will react — as illustrated by the Grameen Bank and the elite reactions to it, different from what one would expect from experience and the literature. This is why experimentation is so important: it can show us, as well as the elites, that things may not be as bad in reality as we think they will be.

As distinct from many rural projects, finally, the Grameen Bank was linked from the start to a major urban centre of national power — the Bangladesh Central Bank. Though Grameen is now an independent financial institution, it found its first institutional home in the Central Bank, as an experimental project. When Grameen became its own bank, the link to the Central Bank continued informally, partly through the three Central Bank professionals who went on extended leave to take managerial positions with Grameen. As in the case of many organizations with links to power, one tends not to notice them, because they are often buried in the early history of the organization, and because leaders of these organizations like to stress their independence from the establishment, and not their connections to it.

Traits of the trade
The traits shared in common by our set of organizations suggests that their performance was influenced by the kinds of economic activities their clients engaged in. Something outside the control of these organizations, in other words, helped them perform well. This 'something' falls into seven categories.

First, the clients of these organizations were already producing what they were receiving assistance for (dairying, garbage-collecting, food hawking, food preparation, cigarette rolling). Or, in the case of activities newly undertaken with the organization's assistance, these were well known in the area and easily mastered (installation and operation of shallow tubewells, water standpipes and rental houses).

Second, though clients always belonged to groups, some formed by the assisting organization (credit groups, dairy coops, garbage collectors' association), the group did not necessarily engage in collective ownership or work. In the cases where the assisting organization did introduce collective ownership (landless pumps, group standpipes, rental housing), ongoing work requirements after the initial installation period were minimal.

Third, the assisted activities did not show economies of scale, so that they did not face competition from large-scale capital-intensive industries (dairying, garbage-collecting, shallow tubewell irrigation *vs* handloom silk production, cigarette-making, garment manufacture).

Fourth, supplies of basic inputs were assured (garbage for garbage collecting, water for shallow tubewells, produce for vending, fodder for cattle, though fodder supply was sometimes a significant problem for the poor).

Fifth, sales markets were already securely in place, though they were not necessarily free markets (dairy products, garbage collection services, water for irrigation).

Sixth, many of the products or services supported were in scarce supply and had high social value in economic and distributional terms (irrigation water, garbage collection services, pork and milk supply, standpipe water and rental housing in squatter settlements). This meant that consumers also benefited from the expansion in supply of these activities, in addition to the providers assisted by the project. The high social value or 'externalities' of assisting these providers is reflected in the fact that some of these services are traditionally provided or subsidized by the public sector (garbage collection, irrigation water, potable water, low-cost housing). Indeed, for most of these services, there had been a history in all four countries of public sector activity that was inadequate. The activity under our programmes, then, represented a kind of *ad hoc* 'privatization' or decentralization of these services, though nobody portrayed things in these terms.

Seventh, powerful consumers of these services themselves often played a role in bringing about support for the project (eg the Indian dairy parastatal as the purchaser of milk supplied by women producers). Or, these consumers had enough self-interest in seeing supplies increase that they did not stand in the way of organizing for that purpose among the poor (eg the land-owning employers as purchasers of irrigation water from groups formed by their landless employees).

Though the last two findings of these seven came as a surprise to me, the rest seem to reflect good common sense. Yet many LEIG programmes choose economic activities and ways to support them that do not reflect this sense. Many programmes, for example, are more ambitious with respect to their clients' income-earning activities. They may try to introduce activities that are new (Tototo and crafts production) or that generate opposition from elites (Proshika and fish ponds). In choosing certain sectors, moreover, LEIG programmes often take on a difficult battle against scale economies in the sector which, though perhaps created by past government subsidization of large producers, have already led to large-scale, capital-intensive, and competitive production (handloomed textiles, leather footwear, garments, cigarettes). In our set of activities, there were no scale economies constantly threatening to overwhelm the assisted activities, and against which a constant and often losing battle had to be fought.

Many LEIG programmes promote collective enterprises (eg Grameen Bank's mustard oil mills, EQI's composting plant and garbage-collectors' firm, PRADAN's community-enterprise programme) because they believe that the poor are locked into low-income occupations and that collective production, often of something new, is the only way to get them out. The designers of these programmes often look for their inspiration to community traditions of cooperation around certain tasks — the building of a school, a road, a church, or a soccer field. In contrast to these latter endeavours, a large number of the collective production ventures promoted by assisting organizations do not succeed, or do so only at a high cost and with benefits to only a small number of participants. One reason for these disappointing outcomes is that the traditional collective tasks named above have a beginning and an end, in contrast to the work requirements of LEIG-promoted collective production, which is usually of an *ongoing* nature.

Collective work obligations often lead to disputes among cooperators about their relative work loads, and about who is working hard and who is slacking off. Also, collective work requirements fall hardest on the poor, since they are least able to take time away from their current employment; and most collective ventures do not begin to pay a return for a long period of time, let alone enough of a return to live on exclusively. The work requirements of our collectively-owned activities, in contrast, were more like those of traditional collective patterns. They involved a discrete task at the start, with a minimal amount of sustained work afterwards — the installation of a tubewell and the digging of canals, the installation of a standpipe and the construction of rental housing.

LEIG organizations usually recognize the importance of markets, but they often approach the matter by trying to set up their *own* marketing outlets (Tototo, Mahila Vikas Sangh). Since nonprofit organizations have no particular comparative advantage in marketing, which itself often involves economies of scale, these attempts at creating marketing outlets frequently fail; or, at best, they benefit a limited number of producers. In our cases, in contrast, the market was already in place, even when clients were producing the service for the first time (irrigation water in rainfed rice-growing areas, potable water and rental housing in squatter settlements).

Problems of input supply also tend to be overlooked in LEIG programmes, attention usually being riveted on production processes and sales markets. In our set of activities, the supply of the major input was unusually secure (water for standpipes, housing stock for rental, garbage for garbage collection), or variations in supply were predictable (irrigation water for tubewells, fodder for dairy cattle).

We tend to think of consumers as atomistic and faceless and, therefore, of little relevance to our attempts to increase production, just so long as their presence is attested to by a given volume of sales. When we do think of consumers as powerful, we view them as persons or institutions from whose clutches we want to help our clients get away, a classic example being the apparel manufacturer who subcontracts out to women working at home at piecework rates (SEWA). In our cases, however, powerful consumers played an important role in *supporting* improved producer conditions, out of their interest in seeing supplies increase (the dairy parastatal's support for women dairy coops and for a training institute in rural management, the Cairo governorate's holding back from banishing the Zabaleen donkey carts, the Bangladesh rice farmer's donation of a small plot of land for installation of the tubewell owned by a group of his landless employees).

When powerful consumers did not play an active role in supporting increased supply, they at least did not oppose programme activities. As noted above, Grameen Bank did not get much trouble from local landowners for organizing landless labourers, partly because these elites felt that there was something in it for them. Powerful consumers or parties interested in seeing increased supply of an input, then, can be forces of support, just as much as they can oppose or exploit.

What kind of lesson?
What is the lesson to be learned from the traits shared by these better-performing programmes? I should say, first, what the lesson is *not*. Most importantly, I do not see these traits as a checklist for prerequisites or proscriptions. Credit worked well in its minimalist form, for example, because it had certain attributes that made it both 'easy' and demanding of good performance. The lesson of the story is not that LEIG programmes should do credit rather than other things, but that some tasks and their environments are easier than others and, at the same time, more demanding of good performance. Programmes should be designed with this in mind, with tasks being chosen or avoided for reasons of this nature.

Though this statement about lessons seems obvious, we tend to design programmes in terms of what we think is needed for the clients (increased skills, access to capital, reduced dependence), rather than in terms of what is needed for the organization to be able to function passably well. We often act, in other words, as if the problem is only to figure out how to increase people's incomes, but that is only the half of it. Organizations are often just as handicapped as the poor in trying to do what they want.

Rather than being prescriptive, this list of traits is both cautionary and constructive. It is cautionary in that it shows that some of our standard approaches to programme strategy and organizational design do not work well, and explains why. Providing business assistance to poor borrowers, for example, has become an unquestioned part of the way many planners think about microenterprise credit. But our study shows the better-performing credit programmes as consistently *not* providing business assistance. The lesson is not that we should never provide business assistance, which is to exchange one set of rules for another, but that we should pay attention to what works well and what doesn't, that we should be constantly questioning our accustomed ways of doing things, and that doing less often works better than doing more. Similarly, for organizations that want to promote collective enterprises, or take on marketing, or promote new production processes, this list should be interpreted as cautionary, not proscriptive. Some of our better-performing organizations did just these things, after all, though only after travelling along the narrow path described. Finally, I consider this list as constructive because it points to opportunities where LEIG planners often do not expect to find them — monopsonistic buyers, old-fashioned products and markets, well-connected technocrats (including an economist!), acquiescent elites, poor people collectively providing public-sector-like services, support from powerful public-sector actors, tedious surveys of narrow sectors, non-specialist staffs succeeding at providing a specialized service like credit.

The question arises as to whether this small set of cases represents a good 'return' on the Foundation's investment of $21 m in the LEIG area over the last five years. Part of the answer should involve a judgement on the economic return to the investments in credit, requiring some comparative benefit-cost analysis across activities, projects, and countries. Though benefit-cost ratios will not illuminate impacts in important areas like policy and professional thinking, they would help us to understand the actual impact of such programmes on poor people's incomes and the sectors in which results are more robust. A recent AID-funded comparative benefit-cost analysis of five microenterprise credit programmes showed high rates of return for some programmes — at least as high as those obtained on large World Bank infrastructure and rural development projects.[11] That represents a clear standard by which to compare projects in an area where comparison is quite difficult, though I would not want to approve or disapprove of an LEIG programme solely on benefit-cost grounds.

At present, the Foundation has only bits and pieces of impressions about credit impacts, and they are conflicting: some evaluations say that credit has no impact, leaving people in their poverty traps with insignificant incomes, and some report just the opposite. The question is not merely academic because donors, NGOs, and governments are constantly making decisions on programme design based on unverified assertions about credit. Credit organizations, for example, often justify their expansion into non-credit activities on the grounds that credit is 'not enough' to increase people's incomes significantly — the rationale behind Annapurna's move into collective food catering and Grameen Bank's move to collective enterprises and venture capital. If credit *does* have more potential for impact than these other activities, or vice-versa, then funders need to know this, and comparative economic analysis is one way to find out.

The AID study of comparative benefit-cost findings showed that high rates of return had just as much to do with the characteristics of the lending programme as they did with the type of economic activity assisted. The high-return programmes provided only credit (no business or technical assistance), lent through the group mechanism, and operated in low-inflation countries — that is, where real interest rates were positive. Benefit-cost analysis, in other words, can also help us make judgements about programme strategies and organizational design. Since this kind of analysis represents one of the few clear quantitative indicators we can rely on in the LEIG field, and since the methodological path has already been paved by others (also unusual), it would take little additional effort by funders to avail themselves of this opportunity to understand their programmes better.

It is difficult to make a judgement about the return to the Foundation's investment in the LEIG sector without specifying what the 'returns' have been in other sectors where the Foundation works and has a longer history. The Foundation's programmes in agriculture, forestry, and water management are most akin to LEIG because they all carry a poverty focus, at least now, and involve activities that generate income. The Foundation's reviews and discussions of these programme areas seem to exhibit no more of a sense of 'hard' data or comparative economic returns than the LEIG materials. The reviews describe changes in policies, new approaches being tried, small groups being benefited — evidence that is just as qualitative and case-oriented as that coming from the LEIG programme. Reviews of these three areas may *seem* 'harder' and more impressive, because each one corresponds to an identifiable set of professionals (agronomists, agricultural economists, irrigation engineers, botanists, etc), research institutes, and government departments and ministries. And discussion in each of these areas focuses on the way one manages something physical: land, water, trees. There is no such concreteness or professional homogeneity in the LEIG field, a matter taken up further below.

What kinds of results in the older areas of agriculture, forestry, and water have led the Foundation to feel confident about its continued programming there? The answer to this question would point to institution-building at universities and research institutes and to an impact on policies and institutions in the public sector. And it is *this* standard that goes to the heart of the comparison between LEIG and the other areas, rather than the analytical or systematic quality of the results. It is according to this standard, in my view, that the Foundation's approach to LEIG programming might be improved. This takes us into the subject of the following section.

Between the government and the nongovernment sectors

Why does LEIG programming need improving, and how might the Foundation go about doing so? The answer to these questions has to do with:

1   the Foundation's comparative advantage as a donor,
2   the inherent features of income-generating projects in the NGO sector,
3   the path by which the Foundation came upon the NGO sector as an approach to employment problems, and
4   the opportunities emerging from the present historical moment for a different style of Foundation involvement.

Among donors, the Foundation is somewhat unusual in that it has worked simultaneously in the public sector, the nongovernmental sector, and with research institutions. Whereas the Foundation's programmes in agriculture, water, and forestry reflect this history of working across three sectors, its LEIG programme has focused primarily on the NGO sector, with the exception of the recent initiatives of the India programme. In this section, I suggest why the Foundation might want to reduce its emphasis on the NGO sector and take more initiatives in the public sector and research.

Constraints
The Foundation has had good reason for concentrating so much of its LEIG attention on the nongovernment sector.

First, LEIG has no professional home. It does not correspond to a field of study nor does it deal with one particular economic sector. Unlike agriculture, water, and forestry, LEIG expertise or commitments cannot be found in a particular government ministry or academic discipline. For the Foundation, the NGO sector has come to represent an analog to that missing professional home — a place where everyone is committed to the alleviation of poverty and where substantial programme experience in the subject has been accumulated.

Second, the Foundation's recent shift towards the nongovernment sector in the LEIG area arises out of a deep disappointment, shared by many other observers of development in the third world, about the persistence of massive poverty despite impressive growth records in many countries and several decades of state-promoted development. This disappointment has also extended to the poverty-oriented government programmes of the 1970s, which were meant to alleviate the inequities of growth by redirecting public-sector services and subsidies to the poor.

Third, the Foundation was drawn to the NGO sector out of its belief that empowerment of the poor is central to their ability to increase their incomes. Because governments have often repressed the poor when they organize, or simply neglected them, the Foundation has viewed independent assistance in organizing the poor as crucial to their gaining of rights to government protections, services, and subsidies. In Foundation eyes, improving the incomes of the poor is therfore inextricably linked to empowerment, and it is difficult to empower people through government, particularly military ones.

Though the Foundation's affinity for the NGO sector in the LEIG area is understandable, major emphasis on this sector is difficult to justify. *First*, various donors have funded LEIG-type projects among NGOs since at least the early 1980s. The Foundation is not alone in this area and not 'on the cutting edge'. Nor is it bringing to bear on this problem its unique ability to act simultaneously in the government, nongovernment, and research sectors.

Second, NGO programmes in the LEIG area typically do not make significant inroads on poverty in a particular country — either directly in of beneficiary numbers, or indirectly in terms of affecting policy or programmes carried out by larger institutions. The low impact and lack of replication of NGO programmes has to do with certain 'diseconomies of scale' affecting their expansion. The diseconomies take the following form:

1 the strength of many successful NGO efforts arises out of a certain ethnic, religious, or other social homogeneity, which is irretrievably lost when these organizations expand and become less parochial;
2 NGOs compete against each other and the public sector for funding from foreign donors, which means that they are driven to 'differentiate their product' from these 'competitors,' rather than cooperating with them or exchanging ideas about service-delivery models in the cause of getting good programme ideas replicated;
3 because a large share of NGO funding comes from foreign donors, and because NGOs usually prefer foreign funding to local support, distance and mistrust prevails between the government and nongovernment sectors, thereby reducing the possibility that government will replicate successful NGO 'experiments';
4 NGO programmes do not grow partly because NGOs are under no external pressure to reach large numbers of persons, in contrast to the public sector, where political pressure to reach large numbers is high.

As a result of these diseconomies, the path to replication of successful NGO experiments in the LEIG area is somewhat blocked, meaning that the relevance of their experiments to nationwide problems of poverty and unemployment can be quite limited.

Third, history has shown us that in third-world countries with good performance on income distribution, government policies and programmes have played a key role. Conversely, certain government policies regarding credit subsidization, tariff protection, and agricultural development have had major *adverse* impacts on employment. Though the behaviour of government may leave much to be desired in the poverty-alleviation area, in other words, what government does exerts a powerful impact on poverty. If the Foundation wants to have a significant impact in this sector, it cannot afford to stay away from such a powerful actor.

Fourth, our understanding of what works in the public sector with respect to poverty alleviation is woefully inadequate, partly because recent events have cut short the process of learning from this experience. The economic crises of many third-world countries have brought about a reinterpretation of much past government policy as 'bad' — as having laid the groundwork for the crises — even those policies previously considered to have been good. This current disappointment about the performance of third-world public sectors can be seen, in part, as an almost predictable over-reaction to the excessive optimism of an earlier period, when everyone had great faith in the ability of third-world governments and first-world donors to eradicate poverty and bring about sustained growth.

The economic and debt crises of the 1980s have turned a generation of economists away from the study of poverty and poverty-alleviating initiatives to issues of debt, trade, and macroeconomic management. As a result, our ability to make informed judgements about the potential of policy and programmes to alleviate poverty is constrained by the lack of comparative research on what has worked well. We have turned our backs on the public sector without informed enough reason and have put excessive faith in a 'new' sector, the NGOs, which is impeded by its very structure from bringing about the kinds of impacts we hope to achieve.

Opportunities in the public sector

At first glance, the opportunities for significant LEIG programmes in today's world of economic crisis, fiscal austerity, and 'unfashionability' of poverty concerns, would seem quite limited. Upon closer examination, however, the current moment also turns out to provide some new opportunities for LEIG initiatives:

First, the political unpopularity of today's austerity programmes, with their removal of long-standing public sector subsidies on basic goods, their reductions in public-sector jobs, and their general reductions in employment, constitute a serious political concern to today's third-world leaders. This has made them more sympathetic to certain LEIG-type initiatives than they would have been in the 1970s. Though resources were more abundant and poverty alleviation was more in fashion at that time, the informal sector was held in scorn by political leaders and development planners alike, because of their visions of 'modernization' through large-scale industrialization.

Examples of current public-sector gestures in the LEIG area are India's Integrated Rural Development Programme, Kenya's emphasis on the informal sector in its national plan and recent tariff-rebate measure for small manufacturers and Egypt's programmes to fund the acquisition of equipment for artisanal activities and to allow pensioners to take their retirement benefits in one lump sum for the start-up of small businesses. Though all these programmes have major flaws, they are nevertheless reaching thouands of poor persons.

Second, the economic conservatism of the times, with its emphasis on 'getting the prices right' as the answer to most economic and social ills, turns out to harbour distinct sympathy for the small-firm sector in third-world countries. Firms outside the regulatory power and the privileges of the state, in this view, use capital and labour in the 'right' proportions because they face prices for capital and labour that have not been tampered with by the state. That is, they use capital more parsimoniously and labour more extravagantly than large modern firms, with their access to state-subsidized credit and their labour costs 'encumbered' by government-mandated fringe benefits. With respect to small firms producing in the informal sector, then, the interests of the 'right-price sympathizers' overlap somewhat with those of the 'poverty sympathizers.' This convergence, linking the currently unpopular poverty concerns to the powerful conservative economics of today, provides a distinct opening for LEIG initiatives in the public sector.

Third, and related, the current debt crises have forced many third-world countries to reduce imports drastically through devaluation and import controls. Though lower-income groups have no doubt suffered disproportionately from these crises and the related policy measures, some small producers have flourished as a result of the disappearance of cheap competing imports and of local goods produced by large firms dependent on imported inputs. The current situation, in other words, has made it more difficult for third-world countries to pursue growth strategies biased toward large, capital-intensive firms. And from some of the countries experiencing reduced imports, some surprising and useful evidence has emerged on how robustly the small-firm sector can respond when policy changes in its favour.

Fourth, the current popularity of 'decentralization' among development planners translates into more autonomy to local government and to local offices of central-government ministries and parastatals. This opens up the field for LEIG experimentation by allowing a donor like the Foundation to pick and choose from among the most capable and interested local offices of government. This is exactly what the Foundation has done with the women's dairying project in Andhra Pradesh (working through the state office of the national dairy parastatal), the sericulture projects in Bihar and Karnataka (working through the state offices of the national sericulture board), and the initiative with the Principal Bank of Egypt (working through the regional branch in Dumiat).

Recommendations

In searching for and evaluating grant proposals in the NGO sector, the Foundation should place priority on the potential for impact, rather than on institution-building for its own sake in the NGO sector. Impacts can take the form of large beneficiary numbers, influence on policy, or likely replicability by other institutions. In advance, of course, any project proposer can predict these kinds of impacts. From this assessment and others, however, we have learned that certain kinds of project designs and environments are more likely to lead to impact than others. Organizations can reach a much larger number of people if tasks are carried out in certain ways — the minimalist form of credit being a striking example. Organizational leaders with visions of reaching masses of people are more likely to have impact than those who aim to do an excellent job in a few communities.

'Experiments' in the NGO sector should be viewed with particular caution.

Experiments that work well on the small scale characteristic of many NGO programmes usually do not lend themselves to large-scale operation because of diseconomies of scale — in the organizational and political sense, as well as economic. In order for an experiment to be replicated, it is not sufficient that it only be 'successful'. The experiment must also be conducted in an environment where the institutional capacity for replication is already in place; or the links of project leaders to centres of power must be strong enough so that the experiment has a path along which it can later spread to broader institutional networks. The Grameen Bank is an example: leadership was closely tied to important elites, including the country's Central Bank, in addition to the fact that the organization's founder was determined to follow a 'franchizable' model of service delivery that could be repeated throughout the country.

One of the obvious ways of choosing a setting with the potential for replication is to fund NGO projects that have some relationship to government programmes. This can take various forms: programmes can help a certain class of clients to gain access to government-subsidized goods and services (Working Women's Forum and credit), they can effectively pressure government for changes in policy that will result in increased incomes to large numbers of persons (SEWA achieving reduced police harassment of vendors), they can be given the responsibility for implementing certain parts of large government programmes (MYRADA and India's Integrated Rural Development programmes), or they can help provide a missing ingredient to government programmes that are not working well (Proshika's rehabilitation of defunct government-owned tubewells in Bangladesh and sale of them at subsidized prices to landless pump groups).

To suggest a link to government as a criterion for funding NGOs may seem a constraint on the Foundation, and inconsistent with the very character of the nongovernment sector. But comparative research on NGOs shows that in many countries they have been most important in sectors where a substantial share of their funding comes from government, and where government has been interested in allowing them to play a complementary role in providing services.[12] Even in the US, where private philanthropy is high, government funding still accounts for roughly one quarter of NGO budgets — the share being even higher for social services, community development and health care in third-world countries. The health sector is a good example of public-private complementarity, because NGOs have made important contributions to health there. In most such programmes, NGOs and government actually 'jointly produce' the service, though neither side might describe it that way: governments supply vaccines and medicines, and official certifications to service providers, while NGOs supply the outreach. Neither could operate without the other.

In that NGOs receive public-sector support in countries where they have been important, the largely foreign-funded NGO sectors of many third-world countries can be seen as somewhat of an aberration. The Foundation could help them develop the public-sector connections they need to grow, and to have a greater impact, by requiring of the NGOs it supports some kind of matching commitment from government. The commitment need not be financial — it can take the form of office space, vehicles, seconded staff — as long as it creates the link and hence the potential for replication.

The Foundation could make a unique contribution in the LEIG area if it broadened its programme to include the public sector. As a small donor, of course, the Foundation is not in a position to make a significant contribution to large public-sector programmes. But it does have a unique role to play in supporting experimentation in the public sector, as it has with its women's dairying project in India and its initiative with the regional branch of a government bank in Egypt. Governments find it politically difficult to initiate and fund these experiments themselves, because they can be accused of favouring certain geographic areas.

Though government bureaucracies often act insensitively to the poor and may seem incapable of carrying out poverty-alleviating programmes, an LEIG programme that seeks to have impact should address the challenge of discovering programme designs and methods of service delivery that *can* work in these organizational environments, or that attract skilled and committed people to them. The Foundation should draw on its skills in 'networking' to find the committed, competent, and powerful professionals in the public sector and to locate experiments in their departments or branches. This kind of search should not be limited to the 'social ministries,' since they usually are weak, have low budgets, and follow a welfare approach to their task. Construction ministries are an opposite example: they are powerful, run by skilled technocrats, and their spending and contracting have significant impacts on employment. Powerful parastatals are another example, like India's federated system of cooperatives, where the Foundation's women's dairying project was located.

The Foundation's long history of relating to professionals in third-world governments, along with its more recent experience with the NGO sector during the last six years of LEIG programming, have placed it in a unique position to bring together NGOs and government for exchanges about some of the more successful NGO experiences. Through this kind of interchange around concrete experience, it may be possible to reduce some of the mistrust between government and NGOs — a mistrust that prevents a complementary relationship between NGOs and governments from evolving. In supporting such interaction, of course, the Foundation will be limited by the fact that there are strong and rational reasons for the distrust, and that cooperation for cooperation's sake will often not be in the interest of either party. The Foundation can identify situations, however, in which cooperation might be of mutual interest.

The Foundation should take advantage of some of the new opportunities for LEIG initiatives created by the environment of austerity. Though some of the 'new' policy wisdom has favourable implications for the informal sector, as noted above, the prevailing economic conservatism and the related decline of interest in issues of equity have led to the disappearance of employment and equity as prime objectives of policy. The Foundation might want to provide support to policy-making units on these issues, so that thinking about them becomes less of a 'luxury.'

Research

In the 1970s, poverty alleviation was of much greater concern to economists and project designers than it was beforehand, or today. This was partly because the subject became prestigious in the field of development economics. One of the reasons that poverty issues gained such prestige is that the leader of a powerful institution, the World Bank, decided to invest large amounts in research on the relationship between growth, policy, and income distribution. Giving prestige to research, of course, is not all that it takes to turn the attention of politically powerful decisionmakers to a subject. But it helps.

One result of the fall from prestige of equity-oriented research and policy is that development scholars and professionals with such interests today have no institutional home — research funds, graduate students, colleagues working on the same subject. They do not have the kind of professional support that the field of economics today provides, for example, to economists doing research on issues of debt, trade, and macroeconomic policy. Partly as a result, students and scholars still interested in LEIG issues tend to be found mainly in the non-economist social sciences. And economics has come to be thought of as a discipline that is inhospitable to poverty concerns, even though it was in the forefront of research on the subject in the 1970s.

The field of economics is becoming more and more powerful in determining how policy is made. It also provides some of the important analytic tools necessary to understand the impacts of policy and programmes on poverty. If LEIG concerns continue to remain as intellectually peripheral in economics as they are today, it will be difficult to command the kind of attention that is necessary to attract powerful persons and institutions to the task of changing policies and adopting effective programmes. For all these reasons, the field of economics cannot be avoided by those with LEIG concerns — just as the public sector cannot be avoided if one wants to carry out a programme that has significant impacts on poverty.

LEIG needs research attention because relatively little comparative analysis has been carried out on the 1970s experience with public-sector poverty-alleviating programmes in the third world. Though there is a rich literature on the failures of that period, there is very little to help us understand the successes, and the common traits they share. The record is not only incomplete but, because of prevailing intellectual fashions, it is often wrong — good illustrations being the until-recent misinterpretation of the East Asian growth experience as resulting from a 'non-intervening' state, and the mistaken judgement that government parastatals, particularly in Africa, are always a failure.

There is still much comparative research to be done on what has worked and what has not in the public sector. If the Foundation wants LEIG concerns to be taken seriously, and if it wants to help policymakers and programme designers to make informed decisions in this area, it should be funding more research. The research should have a somewhat narrower and different focus than that of the past. Past research on third-world poverty falls into two categories:

1   cross-country and longitudinal studies on the relationship between economic growth and income distribution (including policy effects); and
2   studies of the 'anatomy' of poverty, including analyses of the adverse effects of growth and many government programmes on the poor.

One of the results of our learning so much about the adverse effects of change on the poor is that, in a certain sense, we have become incapable of acting — pessimistic about things working out and worried that we will harm the very subjects of our concern. This is why we now need to add to our understanding of poverty a better sense of what works institutionally in terms of service delivery and what kinds of interventions bring about significant changes in people's lives.

The Role of Microenterprises in Rural Industrialization in Africa

MARIA NOWAK

Introduction

Confucius' observation, 'It's hard to find a black cat in a dark room, particularly when the cat isn't there', readily applies to present-day development policy.

The economic and financial crisis afflicting the third world in general and sub-Saharan African nations in particular is also a crisis of abstracted models and reasoning. Today's reality, as experienced by the overwhelming majority of economic actors, is no better understood than that of seventeenth century Flanders, the favourite field of study for European proto-industrialization.

Despite the emphasis which the World Bank's 1979 World Development Report put on rural microenterprises they have been largely obliterated from the minds of donors by problems connected with structural adjustment. However, they are beginning to attract renewed attention with the rise in unemployment, a problem which neither agriculture, industry nor a sluggish public sector is capable of resolving. Rural microenterprises represent spontaneous adjustment par excellence.

Anchored in concrete facts, my paper on microenterprise is based primarily on sub-Saharan Africa, drawing on the experience of other continents for clarification.

Given the absence of reliable statistics, the paper will attempt to isolate and identify different facets of reality. Only by enhancing our knowledge of reality can we assist spontaneous economic growth without running counter to its internal dynamics.

Informal or real economy?

Importance of rural microenterprises

While economic science has been refining its analytic and measurement tools for the past 50 years, the economy has taken a perverse pleasure in eluding scientific analysis.

Hidden in the virgin forest of the informal economy, rural microenterprises

---

MARIA NOWAK is Chief, Division of General Studies at the Caisse Centrale de Coopération Economique in Paris, France.

are no exception to this rule. Most studies are conducted at the agricultural subsector level. Baseline surveys, which have become increasingly rare in Africa since the 1960s, concentrate on farming, making no attempt to investigate nonfarm activities. And yet, such activities, formerly associated with subsistence economies, seem now to be growing in importance as the result of a variety of different factors such as the population explosion, the increasing scarcity of farmland, volatile markets, and the inability of the formal sector to generate employment.

According to data compiled by Peter Kilby and Carl Liedholm[1] on 18 less-developed countries, the primary occupation of 14 to 49 per cent of the rural labour force lies outside agriculture. Indeed, the percentage share of non-farm employment and income is even higher insofar as these figures overlook secondary occupations and female labour.

The patterns uncovered by these authors are largely confirmed by studies conducted in other countries. Surveys in Madagascar and Niger show farm income accounting for no more than 50 per cent of total rural household income. At Saa, in Cameroon, 72 per cent of all heads of rural family units have sources of income, enabling them to double their primary earnings.[2] A nationwide survey of rural household budgets and consumption conducted in 1982/83 in Rwanda showed handicraft production accounting for 20 per cent of household cash income, compared with 27 per cent from commerce, 11 per cent from services and other sales, and a mere 19 per cent from agriculture.

In Thailand, only 37 per cent of average peasant income is actually derived from own farms. The remainder is divided between nonfarm income (80 per cent) and earnings from work performed on other farms.[3]

The phenomenon of diversified rural activity is not confined to low-income countries. In the US, the share of farmer income corresponding to net farm earnings fell from 58 per cent in 1960 to 36 per cent in 1982. In Japan, a nation where farming is small scale, 75 per cent of farmers' income came from nonfarm sources. The difference is that, in third world nations, nonfarm activities are almost exclusively informal, while in the industrial countries, a large percentage of such activities lies within the formal sector.

Characteristics of rural microenterprises

The foregoing data dispel our traditional image of the peasant devoting most of his time to working the land without, however, giving us a clear view of rural activities.

The general definition of a microenterprise as an entity employing less than five persons and generating income from nonfarm production, services and trade encompasses a wide range of activities filling all the gaps left by agriculture, including:

1   year-round or seasonal enterprises tuned to the agricultural cycle;
2   full or part-time enterprises (in rural areas, we rarely find tradesmen or

shopkeepers who are not also farmers);
3   individual or family enterprises or enterprises employing full-time or casual outside labour;
4   fixed or itinerant enterprises, particularly petty trading;
5   enterprises with a sole line of business or with multiple lines substituting for one another, according to market needs, or clustered in order to share risks and avoid standing out from the social milieu.

Microenterprise covers a broad range of activities, the most common of which are listed in Table 1.

Table 1 Rural activities in Africa and Madagascar

Products	Services	Trade and commerce
Wood & byproducts	Health	Grain, storage & resale
Housing, construction	Hairdressing	Other farm products
Metal products	Mechanical repairs	Livestock
Skins, horns & byproducts	Radio repairs	Farm inputs
Textiles, garments	Wood gathering	Staples, etc.
Agro-based food products	Transportation etc.	
Pottery, wicker products		
Art, handicrafts		

Grass roots strategies

Rural microenterprises are associated with a broad spectrum of peasant strategies ranging from mere survival to development.

Strategy of survival

The oldest of all strategies as regards small-scale rural enterprise is that of survival, with primitive forms of cottage industries associated with hunting and fruit picking going back before the advent of farming. *Robinson Crusoe* is merely the western version of this myth. This type of strategy is frequently followed by rainless peasants in sub-Saharan Africa, as well as landless peasants in Asia.

Data collected by Peter Kilby and Carl Liedholm on five Asian and African nations show a negative correlation between farm size and the portion of household earnings represented by nonfarm income.[1] On farms in the smallest size category, nonfarm income generally accounts for over 50 per cent of household earnings, rising as high as 70 to 88 per cent in the specific case of Asia.

In Africa, where land scarcity is not yet as acute as in Asia, the importance of small-scale rural activities is not as closely related to farm size. These sources enable households to supplement their income from relatively low-yielding land, mitigating the effects of adverse climatic factors and the impact of highly unstable producer prices.

In the Sahel, earnings during the long dry season often surpass farm income. Although it is becoming increasingly difficult to do so, men can still work in the city or on coastal plantations. Women, however, have no choice but to remain behind with the children and elderly and try to survive through petty trading and crop processing.

Strategy of development
While rural microenterprises are rooted in ancient traditions, in many ways they are also vehicles of progress:

1 they facilitate capital accumulation, often through price speculation conducted by storing the newly harvested grain and reselling it several months later at triple its original value. This, in turn, is accomplished through petty trading, requiring little investment. In a subsequent stage, the capital is invested in the production of goods. This transitory phase of petty commerce recalls the historical development of trading activity in Europe;
2 they facilitate the acquisition of management skills, especially important in an environment lacking a strong entrepreneurial tradition, as well as technical know-how, perfected with each succeeding generation through trading and transfers of urban technology. At Saa, six out of every ten microentrepreneurs learned their trade in the city;
3 they enable the general population, and particularly youth and women, to acquire greater economic independence from the powers that be;
4 they introduce new consumption models and needs.

Multiplying through division rather than expansion, they reshape and vitalize the rural economy while waiting, like their counterparts in more advanced areas, to establish direct linkages with the formal sector, for which they may become subcontractors.

Role of rural microenterprises
Rural microenterprises are the pollinators of the development process. In less-developed economies characterized by market fragmentation, heterogeneous cultures and training levels and constant interruptions of flows, compared by François Perroux to wadis that vanish in the desert, they are the essential point of contact and articulation between the past and future, between agriculture and industry, between city and countryside, as well as between modes of production and consumption.

Link between past and future
While found at different levels of development, survival and forward-looking strategies are actually closely interrelated.

In Africa, sons of blacksmiths, belonging to a traditional caste whose members mined local iron ore for centuries before adapting to the use of scrap iron, learned welding, allowing them to progress from the production of simple manual tools to the manufacture of more complex equipment.

This social sub-stratum is of equal importance in other countries. Thus, Vittorio Capecchi stresses the influence of the traditional sharecropping system in the northern Italy on the development of rural microenterprises which provided the peasantry with important management skills.[4]

Jean-Raphaël Chaponniere highlights the invisible linkages between intensive rice growing and modern technologies requiring sustained concentration and strict coordination of multiple tasks. In Taiwan and Korea, 'the same young girls attentively fitting together components in a present-day assembly-line, at one time used to carefully transplant rice plants from seed beds into rice paddies'.[5]

But mental attitudes can also work in the opposite direction. According to Gourmantché tradition (Eastern Burkina Faso), destiny and fate are a routine, inevitable cause of failure. To defuse destiny and prevent the abandonment of an entrepreneurial activity on the mere grounds that 'you can't fight God's will', the Association for Productivity which lends to rural microenterprises warns borrowers in advance of examples of mismanagement for which they will be held personally accountable.

But while rural microenterprises are rooted in tradition and their development appears to be associated with a long and patient process of maturation of attitudes and capabilities, they are also vehicles of culture shock which, in essentially self-sufficient agrarian societies, introduces the ferment of change and the dynamics of an industrial economy.

The Emilia Romana region of northern Italy and the Wenchou region of China are excellent illustrations of this phenomenon. While their experience is not transferable by any means, still, in different forms and at different levels of development, all societies seem to carry within them a dynamism which seeks merely to unfold a process of 'organic growth', the advantage of which is that it avoids oversized production units and lays the foundation for sound management.

Meeting point for agriculture and industry
In the ongoing debate over the respective roles of agriculture and industry in the development process, rural microenterprise is still the 'no man's land' of economic theory and policy.

1 as far as industrial development is concerned, dreams of an economic 'take-off', the concept of 'industrial poles' and policies favouring large-scale projects, 80 per cent of which are currently inoperative according to an African study, have largely evaporated over the past twenty-five years. Haven't we confused the point of arrival with the point of departure, as suggested by Pierre Judet? Can we create industry without a prior industrial fabric?[6]

2 results in the area of agricultural development have been equally disappointing. Producers of cash crops are reeling from the effects of slumps and wide swings in world crops market prices. In 1986, the cost to the Ivory Coast of the slump in cocoa prices equalled the total value of aid channelled to the entire continent through the Special Facility for Africa. The production of food crops has been stifled by food surpluses in the industrial countries, while Africa is currently dependent on outside sources for over 15 per cent of its food supply, a figure expected to rise to 40 per cent by the year 2000.[7]

In this desolate landscape, the emergence of even the most tenuous new forms of production is grounds for optimism, particularly since rural microenterprises facilitate a smooth transition from farming to industrial activity, with important spin-off effects on agricultural productivity and output.

Increasing agricultural productivity Rural microenterprises supply agriculture with part of its equipment. This includes not only traditional implements but also ploughs as well as transportation and processing equipment. One cannot conceive of the modernization of African agriculture (animal traction, mechanization, irrigation) without a network of artisans conducting maintenance.

The prices charged by these small-scale enterprises are often highly competitive with those of state enterprises, even if quality is not always the same (see Table 2).[8]

Table 2 *Prices of farm equipment in Madagascar (in Malagasy Francs)*

	State enterprises	Independent artisans
Hoes	970 to 2,000	800 to 750
Ploughs	25,000	8,500
Seeders	100,000	40,000
Decorticators	1,000,000	225,000
Wheelbarrows	30,600	25,000

In Senegal, experience gained in repair-work has enabled artisans to copy imported equipment. The frame of an imported millet mill costs 1–1.5 m CFAF. Produced by the national manufacturer, it sells for 400,000 CFAF, built by artisans, the cost is between 200,000 and 300,000 CFAF. (*Promotion de la production d'équipements ruraux par les petites entreprises du secteur metal* Direction de l'artisanat, Senegal, July 1986).

However, due to a series of obstacles, depressingly similar from one country to another, microenterprises fill only a minimal share of market demand (between 5 and 10 per cent of the demand for farm equipment in Madagascar).

It is to say the least disconcerting to note that a mere 10 per cent of Burkina Faso's 500,000 to 600,000 smallholdings have ploughs manufactured by state enterprises which are sold on five-year credit through a long, tedious process involving farmers' groups, regional development offices and the agricultural bank Caisse nationale de crédit agricole, while ploughs produced by the few artisans with welders are bought for cash or on six-month credit. Even if animal traction is not a viable investment in the driest part of the Sahel, the order of magnitude is the same and the percentage of farms equipped remains very small.

The use of animal traction, the introduction of which in West Africa during the 1960s was a slow and difficult task, is nowadays an accepted and desirable farming practice. The adoption of new technology often takes a roundabout course, resurfacing like an underground river where you least expect it.

In Niger, the peasants scrapped their ploughs because they lacked harness to attach them to the animal. In Guinea, where the Sekou Toure regime forced peasants to buy animals on credit, the farmers turned around and sold the oxen in Sierra Leone, paid off their ploughs and left them lying under a mango tree. Nowadays, they use the ploughs without having to be prompted and even try unsuccessfully to buy new ones. The supply of farm equipment is so limited that, as recently as May 1987, there was not a hoe to be bought in any village market after 10 am.

In surveys conducted in Madagascar, the peasants ranked their needs as follows: equipment, followed by credit, with agricultural extension in last place. All interviews conducted in African villages confirm the priority accorded to equipment and credit over extension services.

In addition to equipment, rural microenterprises also supply other farm inputs such as improved seeds and plants, fertilizers and pesticides. Long victimized by state monopolies, nowadays these enterprises are likely to be bullied by traders and moneylenders who, operating with large reserves of capital, keep the microentrepreneur in a state of dependency.

The role of microenterprises in supplying farm inputs could easily be a hundred times what it is now. This would be a more reliable means of improving agricultural productivity than the army of extension agents offering the peasants nothing more concrete than a technical message of very limited value, particularly as regards food production. To illustrate this point, in Madagascar, a simple rotary hoe produced by local artisans for weeding rice fields enables a farmer, working alone, to weed 15 ares a day (approximately 1,800 square yards), ie six times more than by hand, and from a much more comfortable upright position to boot. Studies by Dobelman (IRAT) have revealed that timely weeding can mean significant improvements in yields. Compare the following figures:

- 4.6 tons/hectare for rice fields weeded in a timely manner
- 4.0 tons/hectare for fields weeded behind schedule
- 3.3 tons/hectare for unweeded fields.

Adding value to agricultural output Microenterprises have equally important downstream effects on agricultural output, ensuring marketing and transportation services of fundamental importance in an African economy with fragmented markets and inadequate infrastructure. They add value to agricultural output through processing activities which have expanded gradually from the household to the village level. Ten or 15 years ago, very few private or group-owned grain mills or oil presses could be found anywhere in rural Africa.

Demand for the finished product serves as a production incentive: in the Ivory Coast, buoyant sales of attiéké (cassava meal) pushed local market women who prepared and sold it into creating an upstream production system, leasing land and hiring labourers to grow the cassava.

The technological revolution in food processing in industrialized countries could be a godsend for low-income countries, enabling them to incorporate additional labour in their fruit and vegetable exports. The biotechnological revolution is only beginning. The use of crop residues for fuel or animal feed could be significantly expanded. One way of reducing Africa's dependence on international markets for primary products is to upgrade its agricultural goods. There are numerous options for future departures in this area.

Linkages between modes of production and consumption
One of the objections most often raised against development of rural microenterprise is the narrowness of the market. This argument is based on a static view of the economy. If markets were not expandable, there would be no such thing as development.

The few existing surveys of rural budgets and consumption show that locally manufactured products have the highest elasticity of expenditures. In Sierre Leone and Nigeria, a 10 per cent increase in income leads to a 13–14 per cent rise in expenditure on local goods and services (other than food), as compared with only 11 per cent for imports.[1]

In fact, progress from a less developed to an industrialized economy is characterized by interaction between modes of production and consumption. Either one may be intensive or extensive. Intensified production reflects an increase in per capita fixed capital. Intensive consumption is associated with wider use of durable goods, while extensive consumption is limited essentially to traditional products.

According to the production/consumption grid developed by C. Courlet, Africa's modes of both production and consumption are still extensive, while Asian nations with their high levels of rural industrialization have progressed to the intensive/extensive stages, evolving towards the intensive/intensive mode of industrialized countries.[9]

Under present conditions, market size is limited by low household incomes. However, by creating a local trading network, the development of rural microenterprises has an expansionary effect on the local market. The experience of the Grameen Bank in Bangladesh proves that one group's income is invariably another group's market.

This line of reasoning can be carried even further. Studies of certain areas show negative price elasticities of supply of agricultural commodities when farmers are unable to secure needed consumer or capital goods on the local market.

In Mozambique, consumer goods imports financed by a French loan (CCCE) helped increase the production of cashews, which farmers were not bothering to harvest as long as there was nothing they could do with the money.

In many regions of Africa and particularly in areas where the recent introduction of one or more cash crops has produced a sharp rise in cash income, money is being squandered on beer for want of other goods and services available on local markets. Thus, growth does not necessarily go hand in hand with development. Development must proceed unavoidably through intensification of local trade.

Relations between city and countryside
All third world countries face the problem of uncontrolled urban growth, which in turn creates infrastructure, supply and employment problems. At the beginning of the century, only one-tenth of the world population lived in cities. By the year 2000, industrialized countries will be 80–90 per cent urban and third world nations, whose populations are growing at a much faster pace, will be close to the 50 per cent mark. The population of the third world, measured at approximately 3.7 bn in 1985, will swell to 8.9 bn by the year 2100, with the population of South Asia doubling, that of Latin America tripling and the population of Africa experiencing a five-fold increase. It is impossible to resolve this problem without taking a spatial view of regional development, placing greater emphasis on infrastructure in secondary population centres and rural areas. But, apart from such a policy, the only possibility of slowing down the rural exodus is through creation of rural nonfarm employment.

The most spectacular results in this respect are those achieved by China, whose rural industry presently employs 20 per cent of a rural labour force estimated at 370 m workers, and accounts for 25 per cent of total industrial output. This rapid expansion in recent years is directly linked to the breakup of collective farms. The rural population engaged in nonfarm activities tripled during 1980–1986, from 25 to 75 m inhabitants, while the number of enterprises rose from 56,000 to over 12 m and the gross value of production increased five-fold with rural industry responsible for half the increase in rural income over the five-year period.[10]

On an entirely different level and without having thus far achieved results nearly as spectacular as those reported by China, a small African nation, Rwanda, has taken a similar approach, instituting a decentralized rural industrialization strategy in 1984. Rwanda's three-pronged approach has focused on:

1   creation of rural employment,
2   development of industries with forward and backward linkages vis-a-vis the agricultural sector; and
3   reduction of the trade deficit through creation of import substitution and export-oriented industries.

The wisdom of this approach lies not only in shielding Rwanda from the effects of a bankrupt industrial policy which, according to its President, 'dreams only of large industrial units through deceptive parachuting of turnkey factories costing more than they earn', but also in its deliberate effort to promote balanced development of urban and rural areas and thus ensure social harmony.

Already in 1940, long before Michael Lipton's studies of the urban bias, Gandhi was saying 'The exploitation of the villages is, in itself, a form of organized violence. If our society is to be founded on nonviolence, then we must give our villagers their proper place'.

Urban-rural trade clearly plays a catalytic role in this spatial balance. Thus, rural microenterprises prosper first and foremost in peri-urban areas.

Support for the spontaneous dynamics of the economy

In his travels to neighbouring planets, Saint-Exupéry's little prince meets a king who commands the sun to set, taking care first to confirm the time of day — an elementary wisdom which should also apply to the development process. Experience has shown the futility of going against deep-rooted social currents, of compressing stages of evolution and of trying to centralize and programme decisionmaking by all economic actors.

Evaluations of integrated rural development projects by the World Bank and other donors over the past twenty years reveal a semantic confusion at the project design level. While the criterion for project design was that 50 per cent of benefits should accrue to poor farmers, in the minds of development officials, the objective was to mount multisectoral, multipurpose operations. As a result, the projects benefited governments, more than they did the peasantry and, in Africa at least, over 50 per cent ended in failure. Clearly, it was a mistake to attempt to replicate the complexity of economic life. Would the results have been the same if, instead of erroneously applying the rule book, developers had placed more emphasis on familiarizing themselves with rural reality?

A different view of the economy

There are different ways to read the economy. Engineers approach it by subsectors, economists via market models and economic aggregates. In industrialized countries, their judgements serve to back up political decisions in the face of public opinion.

But in the grand theatre of development, for want of alternatives, this adjustment does not occur. Experts play the leading roles, while economic agents are merely extras, even though they are the ones assuming all the risks. (This brings to mind a passage from Ionesco, 'Reason is but the madness of the mighty. Madness is but the reason of the weak'.)

The failure of all technocratic development policies and the spontaneous emergence of new patterns of production, whether in response to the economic crisis or merely to the easing of government-imposed constraints, as in the case of China, shows the development potential inherent in the rural milieu and its ability to adapt to the constraints and opportunities of the environment.

The evolution of economic concepts and methods is, by nature, slower than change in real life. Economic actors fight to survive and better themselves, while we fashion moulds in which to pour them, according to a principle formulated by Jean Cocteau: 'Since we've been overtaken by events, at least let's try and organize them'.

The growing gap between economic theory and reality has, however, produced new schools of thought. Leading the way in France are studies of the informal sector by Jacques Charmes and Philippe Hugon, of ecodevelopment by Ignacy Sachs, of spontaneous development by Marc Penouil, and of new forms of industrialization by Pierre Judet.

In Italy, the spectacular development of the Emilia Romana region over a twenty-year period from an area with a poor agricultural base to a rich industrial one, attracting a net in-migration, enabled Italian economists Vittorio Capecchi and G. Garofoli to observe the growth of flexible small-scale industries rooted in local agrarian structures and cultural and political traditions, while drawing on increasingly diversified technologies and markets.

Based on observations of industrial reality in various advanced countries, Michael Piore and Charles Sabel of MIT, in their book *The second industrial divide*, develop an alternative system of industrial organization replacing the old Ford model of economies of scale, job specialization and division of labour.

This system, based on small production units, made possible by technological innovation, is a response to the instability of the economic environment facing to-day's entrepreneur as well as to the inability of the overly cumbersome and rigid classical industrial apparatus to resolve the problem of employment.

Thus, taking into account regional specificities, varying levels of development, and differences in opinion from one researcher to another, the study of informal economies transcends the sphere of interest of economists regarded by their colleagues engaged in more sophisticated research on the formal sector as 'journalists, dissidents or poets', and is becoming increasingly acceptable.[11]

Market economy models detached from social reality have proven partially, if not totally, inadequate in dealing with the development problems of dual economies and their imperfect markets. We are duty-bound to broaden our vision by attempting to grasp the living complexities of present-day reality. Only through a better knowledge and understanding of reality can we avoid commanding the sun to rise before daybreak and effectively support, rather than ineffectively supplant, individual initiative in the development process.

Policies in aid of microenterprise development
Rural development is a long-term, systemic process of change in which it is futile to attempt to control all intervening factors. We can, however, create more favourable conditions for microenterprise development and replace extension and assistance policies by self-development policies at the grass-roots level.

Creating a favourable environment
There is no magic formula for the transition from multiple rural occupations to rural industrialization. Such a transition is invariably the result of a unique set of circumstances. However, certain obvious bottlenecks must be eliminated.

Mimetic bias Industrial policies have systematically promoted the formation of large-scale economic units relying on capital-intensive technologies:

1   overvalued exchange rates have facilitated imports of capital goods at much lower prices than would have prevailed had these rates accurately reflected real domestic price levels;
2   interest rates fixed below the cost of money (becoming negative during inflationary periods) have encouraged heavy investment over labour-intensive systems of production;
3   investment codes have provided for capital goods to be imported duty-free or at preferential rates, granted temporary income tax exemptions and allowed for accelerated depreciation of fixed assets;
4   wage policy and social legislation have favoured a small minority of formal-sector wage earners representing a maximum of 5 per cent of the African labour force, while limiting employment opportunities in the formal sector.

Obstacles to rural microenterprise development Compared with the privileges bestowed on the formal sector, the informal sector has been ignored and neglected. Rural microentrepreneurs from Senegal to Madagascar face the same problems:

1   inadequate supplies of raw materials: in order to make a pitchfork worth 6.5 kg of beans, a blacksmith in Rwanda must first spend three or four days in the city combing repair shops for an old car axle and then haul it back to his shop in the country. Import permits are not available to artisans and small enterprises who must go through intermediaries having little interest in small orders. Customs duties are as high as 40 per cent. Thus, a regulatory solution will not suffice. The rural climate of scarcity makes it essential to organize the supply process. In the absence of intermediaries, this can be done by giving start-up aid to trade organizations;

2   primitive, insufficient equipment: tradesmen in African villages continue to rely on primitive tools. Blacksmiths work with only an anvil, tongs and hammer. Several carpenters often share a single plane. Wood supplies may be limited by a lack of saws. Many microentrepreneurs do not even own the equipment they use, whether it be a sawing machine or refrigerator; it remains the property of an official or trader who supplies capital under conditions approaching those of traditional sharecropping arrangements. A survey of tool and equipment ownership in Africa would reveal a number of anomalies. We found a shoeshine boy in a small rural centre in Burkina Faso turning over half his income to the owner of his box of brushes and polish. The box couldn't have cost more than 2,000 CFAF ($6 to $7). With his daily earnings of 200 to 400 CFAF, he could have paid back a loan in two months' time and doubled his income. The solutions to these elementary, yet significant, bottlenecks are simple: adequate market supplies of essential equipment, creation of technical advisory centres to advise tradesmen on the availability of equipment and investment credit. In any case stronger artisanal trade groups are a prerequisite;

3   little or no working capital: most microentrepreneurs are forced to rely either on agents or on middlemen who eat into their earnings;

4   fierce competition from imports sold at clearance prices. How can we expect to develop small clothing workshops while continuing to flood Africa with a torrent of second-hand goods, the very symbol of pauperization? (It should be noted however that the choice of remedies requires careful study. In Rwanda, which imports twice as much used clothing as the average African countries, re-exporting part to its neighbours, repair and distribution of the clothing creates slightly less employment but slightly more value added per unit of sales than do local petty tailors.[12]) Nowhere in the world, including East Asia, has an industry prospered without at least some measure of protection;

5   insufficient rural infrastructure: just as the mimetic bias in the choice of technology has favoured the formation of large-scale production units, the urban bias has favoured more glamorous public works projects, to the detriment of rural infrastructure. Building of secondary and access roads, establishing telecommunications service in rural villages and towns and bringing water and energy to rural microenterprise and industry are among

the prerequisites for development of microenterprise and industry. Local government obviously has an important role to play in this area;
6 marketing: while sales of locally consumed goods and services pose no particular problem, efforts to expand exports immediately run up against a number of marketing problems. In advanced countries, the tailoring to world markets of goods produced in rural workshops with flexible product lines is ensured by state-of-the-art computer and telecommunications technology. Africa is not yet at this stage, nevertheless it is making rapid progress in this direction. As in the case of raw material supplies, the successful marketing of products produced by small-scale rural enterprise requires coordination of output and its adaptation to external demand. Here again, the development of trade organizations should facilitate better control of product quality and quantities.

Criticisms of the informal sector usually focus on its profiting from economic distortions (this is especially true of border trade and black market operations) and lack of any contribution to the national budget, but it is up to the central government to correct such distortions, better adapt its system of taxation and ensure that rural microenterprises exploit positive rather than negative elements of their economic environment.

Recognizing the right to economic initiative Despite considerable rhetoric about satisfying basic needs, fighting poverty and, more recently, growth with equity, in many third world nations misery is still on the rise, fuelled by high rates of population growth and structural adjustment policies, which do not always have a human face.

This rise in misery, which also reflects a major failure of foreign aid, cannot be checked through assistance and charity. However, it could certainly be attacked more effectively if, apart from an environment more conducive to self-help and microenterprise development, socialist and market-oriented governments alike would recognize the individual's right to economic initiative by providing access to capital, training and technology.

Access to capital In view of the importance of non-agricultural activities, lack of access to capital is as much an obstacle as is lack of access to land.

The amount of capital needed to start a rural microenterprise is negligible, considering the minimal investment in plant and equipment. Women open small businesses with $80–100. Tradesmen equip their shops with $300–400. With $4,000–5,000, they can buy modern equipment, including a generator.

However, capital is a scarce commodity. If bank failures are currently legion, this is certainly not the fault of small-scale producers who, outside from isolated projects, have never even shared in the benefits of banking. Microentrepreneurs obtain their capital by working on plantations, joining forces with officials or traders, participating in a 'tontine' group, or borrowing from a moneylender. And money is expensive. In Cameroon, tontines with a face value of $300–1,500 in rural areas are auctioned off at double the nominal value.[13] In the Ivory Coast, the informal interest rate is 25 per cent per month; in Burkina Faso, it is as high as 500 per cent a year. Compared with nominally inexpensive (12 per cent) but virtually inaccessible goverment credit, a farmer-operated savings and loan association in Mali pays 20 per cent interest on savings and charges 40 per cent interest on loans to member farmers. The profitability of dry season activities makes it possible to amortize the loans and pay a relatively high rate of interest.

Solutions to rural credit problems are well-known and follow two differing approaches:

1 largely self-managed village savings and loan cooperatives attract deposits from their members, redistributing a portion and placing the remainder with a central facility which refinances if necessary. Such cooperatives operate in a large number of countries, with varying degrees of success. Between 1970 and 1985, Zimbabwe's Savings Development Movement created 5,500 savings clubs with 140,000 members, the majority of them women. Ghana's and Cameroon's credit unions, Burkina Faso's savings and loans associations and Burundi's people's banks were all inspired by the germanic Raiffeisen system, applied by France's Credit Mutuel (mutual savings bank) and Canada's Caisses Desjardins.

However, these cooperatives have not been entirely effective in satisfying the credit needs of microentrepreneurs. Their creation is a slow process and they have proven more successful in attracting savings than in distributing loan funds. Ignoring the old English adage, 'loans make deposits', they require that borrowers have savings accounts and, in principle, lend only to members able to put up collateral for their loans. Thus, very little of the savings is invested in rural areas, most of it ending up in the banks;

2 in the second approach, specialized agencies or bank windows, drawing on outside sources of funding, lend to smallholders or landless peasants, enabling them to mount productive activities. The model for this credit scheme is Bangladesh's Grameen Bank, formed in 1983 in a pilot operation mounted by Professor Yunus. Today, it has nearly 400,000 members, with a default rate of under 2 per cent and a 50 per cent annual growth rate. The secret of its success lies mainly in the following three elements:

(**a**) an in depth knowledge of the milieu, ensuring the adoption of procedures responsive to its needs and constraints. Launched in 1976, the pilot project has grown steadily. Management training, conducted almost entirely in the field, lasts a full year;

(**b**) giving freedom of choice to borrowers, who assume full responsibility for their respective undertakings, expanding them in stages according to their resources and capabilities. This represents a radical means of preventing failures and avoiding the market problems invariably created by central planning;

(**c**) financial discipline based on solidarity groups, autonomy of branches, commercial interest rates and the mandatory opening of group savings and emergency funds.

A recent mission to two Sahelian countries whose members included the Assistant Manager of the Grameen Bank showed that it would be possible *a priori* to overcome the obstacles (while also profiting from the advantages) posed by the local context and establish a system responsive to local financing needs, based on the foregoing principles. To be sure, the transplant could easily end in failure if it relied on a simple mass replication without first adapting the various elements. But, since the worst is not certain, one might as well hope for the best, namely that the system developed by the Grameen Bank will take root in Africa.

This optimism is further justified by the results of a number of credit programmes for larger-size microenterprises operating in different countries, eg USAID-supported schemes in Burkina Faso and Senegal.

Access to training In his study of food security for Africa, Dr Swaminathan, one of the architects of India's green revolution, observes: 'In rural areas, new technological opportunities need not bypass the poor if steps are taken immediately to train rural women and men in the intelligent and effective use of emerging technologies such as biotechnology and microelectronics. In fact, rural development should be defined as the conversion of all unskilled persons into skilled ones.

Without denying the merits of such an ambitious undertaking, one cannot help but notice how far we are from attaining this goal. What do we find in most African nations? On the one hand, inadequate education systems crank out graduates who take their place in the ranks of the unemployed. On the other hand, a young generation performs feats of valour, migrates to the town and then leave their country in search of basic technical training. Training is indeed a scarce commodity. African apprentices, like other apprentices, work for their masters, but, more significantly, a large percentage pay for the right to work as apprentices. At Saa in Cameroon, the average price paid by 80 per cent of area apprentices is around $250.

Vocational training centres are accessible only to a privileged few, whose hope upon graduating is to find salaried employment and who, in the interim, receive free lodging and a daily food allowance. Scanning the spectrum of technical training projects that address basic needs of the rural areas, we come, first, to the Nyabusindu government-operated smithy to Rwanda which trains blacksmiths and provides them at the end of the training with the basic equipment required to practise their trade. Technical training associated with agricultural development projects yields excellent results. In southern Mali, the Compagnie Malienne de Développement Textile (CMDT) trained 192 blacksmiths during 1970–75 and helped them get started with equipment loans. This resulted in a tripling of local production of farm machinery and equipment and ensured vital maintenance and repair services. The net income of the blacksmith quadrupled in three years.

A number of institutions and NGOs (particularly INADES) are doing remarkable work in the area of functional literacy and management training. But despite government and ILO-sponsored efforts in this area, we are still several light years short of China's SPARK programme which provides training for a million young cadres each year to support the modernization of small-scale rural enterprise under the Seventh Five-Year Plan.

Access to technological information The third and last part of the triptych is research/innovation.

A 'symphonic' system of agriculture, to use the eloquent term coined by Dr Swaminathan as a pleasant change from 'integrated rural development', should provide for environmental conservation, processing of crops and their residues, and improved use of the biomass. This implies a need both for interdisciplinary research and for access by the rural population to usable innovations.

Contrary to what we sometimes see on African television, what is needed is not films on the use of weather forecasting models by farmers in the American Middle West, equipped with their own microcomputers. We can thank our lucky stars that African farmers, who do not have television, missed hearing the concluding 'let's hope our farmers will soon be able to take advantage of this'.

The immediate goal is to provide rural microentrepreneurs with currently inaccessible, compartmentalized information often available in-country and, at any event, from international sources, through support units operating within the framework of trade organizations.

This information will be propagated not so much by experts with doctoral degrees but rather by skilled artisans who, though scarce in Africa, can still be found in some parts of Europe and, to a much greater extent, in Asian countries such as India and China, representing vast stores of appropriate technology. A project mounted in Rwanda with assistance from ITAC brought technical assistance from French craftsmen to trade organizations in Rwanda in woodworking, metalworking and the processing of animal hides and horns.

Only by supplying the missing links in terms of the organization of the business environment, access to credit, training and technical innovation can we hope to improve the absorptive capacity of the African economy, which suffers less from an overall shortage of capital than from the difficulty of investing it productively.

Conclusion

Echoing Confucius, Alfred Sauvy in his book, *Black Labour and Tomorrow's Economy*, asks himself 'Can light come from darkness?'

Rural microenterprises in the third world are but one illustration of how economists have lost control over the economy, whose object after all, is nothing other than to create wealth for the satisfaction of human needs. Given the enormous mass of unmet needs multiplying at the explosive rate of population growth plus the immense potential of unutilized labour, our adjustment policies are merely an expression of impotence.

By creating even the most minimal value added, multiplied many times over, and breaking down rigidities in the economic system, rural microenterprises make a valuable contribution to growth while also ensuring a more equitable distribution of income. Actually, the value added created by these enterprises is more significant than one might think. Surveys of Tunisia's informal sector by Jacques Charmes show that capita value added in the formal manufacturing sector is only 1.2 to 1.7 times greater than in the informal sector.

Do not let the search for private operators to take over bankrupt state enterprises, distract us from the needs of the true private sector, 90 per cent of which, in Africa, comprises rural and urban microenterprises.

Such a policy would not be costly. It relies on trade organizations much more than on cumbersome administrative supervision. In lieu of requiring subsidies, it involves lending at commercial rates. Only the costs of infrastructure, research and training remain essentially a government responsibility.

Given this level of cost, the benefits to government are considerable. At a zero level of development, multisector rural activity would limit the impoverishment of marginalized rural communities and reduce the burden this places on the nation-at-large. At more advanced level of development, rural industry generates more wealth per capita than agriculture and becomes not only a means of saving foreign exchange but also a source of revenue for national and local government. In China, taxes levied on rural enterprises represent two-thirds of rural revenues, notwithstanding tax exemption of new enterprises during their first two years of operation.

The last and certainly most convincing argument for such a policy in the light of population growth and ever more limited financial flows is that the cost of creating a job in a microenterprise ranges between $300–10,000 as compared with anywhere from $100,000–250,000 in a small- to medium-scale enterprise.

'Lost among the ranks of those of humble birth, I had to deploy more science and calculations merely to survive than was used in the past hundred years to govern all of Spain', cries Figaro, in a comedy by Beaumarchais which presages the French Revolution. Two hundred years later, this cry remains a disturbing reality for third world microentrepreneurs. If only one idea remains from this conference, I hope it will be that of the right to economic initiative for all in the development process.

PART II

Informal Credit Markets

Informal Credit Markets in Support of Microbusiness

ANAND G. CHANDAVARKAR

Introduction

This paper analyses the role of informal credit markets (ICMs) in relation to microbusinesses (MBs) in developing countries, and attempts to draw relevant conclusions for policy. The ICMs may be defined as all legal but officially unrecorded and unregulated financial activities and transactions which are outside the orbit of officially regulated institutional finance. For our purposes, we exclude the so-called parallel or black money markets and their role in the shadow or underground economy. The term microbusiness is used to indicate, broadly, microenterprises (typically fewer than ten employees) engaged in unincorporated income generation in non-farm activities under an owner-manager, as distinguished from small-scale enterprises, ie incorporated businesses in the formal sector (typically fewer than 50 employees) under an owner-manager. This dichotomy between MBs and small-scale enterprises broadly conforms to the usages of national and international development and donor agencies. But both micro- and small-scale enterprises share common characteristics and problems, notably of limited access to institutional finance, except for a small minority of established firms of good standing.

Since ICMs are unregulated and unrecorded, they necessarily escape the scrutiny of official statistics. Consequently, it is virtually impossible to analyse the relationship between ICMs and MBs in terms of time-series or cross-section studies. Nevertheless, the available empirical evidence based on qualitative studies, ad hoc sample surveys, and stylized facts are an adequate base for formulating feasible policies by national, international and donor agencies in order to enhance the efficacy of ICMs in relation to MBs.[1,2,3,4,5] As much as the informality of the ICMs it is the ignorance, prejudice and even the hostility of central banks and governments to this sector which accounts for both the sparseness of information and the total lack of a positive policy stance on the ICMs. But as in other spheres of economic policy, action on ICMs need not and cannot always await the full availability of information!

ANAND G. CHANDAVARKAR of India, a consultant, was formerly with the International Monetary Fund, Washington D.C. USA.

ICMs: composition and characteristics

ICMs are by their very nature heterogeneous as they cover the lending, borrowing, brokerage, and remittance activities (often based on verbal contracts and understandings) of a wide variety of lenders. Typically, ICMs comprise professional and non-professional money lenders (often relatives and friends), private bankers-cum-merchant middlemen, pawnshops and finance firms, personal and business fixed fund and rotating savings and credit associations (ROSCAs), landlords, the more prosperous agriculturists, and all sources of suppliers' and trade credit. Nonetheless, ICMs share some typical characteristics, notably, predominance of cash transactions, freedom from official registration and regulation, ease of entry or exit, small scale of operations, multiple-interest relationship (financial and socio-cultural) between lenders and borrowers, and above all the informality which is their primary economic rationale and the basis of their substantial competitive advantages over the formal financial institutions (FIs). But it would be misleading to treat ICMs as an enclave or as a sector because given the high fungibility of finance even in developing countries they are part of continuum with the formal financial sector and have strong functional links with it, competitive as well as complementary.

ICMs can be disaggregated according to the ownership pattern and activities of the lenders, the nature of transactions, and instruments. First,

Table 1: Informal savings and loan associations in Africa

Country	Local name	Remarks
Liberia	Esusu	
Gambia	Osusu	
Sierra Leone	Asusu	
Senegal	Tontine	
Ivory Coast	Diaou moni, wari moni	
Ghana	Nanemi akepee	
Benin	Ndjonu, tontine	Fund does not rotate
Nigeria	Esusu, isusu, dashi, adashi, oha, bam	Some groups have both a rotating and a nonrotating fund
Niger	Asusu	
Cameroon	Njangim djanggi, tontine, credit rings	
Zaire	Ikelemba, kitemo, osassa	
Ethiopia	Ekub, ikub	
Uganda	Chilemba	
Zambia	Chilemba	
Zimbabwe	Chilemba	

Source: Adapted from Miracle[2]

Table 2: Rotating savings and credit associations in Asia

Country	Local name
India	Chit funds, kuries, etc.
Indonesia	Arisan
Korea	Mujin
	Rye
Malaysia	Tontine
	Hui[1]
	Kuthu[2]
Philippines	Paluwagan
Singapore	Tontine
	Hui[1]
	Kuthu[2]
Sri Lanka	Cheetu[2]
Thailand	Pia Huey[1]

[1] Hui or Huey is a generic term for ROSCA in Chinese. Some of the Caribbean countries have similar associations like the partner system in Jamaica and the susu in Trinidad.
[2] No interest element.

there are the proprietary groups (individuals or family businesses) such as money lenders (professional or non-professional), private bankers, pawnshops and pawnbrokers. Money lenders operate with their own capital, do not usually accept deposits and combine money lending with the functions of landlords and merchant-middlemen. Private bankers too largely use their own capital in lending but supplement it by borrowing from the formal sector and accept deposits on a limited scale. Their lending operations are through book entries for lines of credit or short term credit instruments (eg discounting of postdated cheques, indigenous bills of exchange sight and usance like the Hundi in the Indian subcontinent and the cek putih in Indonesia, promissory notes, truck receipts, travel vouchers, etc). The most common instruments of borrowing in India are demand notes which do not require revenue or judicial stamps unlike the term bills. ICMs provide funds for purposes which banks do not finance sufficiently (eg wholesale trade), or which require more speedy finance than banks can provide (eg exports); and for those borrowers who find it difficult to produce acceptable collateral (eg restaurant owners, laundries, bakeries, film financiers, building contractors, etc). Unlike rural money lenders, who give consumption credit, urban ICMs confine themselves to business credit.

The other important proprietory lenders are private pawnshops (largely in South East Asia) licensed by government under legislation like the Pawnbrokers Act in 1972 in Malaysia and the Pawnshop Acts BF 2505 (1962) and BE 2517 (1984) in Thailand. These pawnshops customarily lend small amounts for consumption purposes and occasionally for business against the collateral of portable household effects which are not usually accepted by

Table 3 Uses of funds by informal savings and loan associations: Africa

Use	Sierra Leone	Liberia	Ghana	Benin	Nigeria	Niger	Cameroon	Zaire	Congo (Brazzaville)	Ethiopia	Zambia	Malawi
Trade[1]	X			X	X		X	X		X	X	
Acreage expansion		X		X	X		X	X				
'Property'		X		X								
Buses, trucks or taxis				X			X	X		X		
Bicycles for business					X							
Canoes			X									
Palm groves					X							
Fish nets			X									
Grain grinding mill				X								
'Tools'					X							
Seed					X	X				X	X	
Fertilizer			X				X					
Hire labour			X							X	X	
Roads, schools or hospitals	X											
Livestock					X		X			X		
Education				X	X		X			X		

Use								
Bridewealth	X			X		X		X
Taxes			X X X					
Collateral for loan								
Build houses (use unspecified)		X		X X	X X	X X	X	
Improve houses²		X						
Litigation			X					
Travel (purpose not specified)								
Food or clothing	X			X	X X	X	X	
Bicycles (use unspecified)				X X				X
Sewing machines				X X	X X			
Radios	X			X				
Jewellery								
Ceremonies (including funerals)	X X		X	X X	X	X X		
Parties and other entertainment	X						X	
Medical expenses		X		X				

1 Includes 'buy trade goods', 'finance new business', and 'build rental houses'.
2 Provision of a metal roof specifically mentioned for Benin and Cameroon.

Source: Miracle²

commercial banks. They are not a significant source of finance for MBs. The amount lent depends on the appraise value of pledged collateral and the rates of interest are subject to legal ceilings (2–3 per cent per month in Malaysia). In Thailand pawnshops operate under an annually renewable licence. They normally lend up to 80–90 per cent of the appraised value of gold and jewellery; diamonds up to 60–80 per cent; electrical goods about 50 per cent. Interest rates range from 1.25 per cent per month (2,001–10,000 baht) to 2 per cent per month (up to 2,000 baht).

The mutual units in the ICM sector comprise fixed fund associations and the rotating savings and credit associations in Africa, Asia and the Caribbean (Tables 1 and 2). They are usually organized among socially cohesive groups on the principle of rotating access of each member to a continually reconstituted capital fund based on fixed contributions from each member and/or distribution at fixed intervals and as whole to each member in turn by lot, agreement, or bidding (auctions).[6] The auction system is popular in the urban areas of Asia but virtually non-existent in Africa. The basic principle of a ROSCA is that of an instalment system for deposits and loans designed to pool small savings. Generally, the holder of the first position in a sequence of ROSCA, who is usually the organizer, is a pure borrower and the last a pure saver. As a rule, the longer the loan (ie the earlier the borrower's position in the sequence) the higher the rate of interest to be paid. However, interest rate calculations are not always explicit or rational. ROSCAs show considerable flexibility in resolving conflicts of interest between the early recipients' preference for credit and the concerns of late recipients for the safety of their savings. This is achieved through various devices such as contributions in kind or increasing contributions over the cycle. Potential borrowers can take more than one share, or participate in more than one association at the same time, which provide for variable contributions (eg as in the djanggi in Cameroon). By joining a ROSCA with a cycle of specific contributions members can opt for a payment-repayment schedule suited to their individual cash flow pattern. Unused funds may be deposited in a FI — a good example of the linkage between informal and formal finance. ROSCAs provide unsecured loans, although there are exceptions as, for instance, the chit funds in India which insist on securities, promissory notes, or cosigners to ensure that early borrowers continue their contributions. ROSCAs in Africa show a varied combination of production and consumption credit and are more supportive of MBs than of small-scale enterprises (Table 3). Thailand seems unique in its division of personal and business ROSCAs, with the latter being more important as an element of urban ICMs (Table 4). ROSCAs are like miniature credit unions based on the 'mutuality' principle, since all gains accrue to participants. They mobilize traditional social relationships to fulfil economic functions and are apt examples of an intermediate financial technology and of the 'Economic Theory of Clubs', i.e. of voluntary economic entities intermediate between the purely private good and the purely public good.

Table 4: Thailand: comparison of the sources of funds (per cent)

Sources of fund	Personal rotating credit	Business rotating credit	Cheque discounting
Own income	87.8	23.3	53.2
Friends and relatives' income	6.4	–	–
Borrowing from financial institutions	–	47.5	21.7
Borrowing from friends and relatives	1.0	4.1	3.5
Borrowing from abroad	–	8.4	–
Cheque discounting	–	6.0	–
Funds taken out of rotating credits	2.0	9.0	5.2
Cashing cheques due	–	–	14.2
Other	2.8	1.7	2.2
Total	100.0	100.0	100.0

Source: Bank of Thailand Staff Estimates

The proprietary and mutual lenders typify the role of ICMs as an autonomous sector which historically antedates the advent of formal finance in developing countries. In contrast the ICMs consisting of fringe banking institutions such as private financing firms, represents the 'reactive' component of informal finance inasmuch as it manifests the responses to the monetary controls over, or deficiencies of, the formal sector. A good example of the latter aspect is the proliferation of private financing firms in Kerala in India in recent years as a response to credit restrictions on commercial banks and the closure of credit unions in implementation of the Kerala Chitties Act 1975. These firms offer a much higher rate of interest (payable monthly) than the commercial banks on deposit in the form of promissory notes encashable at short notice. The interest on deposits above the legal maximum of 9 per cent and on loans above the legal limit of 12 per cent under the Kerala Money Lenders Act is said to be paid in unaccounted money from the underground economy. The firms lend only to local MBs in 3-month or 100-day block loans or daily repayment loans (both given after deduction of the interest in advance) which are repayable in 100 daily instalments. They are given on the guarantee or recommendation of a partner on the strength of a promissory note with two known sureties or for larger amounts on equitable mortgage deeds and other collateral. Some firms even accept postdated cheques at the time of issue in order to ensure timely repayment of loans.

The operations of lenders in the ICMs acting as principals and dealers are sustained by an extensive network of brokers, couriers, and assorted middlemen who are 'market-makers' as well as the links of ICMs with formal finance, like the 'compradores' in South East Asia, shroffs, and guarantee brokers of commercial banks in India.

Reciprocity of savings, credit and remittance facilities

The experience of savings banks, credit unions, informal savings and loan associations, suggests that the efficacy of savings mobilization depends in large part on whether 'they can profitably lend to the same clientele from which deposits are mobilized'.[7] This lack of reciprocity also explains the relative unpopularity of post office savings banks (eg in India) which do not extend credit and have become passive collectors of deposits to support the government budget. The potential benefits of reciprocity like economies of scope, lower loan default rates and increased savings mobilization outweigh any possible losses of economies of specialization. The success of the ROSCAs in India and Africa in combining credit and savings facilities is a notable example of the significance of reciprocity.[1,2,8,9]

In India the popularity of one important ROSCA (the chit funds) is explained by the fact that the subscriber is entitled to borrow from it by offering discount at the auction (Banking Commission, Government of India, 1972). These funds combine savings and borrowing facilities for specific needs, but there is no assurance that the money will be available when needed since there may be other strong bidders and in the event of a tie there is a lottery. The chit fund does not prima facie extend credit to productive enterprises, but, as recognized by the Commission, their removal without offering alternative outlets would create a gap. The problem, according to the Commission, is how to regulate them. There is no information on the operating costs of ROSCAs, overdues and defaults (see Table 5 for procedures for dealing with problem loans in Thailand). ROSCAs have been able to compete successfully with postal savings banks largely due to their combined provision of credit and savings facilities.

ROSCAs are not popular in Latin America where they function mainly as an alternative to instalment credit in financing consumer durables, but they are important in Jamaica where they are known as the Partner system.[10,11] Credit unions, on the other hand, are most popular in Latin America. They have the ability to provide low cost deposit services but having been pushed into a role similar to that of agricultural banks, their competitive advantage as lenders seems to have been eroded creating the same loan delinquency problems as faced by development banks.[12]

The experience of the Grameen Bank, Bangladesh, which has successfully replicated and improved upon the better features of ICMs is amply supportive of the feasibility and desirability of combining savings and credit facilities for the landless poor. In this Bank, in addition to weekly personal savings of 1 taka per person, (30–32 takas = $1 US) each borrower is required to pay a group tax of 5 per cent of the loan received. The weekly savings and the Group Tax constitute Group Funds which individual members can borrow for consumption and investment purposes without the consent of the remaining members of the group. The resultant high marginal rates of savings (25–50

Table 5: Thailand: dealing with problem loans (in per cent)

Recourse	Personal rotating credit	Business rotating credit	Cheque discounting
Go to court	2.8	13.6	24.4
Organizer's responsibility	49.9	36.5	–
Sharing of losses by participant	13.8	12.2	–
Rescheduling of debt	17.4	32.1	44.7
Dissolving the game	2.6	–	–
Liquidate collateral	–	–	24.1
No action taken	–	3.0	–
Other	–	2.6	6.8

Source: Bank of Thailand Staff Estimates

per cent of the additional income generated by the Bank credit) are additional evidence of the high productivity of credit with rates of return ranging from 10–40 per cent on the invested capital. The evaluations suggest that the rates of return are higher for trading and modern industrial activities and lower for traditional processing and artisan-type activities.[13] The Syndicate Bank (South India) has successfully operated a scheme which matches 'Small Savers' to 'too Small Borrowers' the bulk of whom are MBs.[14] The principle of reciprocity of credit and savings is unexceptionable but the question is: Would ICMs be able to provide credit beyond a certain small scale which may not be commensurate with the needs of growing MBs? For instance, the nidhies in South India which cater to housing finance, are unable to satisfy the full credit requirements of their members.

A notable advantage of ICMs are their concomitant facilities for remittance which are cheaper and often even more reliable than those of FIs and the government postal system. In India MBs rely quite often on a functionary (the Angadia) who doubles up both as a broker and courier. Overseas migrants' remittances through ICMs (sarafs) in the Arab countries, and Hundi agents in the Indian subcontinent, are so much more popular in developing countries (eg El Salvador, Bangladesh, India, etc) bcause of lower costs, greater convenience and high flexibility.[15,16] The 'transfer' houses in El Salvador reportedly arrange more conveniently for remittances from the US to El Salvador at a far lower cost while also offering a more attractive rate of exchange to the recipients, a feature common to all ICMs. The remittances of overseas migrants, which are largely channelled through ICMs, to the home countries, have generated an extensive network of economic relationships including financing of MBs. These remittances are used largely for housing, consumer durables, repayment of past debt, and social expenditure, but a fair proportion also finances MBs.[17] A survey for Bangladesh showed that nearly

90 per cent of businesses established by migrant families were financed mainly by remittance money and that migrants were also providing working capital for businesses through the ICMs.[16] There is, however, more scope for diversifying the end-use of remittances since an excessive amount has gone into real estate and consumption or else into other saturated businesses (eg bakeries and taxis in Jordan).

While some of the ICMs (eg ROSCAs, private bankers and finance companies) do provide a link between savings and credit facilities, it would seem that ICMs are better geared to the retailing of credit than the collection of savings which in any event are beyond the scope of deposit insurance and central bank supervision. Consequently, the safety of personal savings with ICMs is not comparable with those held with FIs. ICMs are also unable to provide concomitant marketing and technical assistance facilities to borrowers, although they often supply raw material on credit.

Cost and conditions of informal credit: interest and collateral

It is well known that effective rates of interest in ICMs are generally much higher than in the formal sector (Table 6) and exceed the ceilings under usury laws which are notoriously difficult to monitor and enforce. However, even these high rates of interest, which largely reflect the monopoly and monopsony power of money-lending merchant middlemen and the high risk premium consequent upon the absence of collateral, do not clear the credit markets, which strongly suggests that credit rationing is an ever present factor in the ICMs. Consequently, availability is more important than the cost of credit for the typical borrower like the MBs.

The major constraint on formal credit to the MBs is the inability of the latter to furnish acceptable collateral for institutional credit. The typical MBs borrowers do not possess bankable collateral and even when they do possess them the usually vexatious procedures and restricted hours of work of FIs effectively debar MBs from institutional credit, as the following letter to a leading Indian newspaper by a frustrated customer of a nationalized commercial bank vividly illustrates:

> 'Sir, many may prefer pawn-brokers to the Nationalized Banks for raising loans, for certain valid reasons. The small men cannot wait for a long time to get their loans. For instance, the other day I approached an agent of a Nationalized Bank to pledge some gold articles worth 3 sovereigns. It happened to be a Saturday. The Bank staff told me to meet them again on the following Wednesday at about noon, as the Bank's appraiser would visit that Bank only on Wednesday. Is it possible for person to wait up to Wednesday while he needs money badly on Saturday itself? The pawn-brokers, though they are charging exorbitant rates of interest will lend money as and when it is needed. The Nationalized Banks should make arrangements to enable the small

Table 6 Informal rates of interest by country

Region and country	Date	Lower exceptional	Usual	Occasional	Higher exceptional
Africa					
Burundi[1]	early 1960s				300
Ethiopia	1970		40–60		
Ethiopia (Chilalo)	1971		70	90	120
Ghana	1955		50	70	100
Ivory Coast	1972		150	200	
Madagascar	1962				300–400
	1971		30	100	
Nigeria	1958		20–50	50–70	
	1961	less than 10	10–50	70	
Senegal	1960s		60	80	
Sudan	1972		60	130	200
Asia					
Hong Kong	early 1960s		30–40	60	120
India	1962	8–12	18–37	$33\frac{1}{3}$–50	100–150
Indonesia	1950–57		40		80–100
Korea	1969	36	42–54	72	100[2]
Malaysia	1968		24–36	40–60	133–200
Nepal	1969–71	10	25	50	
Pakistan	1962		20–32	46	100
Philippines	1954–55	102–20	25–30	100	200
South Vietnam	1966–67	12	36	60	
	1972		30–36	60–72	
Sri Lanka[3]	1969	6	26[4]	35	above 100
Thailand	1962–3	11	22–35	40–50	80–150
Latin America					
Bolivia	1961		48	96	120
Brazil	1969	15	29–40	60	
Chile	1964–65	27	85	105	155
Colombia	1963		24	60	95
Costa Rica	1969	12	18–24	35	over 100
Ecuador	1965–66	2	20–27	50	80
El Salvador[1]	1970		25		
Honduras[1]	1971		40		
Mexico	1968		36–72	144	300
Paraguay	1972	18	24–30	36	60
Middle East					
Afghanistan[5]	1963		33		
	1971	18	35	50	
	1971	7	18–24	30	48
Jordan[1]	1971		20		
Lebanon	1972	10	16–20	25–36	

1 No range of data available 2 1967–68 3 About 45 per cent of loans have no interest 4 Weighted average 5 Most loans are free of interest and obtained from family members Source U Tun Wai, *Economic Essays on Developing Countries*, Sijthoff and Noordhoff, Netherlands, 1980, p 180

men to get loans at any time on their working day by pledging their goods, if they are to replace usurious pawn-brokers effectively.'

M Jagannathan *(The Hindu,* Madras, 30 September 1973)

The formalities of institutional finance are a formidable deterrent to MBs, many of whom may even lack the formal education necessary to cope with them. In some ICMs (eg India) a broker undertakes to do any minimal paperwork necessary for recourse to the ICMs. There are, no doubt, some negative aspects to informal credit, notably the fear of challenge by civic and tax authorities and even a certain social odium, which also explains why in a major Indian survey, half the respondents denied even using ICMs![3] Nonetheless, the convenience and flexibility of ICMs seem to far outweigh any such drawbacks. The major strength of ICMs is their ability and willingness to extend credit much more quickly and flexibly than FIs without collateral (except in the case of pawn-brokers and pawnshops) on the basis of personal knowledge and credit appraisal of the borrowers. A classic example of 'character' loans as a technique of transformation of intangible collateral into tangible credit. The unsecured credit of the ICMs has several advantages for the borrowers. Firstly, it does not tie up inventories in collateral. Secondly, it meets the needs of many MBs which do not generate acceptable collateral (eg laundries, restaurants, construction contractors). There are, of course, some forms of secured credit in the ICMs, like those given by firms purchasing the accounts receivable of textile mills in Bombay (India). By and large, informal lenders concern themselves with the overall credit standing and financial position of the borrower rather than with the end purpose of credit.[3] Nor do they supervise the end use of credit being generally content with surveillance of the borrower's overall activity, including even his social conduct which is only possible in a close face-to-face society based on multiple-interest interrelationships. They lend on the basis of the projected cash flow of the borrower rather than asset protection or any of the standard banking ratios. However, in the ICMs in India there appears to be some notional relationship between the net worth of a customer on the credit extended to him which ranges from 25–33 per cent of net worth (among the Shikarpuri and Rastogi financiers). The Gujarati financiers are said to lend on the basis of the cash and stock position of their clients rather than on their net worth. The Shikarpuris, who lend to a more varied clientele than their rivals — also reflected in their higher than average interest rates — prefer to lend to income tax assessees and often ask for tax returns. A major determinant of credit extension is said to be the record of punctiliousness in servicing of loan obligations.

There are also other screening mechanisms in ICMs, which are both legal and prudential. For instance, urban informal financiers in India generally try to avoid infringement of the restrictive state money-lending laws. They do not therefore lend in amounts less than Rs 3,000 (Rs 12.50 = $1 US) or to agriculturists who are specially protected under these laws. In addition, most lenders have informal maximum limits to any one party (eg Rs 25,000 in the case of the Shikarpuris). Borrowers who require larger accommodation can arrange through brokers to put together loans in multiples of Rs 25,000, which is akin to the loan syndications of formal markets. Likewise, in some centres such as Amritsar (Punjab) there are informal limits for overall credit apportionment at least for large clients — one third each from own resources, FIs, and the ICMs. Those lenders who are primarily financiers like the Shikarpuris are more concerned with limits on their own exposure, whereas lenders and brokers from other communities are too specialized in the finance of one or another commodity or product (eg spices, cloth, etc) to be able to limit their exposure in it. Consequently trade credit is a very substantial item of informal finance.

Despite the absence of collateral, the bad debt experience of lenders to MBs in the urban ICMs in India is said to be roughly comparable to that of similar credit to commercial banks,[3] which suggests that collateral requirements of the latter do not make a material difference to the quality of credit. This is also borne out by the remarkable experience of the Grameen Bank of Bangladesh, which extends collateral-free credit to landless customers and yet boasts of a loan recovery rate of about 98 per cent, although the rate of interest (16 per cent) is about the same as charged by FI. The high recovery rate reflects cumulative effects of: the group liability which provides a substitute for collateral; the intensive supervision of credit; and the innovative device of weekly repayments of credit instalments spread over a 50-week period, irrespective of the maturity cycle of the end-use of credit. The Bank, like the ICMs, uses a net worth criterion rather than income or cash flow.

Informal credit and finance of microbusiness

Because of the inherent informality of ICMs it is obviously not possible to present systematic data on their size, flows, and turnover. Even the well-endowed Banking Commission of the Government of India (1972) found it difficult to obtain adequate information on ICMs. The subsequent study on urban ICMs in India based on interviews with one thousand respondents (lenders, borrowers and intermediaries) noted that 'informal credit market actors are notoriously shy about publicity — and the task of convincing them was an arduous diplomatic one'.[18] The available evidence, based on surveys of financing of MBs through ICMs is presented below for selected countries in Africa; Asia; Latin America; and the Caribbean.

The evidence from Africa (Table 7) shows the following broad features.[19] The start-up capital is often minuscule, with a reported mean of about $70 (in 1974–75) in Sierra Leone[20] and for rural industry in Kenya.[21] The initial investment is almost wholly financed from own savings or those of relatives or friends and subsequent investments are financed largely from retained earn-

Table 7: Sources of finance for initial investments by small enterprises in some African countries (percentage of initial investment by source)

	Nigeria					
	Western Region	Ibadan	Ghana	Tanzania	Sierra Leone	Uganda
Own savings	97.7	59.0	90.8	78.0	60.2	77.5
Relatives	1.9	35.0	10.8	15.0	19.5	–
Banks	.02	2.0	10.8	1.0	0.9	0.8
Government	–	–	–	1.0	–	–
Moneylenders	.03	–	–	–	0.9	–
Other	–	4.0	–	6.0	18.3	21.7

Source: Page (1979).

ings, though institutional finance plays a somewhat larger role. There is no information on the rates of interest charged by friends or relatives. The opportunity cost of own savings or funds lent by relatives and friends is difficult to estimate, but Page suggests a real rate of 15–25 per cent. Although most surveys echo complaints of inadequate working capital, the major complaint relates to material shortages.[22]

Interestingly, this pattern is broadly replicated in the Caribbean (Jamaica and Haiti) and Latin America (Colombia), except for the higher average initial investment ($800 in Jamaica with a range of $70–17,000). In Jamaica 90 per cent of the start-up finance for clients with less than 245 employees originated from own savings, with friends and relatives providing another 6 per cent. In Haiti, the banks provided less than 3 per cent of initial investment finance ($100–6,000) for enterprises employing less than 50 workers. The principle source of start-up finance in Colombia has been personal savings, often derived from severance compensation but supplemented by other personal savings, family loans and suppliers' credit.[23] Although the role of institutional finance seems to have increased with the growth of the borrowing units, the share of self-financed capital was above 75 per cent in the two sample sectors (metal-working and food processing) and less than half the firms resorted to any institutional finance mainly because of the paperwork involved and the dislike of indebtedness. Significantly, while the lack of collateral was the main reason for rejection by institutional lenders, social and educational status were reportedly influential in obtaining credit. There was also some association between the extent of ICM credit and the economic surplus generated by the MBs.[23]

The establishment surveys and other information for Asian countries (Korea, Malaysia, the Philippines, and Thailand), point to the following main features. The Korean ICMs are possibly the largest in relation to the money supply among developing countries. The declared volume of indebtedness to the ICMs (reported by 40,677 enterprises of all sizes in response to the Presidential Emergency Decree of 3 August 1972) was 345.6 bn won, close to 80 per cent of money supply and 24 per cent of FI credit.[24] The Korean ICM are substantial lenders not only to MBs but also to the formal sector. Surprisingly, Korea, despite its large and extremely sophisticated ICMs, shows a higher proportion of institutional finance (9 per cent in 1973 of units in the size group 5–49 workers) as the main source of start-up finance than elsewhere.[25] This survey, which covered all manufacturing, showed that the larger the size of the unit the larger the share of FI finance. About one-third of investment was financed from outside sources, much less for the smallest units; one quarter relied on outside sources for working capital, mainly to banks, but also the ICMs (suppliers, friends and relatives).

In Malaysia resort to ICMs by most enterprises normally seems to occur after exhausting all their past internal savings and access to FI credit. But small business units seem to prefer the ICMs despite the high interest rates because of speedy access without stringent collateral requirements.[26] There are no figures for start-up finances for Malaysia but of the new investments in the size group (1–50 workers) 18 per cent obtained some associated bank credit and 20 per cent obtained credit from banks for working capital.[22] More than half of the working capital represented supplier's credit until the size class of over 100 workers was reached, where bank credit became predominant. Bank credit rose sharply with size of enterprise but entrepreneurial characteristics were more important in explaining credit use than establishment characteristics like age and size.

In the Philippines an All-Size Sample Survey found that the modal size of start-ups was 6,000–20,000 pesos (1978 prices) ie $800–2,700, of which 8 per cent was from FIs and the rest from the ICMs. But recourse to institutional credit for both fixed and working capital increased after start-up.[27]

In Thailand the role of the urban ICMs (ie personal and business ROSCAs, cheque discounting liable credit) seems far more important than in the other Southeast Asian countries.[28] The Thai ICMs are notable for the distinctive entity of business ROSCAs and the most extensive resort to cheque discounting practices outside Taiwan. Interestingly, only 23 per cent of the business ROSCA funds came from own funds, supplemented by about 9 per cent from other ROSCA credit and 8 per cent from abroad. About 47 per cent came from borrowings from commercial banks and finance companies. The bulk of ROSCA credit (59 per cent) was used for working capital, 22 per cent of repayment of loans and 8 per cent for lending. About 34 per cent of funds obtained through cheque discounting was used for working capital and 17 per cent each for fixed investment and for coping with cash flow problems with FIs and 15 per cent for inventories.

In India the Banking Commission (1972) reported that the indigenous bankers provided one-twelfth to one-half of all credit to different categories of industrial units. A study of urban ICMs[3] showed that they represented about 50 per cent of that provided by commercial banks and serve sectors or needs to be served by banks at only slightly higher rates of interest. They lend (without collateral) mostly for short-term working capital to small scale enterprises in the upper range (ie with assets between Rs 100,000–1m). In regard to start-up finance, another survey showed that, except in the case of power loom companies, where the funding is financed by the merchant under the putting-out system, trade credit was dominant.

A sample survey of the schemes in Gujarat (India) for assisting small-scale techno-entrepreneurs showed that about 48 per cent of the techno-entrepreneurs raised more than 25 per cent of seed capital from own savings: about 57 per cent sought assistance from families and friends for meeting more than 25 per cent of finance. Money lenders accounted for less than 10 per cent of the amount.[29] Significantly, even when funds were borrowed from families, friends and private sources, the interest paid was close to what the banks would have charged (12 per cent). But the main problem for the new entrepreneurs was shortage of working capital after the ICM financing was used up at a very early stage of production.

Surprisingly, there is no reference in the literature to what is often a major source of the cash flow and working capital problems of MBs — the inordinate delays in payments due by governments and public authorities who do not pay any interest on overdue bills to their suppliers. Although such delays affect all suppliers to governments, they impinge more severely on the MBs. Thus we have the irony of MBs who borrow at high rates of interest from the ICMs because of bureaucratic failures and are then obliged to extend credit at zero rates of interest to governments, while being punctilious in making property, sales, and income tax payments.

Linkages of informal and formal credit

In all developing countries, ICMs have lines of credit with FIs. ICMs cater not only to the MBs and the informal real sector but also supply those credit requirements of the organized sector which cannot be met by FIs. These aspects have hardly been studied except for some studies relating to Korea and India. In Korea, ICMs have been a major source of finance in giving flexibility to a high-growth economy.[30] In India, changes in monetary policy have had a significant effect not only on the volume of credit in the informal sector, but also on the rates of interest in the same direction. A contractionary credit policy has been observed to raise interest rates in the ICMs in India even as an expansionary policy lowers it.[31]

One study of Korea concluded that limitations on the availability of credit tend to affect economic decisions directly instead of through interest rate movements.[32] The results indicate that the main source of investment financing for small enterprises is internal resources and that increase availability of bank credit was unlikely to affect significantly changes in the working capital of either small, medium or large enterprises. The selective credit controls adopted in Korea to provide incentives to the small enterprises did indeed help to expand their investment activity, albeit only slightly. However, the lessons of Korean experience have to be qualified to allow for the fact that since 1965 commercial banks have been required to lend a minimum proportion of their total loans (since 1980 it is 35 per cent for national banks and 55 per cent for local banks) to small and medium enterprises. These minimum lending ratios constitute a hidden subsidy to MBs. Korean experience is even more instructive in demonstrating the linkage of formal and informal finance in savings behaviour. Thus an increase in institutional interest rates after the interest rate reforms of 1965 resulted in an inflow of savings from the informal sector. On the other hand, in Thailand reverse flows of savings into the informal sector have been observed from time to time because of higher rates of interest on chit funds, pyramid schemes, etc.

Conclusions relevant to policy

The following broad conclusions arising from the preceding analysis and evidence are relevant to policy.

Personal savings are a substantial source of start-up finance and seed capital for MBs; the share of institutional finance seems to rise with the increase in the size of MBs. Nevertheless, the share of ICMs in the total finance of MBs is still large. The availability rather than the cost of working capital, short and medium term, seems to be the major financial problem of MBs.

The efficiency of ICMs depends on the reciprocity of savings mobilization, credit extension and remittance facilities. There are viable substitutes for collateral such as group credit and group liability (through entities like business ROSCAs and the borrower groups of the Grameen Bank) but ICMs seem better suited to be retailers of credit than collectors of savings.

When MBs grow in size, their credit requirements cannot be met by ICMs after a certain size and scale threshold. Therefore, they have also to be trained to become eligible clients of institutional finance. This would also enlarge their portfolio of choice between ICMs and FIs and the competition between the two sectors. Likewise, lenders in the ICMs may at some point wish to graduate to institutional status. This process too should be facilitated through appropriate procedures and policies.

The success of institutional lenders in dealing with MBs is strongly correlated to the extent to which they replicate the desirable features of the ICMs (eg flexibility and credit related to personal appraisal and net worth rather than collateral and cash flows).

Insofar as delayed payments by public authorities are a major source of cash flow problems of MBs, government and municipal authorities should be required to expedite such payments and to pay appropriate interest (eg corresponding to treasury bills of similar maturity) on any overdue obligations to suppliers and contractors.

Central banks have been prone to benign neglect and even obstructiveness of innovations by FIs intended to help small savers, investors and MBs (eg the Reserve Bank of India discontinued the Pioneering Investors Agency Service of the Syndicate Bank for small investors in shares with an assured return of 9–10 per cent on the ground of its inconsistency with 'pure banking' business!)

Governments and central banks should create a favourable environment for ICMs (eg by establishing special units in central banks, as in the Bank of Thailand) to study and assist ICMs and offer competitive rediscount and refinance facilities for any documentary credits originating from ICMs and endorsed by approved brokers and intermediaries. Changes in monetary policy affect the cost and availability of informal credit but with varying time-lags.

ICMs have a positive role in the finance of MBs as they provide efficient and flexible credit to productive sectors which are generally not catered to by institutional finance because of cost, risk and related factors. It is unlikely that institutional finance will be able to displace ICMs altogether in meeting the requirements of MBs. Nor is 'such displacement essential' (Banking Commission, India, 1972). The core of a positive policy, therefore, is to enhance the efficacy of ICMs through removal of obstacles to their markets, transactions and instruments. Attempts to merely formalize the informal credit sector would only serve to erode the intrinsic economic rationale of ICMs and their competitive advantages relatively to institutional finance, and would, therefore, be counterproductive. It is fallacious to associate an increase in the scope of ICMs as a case of 'disintermediation'.

Linking Informal and Formal Financial Institutions in Africa and Asia

HANS DIETER SEIBEL

Introduction: The small businessman's self-help bank in Nepal and the three fallacies of microenterprise development

BS of Dhule Gaunda is a farmer in one of the poorest countries in the world, with a per capita income of US$160. As it is difficult in landlocked Nepal to earn more than one's subsistence from farming, he decided to open a small shop, but needed to find the start-up capital. He did not qualify for a bank loan. He initiated a dhikuti of 25 members of various castes and ethnic origins, each one contributing Rs 2,000 per month. As organizer, he was the first to receive the total sum of 25 × 2,000 = Rs 50,000 (US$ 2, 270): his start-up capital. There are only a few microentrepreneurs in western Nepal who were not members, at one time or another, in one or several dhikuti, a rotating savings and credit association (ROSCA) with a sophisticated system of fund allocation by secret tender bidding and with incremental interest charges. Over a two-year cycle, total savings mobilized and credit delivered varying between US$ 50,000 and 500,000 per group are nothing unusual. The dhikuti solves some but not all the financial problems of microentrepreneurs. Participants complain that there is no permanent loan fund which would be available in times of need; bidding makes investment planning difficult; and there is no recourse to sources of refinance.[1]

Yet in developing countries microenterprise policies have been based on premises quite different from the dhikuti case, namely that microentrepreneurs are unable to organize themselves, they are too poor to save and they need cheap credit for their enterprises.

There were three major policy consequences: first, development banks and special programmes were set up for credit delivery, which neglected savings mobilization, secondly credit was subsidized, and thirdly credit guarantee schemes were set up by the state to cover anticipated losses.

The results were, first, that the scope of credit remained severely restricted, as there was no built-in growth factor which would have resulted from internal resource mobilization; small numbers of relatively large loans went to medium and large enterprises; the masses had no access to institutional finance. Secondly, entrepreneurs were demotivated to repay and banks

---

HANS DIETER SEIBEL is now working as an advisor with the German Technical Aid Programme in Jogjakarta, Indonesia. He holds a professorship at the University of Cologne, West Germany.

to screen their candidates and recover their loans, resulting in high default rates and in continuous programme decapitalization; and thirdly subvention led to misallocation of production factors.

Around 1980 a reorientation set in. Mounting international debts, increasing shortages of internal and external credit supplies and a growing dissatisfaction with state-nurtured and seemingly ineffective credit programmes led to a rethinking of development policies, centring around such concepts as self-reliance and self-help, which in financial terms was to include the mobilization of savings. Development assistance was now to promote, not replace, self-help and personal effort.

At first, the new approach still bore the mark of the poverty premise, so self-help groups were to be created through outside initiative and credit was to precede savings mobilization.

At the Third UN International Symposium on the Mobilization of Personal Savings in Developing Countries, held in Yaoundé, Cameroon, in December 1984, cognizance was taken of the widespread existence of financial self-help groups and their savings potential in the informal, or non-institutional, sector. It was concluded that, 'the main means of improving the performance of the non-institutional sector were policies directed to enhancing its links with the institutional financial sector.' (UN 1986:13)

To achieve this objective, it was decided to carry out national surveys of informal financial institutions, to work out models and procedures of linkages between them and to design pilot projects to implement the models.

Problems and objectives of microenterprise development

Microentrepreneurs in development countries may be poor; but they are able to save, and they are capable of forming their own self-help groups. Yet, despite wide variations, they usually face a number of fundamental problems:

1   most microenterprises have no access to institutional finance, technical assistance or special incentive schemes. This usually applies to microenterprises in both the formal and the informal sector. Markets of various types are segmented, with large enterprises in a privileged and small ones in an underprivileged position. Most microenterprises fall into the informal sector where they are ignored at best, or actively discriminated against, with measures ranging from extortion to physical elimination;
2   concessionary financial programmes for microenterprises have largely failed. Economically they are not viable; in terms of impact, they reach but a minute proportion of their target group;
3   in every country there is a wealth of human, organizational and financial resources, but their potential remains largely untapped. Such resources include small enterprises, informal and formal financial institutions, non-government organizations and government agencies and programmes;

4   existing financial programmes for microenterprises face high transaction costs for both lender and borrower;
5   credit programmes for microenterprises too often ignore savings as a means of internal resource mobilization and savings habits as a psychological basis for investment and repayment behaviours.

The solutions suggested in this paper and the guidelines offered for their implementation are aimed at the following development objectives:

1   microenterprises in both the informal and the formal sectors should be included among the target groups of financial institutions and programmes, without discrimination or privilege;
2   financial programmes for microenterprises should be developed by banks along commercial lines. Existing programmes in which market interest rates are charged have proven to be economically viable, to reach large numbers of small enterprises and to be capable of self-financing their own growth. Well known examples, are KUPEDES of Bank Rakyat Indonesia, with 3.6 m loans since 1984 and a long term recovery rate of 97.8 per cent (7/1987); and BKK in Central Java with 4.8 m loans since 1972 and a recovery rate of 97.3 per cent (12/1986);
3   the whole network of human and institutional resources should be used, including self-help organizations of microentrepreneurs as delivery structures of their own making, both for financial and non-financial measures;
4   utilizing these resources, a financial intermediation system is to be built, linking informal and formal financial institutions. Non-governmental and governmental self-help promotion institutions (SHPI) may be included for additional supporting services;
5   financial programmes for small enterprises are to include both a savings and a credit component, with systematic linkages between them.

The target group

The sustenance of the growing population in the developing countries is largely provided by microenterprises. Most of them — usually around 95 per cent — are located in the informal sector, which has been growing, despite the predictions of neoliberal and Marxist theories to the contrary: 'The informal sector has proven a resilient feature of peripheral economies and has actually increased in size and scope in a number of them . . . It has not only occurred under stagnant conditions but also in countries experiencing high rates of industrial growth.'[2]

In urban areas, the major subsectors are trade, crafts and small industries, transportation and catering. In rural areas, agriculture is the major subsector, followed by agricultural processing in cottage or home industries and by trade and crafts, usually as secondary activities.

Microenterprises serve vital functions in a developing economy, supplying low-cost goods and services to the masses; providing basic vocational training to uneducated youths and school-leavers; presenting a proving ground for latent entrepreneurial talent; and providing a buffer during times of recession when larger enterprises fail to cope with foreign exchange and spare-part shortages.

The target group of this paper comprises all microenterprises; but a special emphasis is placed on those in the informal sector participating in IFIs or similar SHOs.

The financial and organizational support system

There are many organizational and institutional resources in developing countries which have great potential for microenterprise finance. What stands in the way of their full utilization is financial market segmentation. There are formal financial markets for the upper 5–20 per cent of the population, which fall under the control of state credit and related financial laws and are usually supervised by a central bank. They comprise central, commercial, development, savings and secondary banks as well as non-banking institutions. There is a small but growing semi-formal financial market, which comprises governmental and non-governmental organizations with their own financial programmes. They do not fall under the credit law but operate with the approval of the state. Informal financial markets comprise financial self-help organizations (SHOs), other SHOs with secondary financial functions and individual financial brokers, such as moneylenders, deposit collectors and trade-, land- or crop-related financial arrangements.

From a policy viewpoint, SHOs are of particular importance. The most widespread type of association, globally, and one which simultaneously falls into the categories of both SHO and of IFI, are the savings and credit associations (SCA).[3] They are found in most Asian and African countries and in most culture areas or ethnic groups within them.[3,4,5]

Their main financial functions are the accumulation and depositing of savings, the granting of loans; and the rendering of insurance services.

They may be found in urban and rural areas, among traders and market-women, farmers, fishermen and small industrialists, wage and salary earners, and even among bankers. In recent decades, many SCAs have expanded their activities to comprise saving and lending, joint work for members or non-members, house building and social insurance services for medical treatment, hospital fees, drugs, funerals, naming ceremonies, marriages, etc. Activities focus around one or several funds, which may be built up from regular contributions, entrance and registration fees, interest from loans, penalties and proceeds from communal production or hired labour. There is a strong tendency towards permanent organizations, some of which have been operating successfully for decades. Distinguishing between rotating and non-rotating associations, and between associations with and without a loan or insurance fund, a typology emerges which tends to follow an evolutionary pattern.

Type I: Rotating savings association
Each member pays a fixed amount at regular intervals. In rotating order, each member receives the total amount at a time. A cycle is terminated when all members have received the full amount at least once, and then the next cycle begins. In most African countries, the concern for self-imposed forced savings is primary. When the credit element looms larger, as in most Asian countries, interest may be chaged on an incremental scale, or competitive bidding may be used, turning the RSA into a ROSCA.

Type II: Rotating savings and credit association (ROSCA)
Each member pays a fixed amount at regular intervals. Part of the contribution is allocated to one member at a time in a rotating order; another part is put into a general fund for loans, insurance etc.

Type III: Non-rotating savings association
Each member pays a fixed or variable amount at regular intervals. The contributions are deposited and paid back to the individual member at the end of the stipulated period.

Type IV: Non-rotating savings and credit association
Each member pays a fixed or variable amount at regular intervals. The income of the association from sources such as contributions, fees, penalties, joint business etc, is put into a fund, which may be utilized for loans, insurance and social services. The fund may be established for a specified or unspecified period. Contributions may or may not be paid back at the end of a stipulated period. Interest rates tend to be high, as they provide an additional source of funds.

Though part of the informal financial sector and lacking legal status, most associations do have a clear organizational structure. Typically, they are headed by an elected executive committee; and there are written rules and regulations. Membership lists are kept and some form of book-keeping is mentioned. Local social control mechanisms effectively prevent defaulting or fraud, which plague so many credit programmes, formal and informal.

Business organizations are an important part of the organizational support system in two respects:

1   as self-managed trade and interest associations, they have the potential of building up or mediating any type of service for their members, including financial services;
2   they may act as informal (and sometimes semi-formal) financial institutions, raising funds from their members and extending loans.

Their number, spread and importance varies considerably, both sectorally and geographically. They are variously called trade, interest, occupational or employers' associations. They may be organized locally, regionally or nationally; they may be voluntary or compulsory; they may be formal, registered bodies or they may be unregistered and they may fall into the formal or the informal sector of the economy, occasionally into the semi-formal sector.

National employers' associations of small entrepreneurs, Chambers of Commerce and Industry with a small businessmen's section and Chambers of Crafts (Chambres des Métiers) — the latter virtually non-existent in the English-speaking world — are typical examples of business organizations in the formal sector.

Guilds and unions of craftsmen, traders and market women, transport and restaurant owners are common business organizations of microentrepreneurs in the informal sector. They may be registered or unregistered. Even when registered, they are typically not recognized by the state as representative bodies.

A few of them have demonstrated that they are capable of building up a system of services for their members; that they can raise funds of their own by mobilizing members' savings; can build up a credit system utilizing their own internally generated funds; and that they can link up with formal financial institutions or establish a financial institution of their own. Yet for the large majority of them, this is an unused potential.

Intervention strategies for a financial intermediation system

Institutional linkages: linking informal and formal financial institutions and self-help promotion institutions

Transaction costs with regard to depositing savings, credit delivery and repayment collection are too high to permit a substantial expansion of the services of existing formal institutions to microenterprises, particularly among the poorer sections of the population. Financial institutions of the formal and the informal sector are largely unrelated. As a result, their potential is vastly underutilized, the financial needs of the micro-entrepreneurs are not adequately satisfied and the financial system remains underdeveloped. Substantial improvements require financial innovations based on an intermediation system built around IFIs and SHOs, which usually exist in many varieties and large numbers. The proposed intermediation system is to optimize the utilization of all institutions in the formal, semi-formal and informal sectors involved in savings mobilization and credit delivery. It is also to include supporting technical and consultancy services.

The intermediation system first encompasses an institutional linkage dimension, with links between IFIs and SHOs as primary intermediaries and banking institutions, in two alternatives, either with direct links between

IFIs, SHOs and banks or with indirect links, mediated by private voluntary or government SHPIs as secondary intermediaries.

It is the ultimate and long-range objective of such linkages to make the individual microenterprise bankable and gain direct access to formal financial institutions. There are three alternative models in an evolutionary sequence:

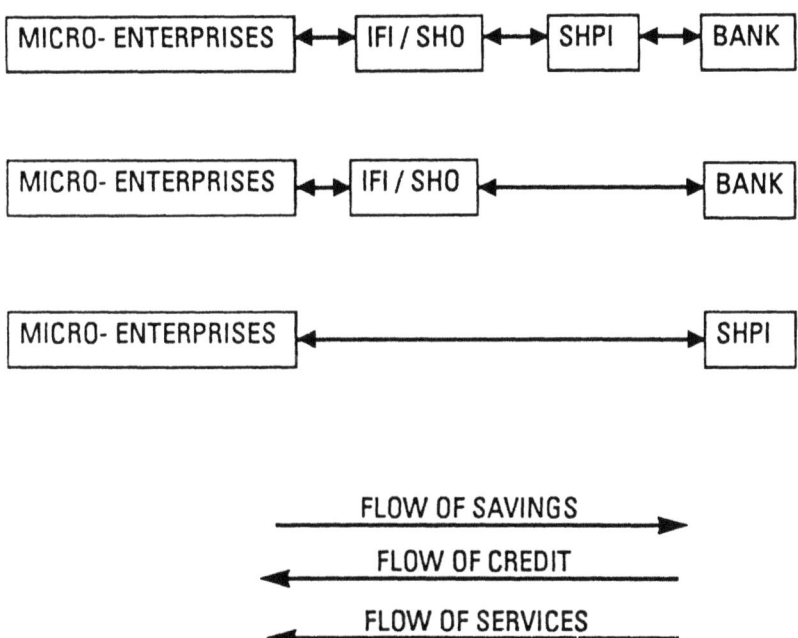

Figure 1: *Alternative institutional linkage models*

In the course of evolution, the role of IFIs/SHOs may change from that of a financial intermediary to credit guarantee group, consultant and referral agency. In the case of the lack of any legal status of an SHO, a bank may prefer a model of direct credit delivery to the microenterprises, with the SHO acting as a credit guarantee group and as an agent of savings and repayment collection.

Financial linkages: linking savings mobilization and credit delivery

As savings without credit lead to demotivation, resource deflection and the inadequate financing of small enterprises, and as credit without preceeding savings leads to haphazard loan spending, to risky business ventures and to poor repayment morale, we propose a model of linking savings and credit: no credit without savings, no savings without credit!

Savings and credit can be linked on two different levels:

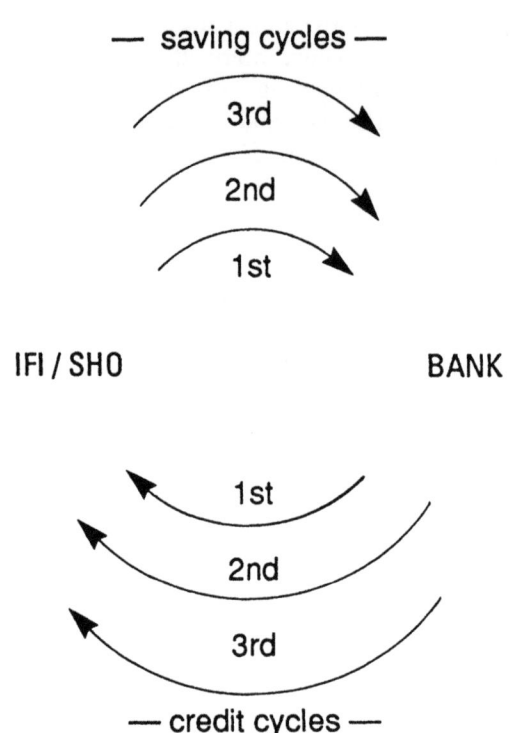

Figure 2: *Dynamic financial linkage model*

1 There may be a joint credit savings scheme in which a loan is contingent upon every individual client meeting specified savings requirements;
2 there may be separate savings and credit schemes, each with its own set of clients. In this case, the bank mobilizes its own resources through a savings scheme but does not require its borrowers to meet any savings requirements.

Both types of linkages are viable and feasible. The second case of separate schemes is well known. The first type would be a financial innovation to most banks. The following presentation is therefore confined to this type.

Sources of savings generated by IFIs/SHOs may include entrance fees, equity share capital, compulsory regular savings, voluntary savings, rotating savings, savings in kind and savings derived from income-generating activities.

These savings may enter into two different cycles:

1 an IFI/SHO may set up an internal loan fund for immediate relending to members; these loans may be used for emergencies, consumptive or productive purposes;
2 a certain amount of its internal funds may be deposited with a bank as

collateral within a contractual loan savings scheme. These loans may be reserved for working capital or investment.

For the internal loan fund, we recommend a fixed ratio between savings and credit. This ratio would be mainly contingent upon the availability of funds.

For the loan savings scheme, a dynamic ratio is recommended. Savings are deposited as collateral, and the amount of credit is contingent upon two factors: the amount of savings deposited and the number of cycles of satisfactory repayment (repeat loans), resulting in augmenting cycles of savings and credit and providing a strong double incentive to save and to repay on time.

For example, after an initial period of regular savings, say of one year, the SHO obtains a loan equal to twice the amount of accumulated savings. After the principal and interest have been duly paid back and the group has continued to adhere to its self-imposed savings schedule, it may obtain a second loan, this time three times its savings. Subsequently, the multiplier may continue to increase by a value of one or by a different point value, provided repayments and savings collection have been satisfactory.

Operational guidelines and procedures

There are ten major operational elements in programme implementation:

1 Working out and testing guidelines for linkages between IFIs/SHOs and banks, with specific provisions concerning obligations, liabilities, bye-laws, savings, credit, accounts, interest rates, book-keeping, collateral, re-insurance, mutual information, termination and liquidation, registration and arbitration;

2 guidelines for relations between IFIs/SHOs and their member-microentrepreneurs;

3 definition and co-ordination of institutional tasks and activities for micro-enterprises and banks and possibly for central bank and for governmental and non-governmental SHPIs;

4 survey and mobilization campaign as a grassroots strategy, which is to gather data and activate the participants at the same time. S&M is a methodological tool to provide banks with the necessary information about IFIs/SHOs, to provide IFIs/SHOs with the necessary information about the bank, its personnel and the linking scheme, to establish effective communication between IFIs/SHOs and bank personnel as well as local authorities and SHPIs, if any, and to initiate the linkage procedure.

5 communication and training measures for national and local policy makers and for participating staff from IFIs/SHOs and banks through national seminars and local workshops;

6 upgrading of IFIs/SHOs to higher organizational levels, institutional skills and financial practices;
7 the institutional adaptation of banks to their environment, 'taking the bank to the people'. This may involve the adoption of practices hitherto characteristic of IFIs ('downgrading of banks');
8 monitoring and evaluation;
9 supporting technical services concerning management and production technology, supply, marketing, finance and training — varying in intensity between phases of limited growth and of more rapid development;
10 providing and co-ordinating sources of refinance from banks, government and donors.[6]

Case studies from Africa
Initiatives from below
Private deposit collection in West Africa
Daily deposit collection is an IFI which mainly operates on markets in West Africa (ajo, anago susu, jojuma, yesyes, etc). The deposit collector may serve between 200 and 600 clients a day, collecting a fixed or variable amount from each, which he enters onto a printed card. By the end of the month he returns the total, keeping the amount of one daily deposit as a fee. As an extra service, clients may obtain short-term loans of up to 50 per cent of the monthly total free of interest. Participants are microentrepreneurs in trade, crafts, restaurants and transportation.

The efficiency of this IFI is far beyond that of any bank. The average length of a savings transaction in Accra und Kumasi was found to be 17 seconds, a lending transaction between 40 and 60 seconds. With time input as the main cost factor, transaction costs were minimal for the itinerant banker and for the client. There are several links to other financial institutions:
1 participants may use half of the monthly returns for the purchase of supplies; the other half is put into a ROSCA;
2 When their turn comes in the ROSCA, they may spend it or put it into a bank account;
3 all daily deposit collectors have bank accounts on which they deposit the collections, usually with a one-night delay because of unsuitable banking hours;
4 in some countries, the ajo or anago susu are registered, tax-paying enterprises. In Accra, 300 of them have formed the Greater Accra Susu Collectors Association, which is registered and keeps its accounts with the National Savings and Credit Bank of Ghana. As the NSCB does not meet GASCA's financial needs, it is now in the process of establishing its own formal bank;
5 in Lagos, Nigeria, experiments were carried out between 1960 and 1980 to organize ajo-participants into co-operative societies and to link them to

banks. By extending credit before sufficient savings were deposited, the self-help principle was violated, and the co-operatives collapsed;[6]
6 in Niger, a model has been worked out in 1987–8 for the Caisse Nationale d'Epargne directly to utilize the daily deposit collection system as a basis for financial services to microenterprises.

Linking IFI and co-operatives in the Congo
Between 1983 and 1985, a first set of eleven savings and credit co-operatives (COOPEC) was set up in the Congo. In Kinkala, a small rural town, a COOPEC of 268 members is located next to the market place. Its members are microentrepreneurs and salary earners. On the market, there are several IFI, among them a ROSCA with 24 members. Monthly contributions are F CFA 2,000. Thus each member receives the total of F CFA 48,000 once every two years. At its own initiative, the IFI has linked up with the COOPEC. The members, who participate in both organizations, now pay their monthly contributions to the manager of the COOPEC, who deposits the F CFA 48,000 in the savings account of the recipient, which in turn improves his credit rating with the COOPEC.[7]

Linking IFIs and commercial banks in Nigeria
Eha Amufu is a rural town of 10 adjoining villages with 30,000 inhabitants, located in the Isi Uzo Local Government Area, Anambra State. There are two commercial bank branches in the district. Self-help activities and organizations have a long tradition among the local Igbo population. Since the money economy started spreading in the late 1930s, rotating savings associations, isusu, have grown in number and importance; they are now ubiquitous. During the last twenty years, most of them have started to build up permanent loan funds, and many have engaged in joint projects.

In conjunction with a survey of co-operatives and IFIs in early 1984, I was approached by several IFI executives. Their problems were the inadequacy of savings for larger investments, lack of refinance and lack of consultancy services for microenterprises. As a result of the discussions, the executives approached the managers of a local bank in April 1984, established the Isi Uzo SHO in April 1985, which is an umbrella organization of 40 IFIs, and concluded a savings and loan agreement with one of the commercial banks: member societies deposit regular savings with the banks as collateral and obtain group loans for on-lending. Between April and December 1985, the first 14 IFIs had deposited N 16,160, and the first ten of them had obtained N 18,000 in credit by August 1986. Isi Uzo SHO is now in the process of using using 5 per cent of its savings to employ its own microenterprise consultant, arguing that the state's extension services are of little practical use.[6]

Initiatives from above

Linking IFIs and business organizations of microenterprises to a savings bank in Togo

IFIs of the rotating type were first noted early this century by the ethnologist Westermann. Today three major types are in existence: rotating savings associations with weekly or monthly contributions (sodzodzo, sodyodyo, abo); daily deposit collection (yesyes, jojouma); and a combination of the two, in which a cashier collects fixed amounts every day from each participant and one at a time receives the total collection at the month's end. In addition, there are two principal types of business organizations of microentrepreneurs: market women and traders are organized in product associations of between 200 and 300 members each, and a relatively small number of craftsmen in employers' unions. They have virtually no access to institutional credit.

When the Savings Bank of Togo, CET, opened a branch in the central market of Lomé, it embarked on a new course of banking for microenterprises, with craftsmen's and market associations and their IFLs as target groups. The craftsmen agreed to deposit their receipts from ROSCA in a group account with the CET. The group obtains a loan from the CET for on-lending to its members, while the savings deposits serve as collateral. A similar system is being introduced among market-women and traders on the central market of Lomé, creating the following links between IFIs and CET:

1 market associations deposit their funds derived from weekly or monthly contributions with the CET:
2 the members of ROSCA within the market associations are to be given the opportunity of depositing their funds with the CET and act as a credit guarantee groups for loans from the bank;
3 participants in the daily deposit system are to be given the opportunity to make their deposits to a CET agent rather than an anonymous collector;
4 the possibility of direct collaboration with the daily deposit collectors is being explored.

The links between IFIs and CET have two major implications: upgrading of the business organizations of the microentrepreneurs and of their IFIs; and downgrading of the CET in the sense of simplifying its banking procedures and of adopting some of the people-oriented practices of the local IFI.[6]

Linking IFIs of rural microentrepreneurs to a development bank in Ivory Coast

There are some 50 to 60 ethnic groups in Ivory Coast which fall into four major ethno-linguistic groups: Kru, Gur, Akan and Mande — varying from highly decentralized and segmentary to centralized and state societies. These socio-political orders are in turn related to culture patterns, value orienta-

Social System (ethno-linguistic group)

	Kru	Gur	Akan	Mande
Descent system	Patrilinear	Patri- or matrilinear, acc. to ethnic group	Matrilinear (except two ethnic groups)	Patrilinear
Socio-political system	Segmentary and decentralized	Segmentary with hierarchy controlled by secret society	Centralized differentiated state society	Centralized (Malinke: state society)
Agents of social control	Decentralized secret societies	Centralized secret societies	The nobles (sacred chair holders)	The nobles
Social stratification	Equalitarian social order: equal opportunities; unstable inequalities as a result of individual achievement	Social classes based on initiation and age groups	Three estates: nobles, freemen, prisoners / slaves	Caste society
Social mobility	Extensive upward and downward mobility; pronounced competition for success	Upward mobility based on initiation into age groups; absence of free competition	Controlled mobility in ec. and religious spheres; absence of socio-political mobility	Mobility in economic and religious spheres within castes; absence of socio-political mobility
Integration into monetary economy	Low degree of integration	Weak and late integration	Early and intensive integration	Moderate to strong integration
Crucial problems	Reconciling individual success with social equality	Unquestioning acceptance of authority and tradition by the young	Reconciling individual achievement with hereditary inequality	Confining individual achievement to caste limits
Development approach	From below: grassroots approach	From above: through secret societies and chiefs	From below and from above	From above and below

Figure 3: *Social systems and intervention strategies in Ivory Coast*

tions and personality traits, varying along such axes as status equality to inequality and achievement to ascription. All these variables enter into a highly complex web of determinants of receptivity to change. (Figure 3)

Major types of IFI are hired work associations with primary financial functions ('Work is money!' as one participant put it), rotating savings associations and non-rotating SCAs. In addition, there is the daily deposit collection system, which is purely urban. There are wide variations according to ethnic groups. The economy of the Mande-speaking Dan and Malinke is entirely dominated by financial and non-financial SHOs. Among the Sénufo (Gur), rotating work associations are universal, while IFI are entirely absent. Among the Agni and Baulé (Akan) as well as among the Guéré and Bété (Kru-speakers), IFIs are important. With the monetization of the local economy as the chief determinant, three tendencies of change have been observed over the past 30 years: from work associations to financial SHOs, from rotating savings associations to non-rotating groups with permanent revolving loan funds, and from mutual assistance and insurance to interest-bearing loan funds. Geographically, IFIs have spread from rural to urban

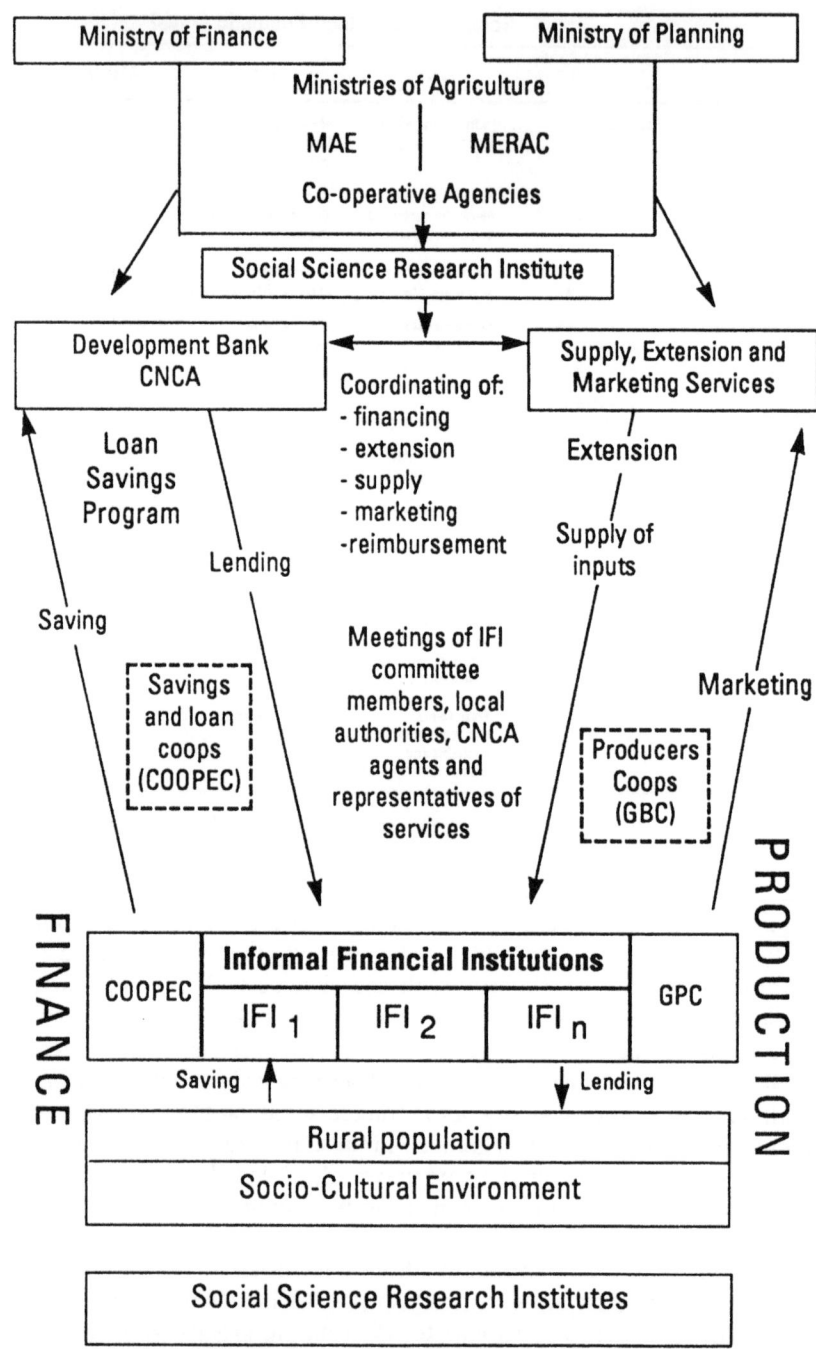

Figure 4: *Mode of intervention in Ivory Coast*

areas where they have made inroads into virtually all occupational groups. Sectorally, they first expanded in two sectors: agriculture and trade. From there, they spread to other microenterprises, paticularly small crafts and transportation. They are also widespread among blue and white collar employees.

The core problem of the Ivorian IFI is the lack of access to refinancing institutions and to financial consultancy services.

Prominent among banks which intervene in rural areas is the agricultural development bank BNDA, which plans to step up its decentralization to reach all 750–900 central villages of the country within the next five years. In this process, a linkage model has been worked out as a grassroots intermediation system for IFIs of agricultural and non-agricultural microenterprises (Figure 4). A prerequisite for successful interventions is the adaptation of strategies to local and regional sociocultural conditions along the following lines:

1 local banking and supporting technical services are linked to indigenous IFIs.
2 local IFIs of microentrepreneurs are promoted within the framework of the relevant socio-political entity, which may be the village, as among the Sénufo, or the quarter, as among the Dan and Malinké, or the household as among the Kru and Guéré;
3 interventions are adjusted to local decision-making and allocative processes, yielding three different types of strategies: a strategy of development from below with broad grassroots participation in decentralized segmentary societies, a strategy of development from above with primary involvement of local authorities and social control agents in centralized societies with restrictions on socio-economic mobility, and a mixed strategy of development from below and above in complex societies with elements of decentralized decision-making and centralized control, or simultaneous achieved and ascribed criteria of role and reward allocation (Figure 3).

Given the variety of IFIs and the diversity of sociopolitical systems, the linking of informal and formal financial institutions can only follow a certain procedure, not a fixed model. Procedural guidelines include,

1 a Survey and Mobilization Campaign;
2 initiation of appropriate participation processes;
3 linking IFIs to the BNDA, involving cooperatives, chambers of crafts and other development organizations as second-tier intermediaries as seen fit;
4 establishing a loan savings scheme for IFIs of microentrepreneurs, to be administered by BNDA;
5 monitoring and evaluating the linkages.[8]

The emergence of microenterprise organizations with their own bank in Rwanda

Rwanda is a country with very limited microenterprise traditions outside of agriculture. IFIs in the form of RSAs are widespread. Rwanda has demonstrated that, in spite of very adverse conditions, effective business organizations of microentrepreneurs can emerge; and that they can establish their own formal financial institutions, by-passing the linkage stage.

Most modern crafts developed after independence in 1962 when the capital Kigali had 7,000 inhabitants. Today, Kigali has some 200,000 inhabitants and a full range of modern crafts. It is also the place of one of the most successful craft development projects, initiated by Jeunesse Ouvrière Catholique and subsequently promoted by the ILO. By 1986 there were 61 unions of 1,600 craftsmen in Kigali plus an umbrella organization, KORA. The guiding principles are self-help, self-organization, self-financing and self-training, plus joint efforts in supply and marketing. Each union follows a policy of savings mobilization, with weekly or monthly contributions depending on the financial capacity of each union. This is paralleled by the emergence of 88 cooperative People's Banks, with savings and credit activities of predominantly small entrepreneurs. The two approaches of craft unions and of savings and credit cooperatives overlap in that KORA has now established its own People's Bank as the housebank of the craft unions, headed by a craftsman. This Banque Populaire KORA is a successful example of upgrading the savings and credit activities of business organizations of craftsmen to a formal financial institution of their own making. In 1985 the approach was extended by the ILO to the provincial towns of Butaré, Gisenyi and Ruhengéri.

Case studies from Asia

There are many varieties and large numbers of IFIs of local origin in Asia, the most prominent among them being perhaps the hui in China and Vietnam, chitfunds in India and Sri Lanka, arisan in Indonesia, kye in Korea and paluwagan in the Philippines. In some countries, indigenous IFIs and SHOs initiated by governmental and non-governmental SHPIs overlap to a large extent. There are many linkage experiences in Asian countries. Here I will comment only on the linkage programme of APRACA, which is the broadest and most ambitious one.

APRACA, the Asian and Pacific Regional Agricultural Credit Association, is one of four RACAs originally promoted by the FAO. Established in 1977 as an association of central banks and agricultural credit institutions, it subsequently shifted its emphasis to rural finance. Under its chairman G. B. Thapa, Governor of the Central Bank of Nepal, and its secretary-general B. R. Quinones, a programme of the promotion of linkages between banks and rural microenterprises was adopted by the member countries at a workshop in Nanjing, China, in May 1986. The main focus of the programme is a financial intermediation system built around IFIs/SHOs, with the double purpose of savings mobilization and credit delivery. While three different approaches have been discerned, upgrading the IFI/SHO of microentrepreneurs, linking IFI/SHO and banks and institutional adaptation of banks to their environment, the linkage programme has been chosen as an approach which may eventually include upgrading and downgrading measures. While the essence of the programme during its first year of existence was close to what has been presented above, the emphasis is not on a particular model of linkages but on the initiation of processes of interaction and dialogue, resulting in appropriate national and local activities to promote the financial system of and for agricultural and non-agricultural microenterprises.

Supported by international consultations, the following procedures have been worked out by APRACA:

1 establishing a national task force, whch may comprise banks, SHO networks and NGOs, in close collaboration with the respective APRACA National Committee;
2 setting up a national survey team; adapting survey instruments provided by APRACA to the national situation; and carrying out a survey on IFI/SHO;
3 analysing the survey results and working out alternative linkage models and procedures;
4 organizing a national seminar of policy makers and representatives of the participating groups and institutions to present, discuss and finalize the survey results and the proposed programme;
5 carrying out a pilot project to implement the linkage programme on an experimental basis;
6 implementing the linkage programme on a national scale.

So far, pilot projects have been designed by Indonesia, Nepal, the Philippines and Thailand, while Bangladesh, India, Pakistan and Sri Lanka are in the survey and programme preparation stage.

Programme activities in the pilot project phase may include:

1 selecting participating institutions, fulfilling linkage prerequisites to be defined;
2 finding operational solutions to the problem of lack of legal status of IFIs/SHOs;
3 selecting institutional linkage models between banks, IFIs/SHOs and possibly governmental and non-governmental SHPIs;
4 selecting financial linkage models, with credit linked to savings, of microentrepreneurs with IFIs/SHOs and the latter with banks;
5 working out interest rates for bank loans to IFIs/SHOs and SHO loans to members, covering the costs of funds, transaction costs and risks, plus an adequate profit margin to finance the growth of the programme;

6 working out collateral and liability requirements, plus possibly a risk management service and a credit guarantee scheme from internal sources;
7 defining loan purposes for members' activities on an evolutionary scale, from emergency, consumption and durables, mainly from IFI/SHO funds, to working capital and investment from combined IFI/SHO and bank sources and group activities, which may include finance (on-lending), supply and marketing and, in some cases, production;
8 working out and testing operational guidelines;
9 defining institutional tasks for a lead agency, IFIs/SHOs, central bank, handling bank and possibly SHPIs;
10 co-ordinating linkage activities on a national and a local level, with loops to the international level;
11 carrying out Survey & Mobilization Campaigns as a grassroots implementation procedure;
12 providing training and communication facilities to national policy makers, trainers, community leaders, bank field staff und IFI/SHO executives;
13 initiating regular monitoring and periodic evaluation activities, measuring the financial performance of the programme and its impact on microenterprises;
14 co-ordinating supporting technical services by other development agencies;
15 assisting IFI/SHO in upgrading to higher organizational levels and improved business practices;
16 promoting banks' adaptation to their environment, by simplifying banking operations and adopting some of microenterprise-oriented financial practices of the IFIs.

Four case studies are presented below, with brief descriptions of participating institutions, programme initiatives, linkage models and project organization.

In *Indonesia*, a country of great cultural and ethnic diversity, most adults belong to one or several IFIs/SHOs of overlapping origins: indigenous, governmental and non-governmental. There is a moderate number of NGOs, some of which work with SHOs and microentrepreneurs. There is a complex, liberalized banking system comprising 116 primary and 5,948 secondary banks and non-banking institutions. The bank with the largest rural network is Bank Rakyat Indonesia (BRI), with 3,499 branches.

Programme initiatives were first taken by the central bank, the Bank Indonesia (BI), by establishing a national task force of BI, BRI and Yayasan Bina Swadaya, a leading NGO.

Two linkage models are to be tested: direct linkages between IFIs/SHOs and banks; indirect linkages, mediated by NGOs and GO-SHPIs.

BI is the lead agency, which plans, supervises and co-ordinates the linkage activities. BI implements the programme through various banks, in close collaboration with NGOs as secondary intermediaries or consultants where they exist (Figure 5).

The pilot project, which competes with BI's own non-commercial working-capital and investment credit programme for microentrepreneurs (KIK/KMKP), started in mid-1988 with technical assistance from GTZ (Germany).

In *Nepal*, a very poor country of considerable ethnic and caste complexity, formal SHOs such as cooperatives were found ineffective, with low repayment rates and little impact on members' enterprises. There are several types of semi-formal SHOs initiated by GO. Large numbers of indigenous IFIs/SHOs of fourteen different types have been identified in a survey. Despite very low incomes, rotating and non-rotating SCA were found to be prominent, within and across caste and ethnic lines. In the past, SHPIs have established their own SHO, ignoring the existing indigenous ones. There are very few NGOs in Nepal. There is an extensive rural banking network of one development bank and two commercial banks.

In collaboration with APRACA-NCC, the central bank, Nepal Rastra Bank (NRB), established a national task force of all banks with a rural network, which also provided the staff of the survey team.

Four models are to be tested in the pilot project:

1 IFIs/informal SHOs as collecting agencies, with direct credit delivery from the bank to the microentrepreneurs;
2 IFIs/informal SHOs as joint liability groups for group projects;
3 IFIs/informal SHOs as joint liability groups for on-lending;
4 IFIs/informal SHOs turned into formal registered groups as on-lending agencies of banks.

The linkage project will be part of the lead bank programme, in which one bank in a given area is designated to co-ordinate the development activities of all banks and line agencies. The central bank will be directly involved in project implementation on the field level, in close collaboration with the respective lead bank and the other participating banks (Figure 6).

The *Philippines* is a country of great social and political complexity, which is only matched by the complexities of its IFIs/SHOs, NGOs and banking systems. In the SHO survey, large numbers of formal, semi-formal and informal groups were identified, with primary and secondary financial functions, of ancient and recent local origin as well as those initiated by NGOs and GOs, cutting across all sectoral lines. Examples, of SHOs with savings and credit activities are indigenous ROSCAs with or without a loan fund, savings and credit clubs, credit unions, privately organized, as opposed to government-initiated, cooperatives, occupational and trade associations, interest associations, religious societies, etc. In addition, there is a very strong NGO sector with numerous umbrella and apex organizations. There are

Figure 5: *Project organization in Indonesia*

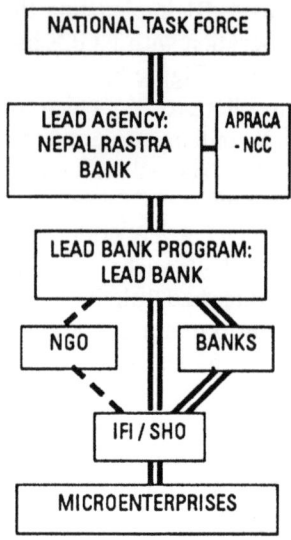

Figure 6: *Project organization in Nepal*

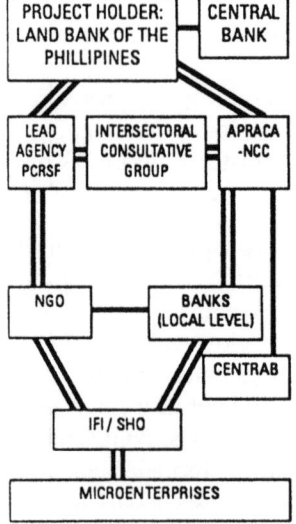

Figure 7: *Project organization in the Phillipines*

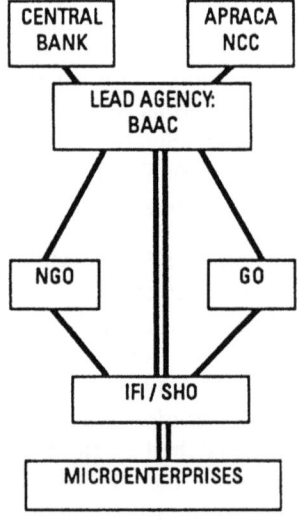

Figure 8: *Project organization in Thailand*

1,020 banking institutions, among them 871 Rural Banks and 116 thrift banks; 1,898 non-bank financial intermediaries, among them 1,143 pawnshops and 82 non-bank thrift institutions.

The first programme steps were initiated from below, which is typical for the Philippines: from SHOs and NGOs who responded to APRACA's call by forming their own network: the People's Council of Rural Savings and Finance, Inc. (PCRSF), with 24 NGO members which comprise over a thousand SHOs with more than 100,000 individuals.

Three models are to be tested in a pilot project:

1   direct IFI/SHO-bank linkages, with NGOs in a consultative role;
2   indirect linkages, mediated by NGOs;
3   linkages of IFIs/SHOs to an NGO central fund upgraded to a banking institution.

There is a complex project organization. Together with APRACA-NCC, PCRSF established the Intersectoral Consultative Group, an informal body for the elaboration and co-ordination of the proposed linkage programme. This body in turn cooperates with the Agricultural Credit Policy Council, ACPC, an interministerial policy co-ordination body for rural finance. The designated project holder is the Land Bank of the Philippines, an APRACA-NCC member with a rural mandate. The project is implemented through two channels: by PCRSF through its member NGOs, some of which are in the process of establishing their own formal financial institutions, and by the Land Bank through local banks and branches. The training of NGO staff and SHO executives will be carried out by one of the member NGOs specialized in that field; training of bank staff by CENTRAB, a bank training institute set up by APRACA in collaboration with the central bank's training institute (Figure 7).

In *Thailand*, a socially and politically monolithic country, there are 6,647 cooperatives and formal farmers' associations, 6,374 semi-formal savings and credit groups set up by the Community Development Department, 21 Saccakorn savings and credit groups initiated by an NGO and a large number of indigenous SHOs, among them rotating and non-rotating SCAs with payments in cash (pia-huay) or kind. Women are prominent in informal ROSCAs. The Government Savings Bank is presently preparing a survey of IFIs/SHOs among urban microentrepreneurs. NGOs are few. The banking system is rather restricted. Among the banks with a rural network, the Bank of Agriculture and Agricultural Cooperatives, BAAC, is prominent, with 582 field offices, which in turn work with 96,000 informal credit guarantee groups.

Survey and programme preparation activities have been initiated and carried out by BAAC in collaboration with APRACA-NCC.

Three linkage models will be tested:

1   IFIs/SHOs as credit guarantee groups and collecting agencies, with direct bank-lending to microenterprises;
2   IFIs/SHOs as full-fledged financial intermediaries;
3   IFIs/SHOs as financial intermediaries, with technical assistance to be provided by GO- and NGO-SHPI.

The project design is straightforward, with BAAC as the lead agency and the main bank, establishing links with IFI/SHO of microentrepreneurs. SHOs initiated by the Community Development Department and the Thai DHRRA Foundation are to be included (Figure 8).

Conclusion: five messages of microenterprise development

How can the rotating dhikuti in Nepal be linked to banks without giving up its substance? There are two requirements of change for the dhikuti: to move from being a temporary to a permanent group and from impermanent to permanent fund formation. The latter may be accomplished without relinquishing the principle of rotation by using bidding gains for fund formation, rather than the lowering of individual contributions. Other than that, their internal structure and functioning will remain untouched: a microentrepreneurs' informal self-help bank, but now linked to a formal financial institution as a source of refinance.

There are of course risks that the linkages may be used, or abused, to gain undue, or premature, control over IFIs/SHOs. However, no government has yet succeeded in gaining unwanted control. If pressures become too strong, the groups will simply go back where they came from — underground.

There are five principal messages to policy makers to be derived from the linkage experience:

1   include both formal and informal sector microenterprises in your target group;
2   develop financial programmes for microenterprises along commercial lines;
3   utilize the existing organizational and institutional resources;
4   build a financial intermediation system, linking microentrepreneurs' IFIs/SHOs to banks;
5   include combined savings mobilization and credit delivery schemes in the programme.

In the implementation, international and national programming and steering units may be instrumental and deserve particular support.

PART III

Finance Services for Enterprises

Financial Services for Microenterprises: Programmes or Markets?

RICHARD L. MEYER

Introduction

For more than two decades, government agencies and donors have pumped billions of dollars into agricultural credit (especially small farmer) programmes in developing countries. Broadly speaking, the objective of these programmes has been to expand the supply and reduce the cost of loans, especially for small farmers. It was expected that, through this 'supply-leading' approach to rural finance, technological change would accelerate, agricultural output would expand and small farmer income would rise.

The great concern today for microenterprise credit is reminiscent of this earlier preoccupation with agricultural credit. The rationale, the approach, the earmarking of funds, the targeting of beneficiaries and the rationalization of poor performance in microenterprise projects are similar to agricultural credit projects. Small business programmes, of course, have as long and chequered a history as do small farmer programmes, but most advocates cast aside that experience in their zeal for microenterprise development. It is appropriate, therefore, to review the now abundant analysis of the small farmer credit experience. That experience can provide a framework for analysing issues relating to microenterprise financing. The lessons learned should help prevent a repetition of past errors and reduce some private costs to the individuals directly affected and social costs for the society as a whole.

Small farms and nonfarm enterprises

A useful point of departure in this analysis is to identify the similarities and differences between small farm and nonfarm enterprises. The similarities are significant. Both are small by definition whether measured in scale of production, capital invested or persons employed. Most employ only family labour. The technology utilized is traditional and may be several generations behind the most modern enterprises of the same type in the country concerned. Incomes and wages are low, frequently below wage rates in the modern sector; therefore, they are often viewed as subsistence operations. Some may sell only a fraction of their total production and are not well

---

RICHARD L. MEYER is Professor of Agricultural Economics and Rural Sociology at Ohio State University, Columbus, Ohio, USA.

integrated into factor and product markets. Likewise, they have limited access to government programmes and evade many laws and government regulations. In fact, many nonfarm enterprises can survive only by avoiding some laws and regulations that apply to larger enterprises.

Both types of enterprises receive little credit from formal institutions, although they may have deposit and saving accounts. They self-finance most of their working capital. Loans from friends and relatives furnish much of their start-up capital. Informal lenders supply short-term loans frequently at interest rates much higher than regular bank rates. The entrepreneurs participate in a variety of self-help groups, many of which have savings and loan programmes. Rotating credit societies (ROSCAs) frequently provide them with a means to save and access to loans for emergencies or selective investments.

Although they are not well integrated into formal financial institutions, small enterprises often engage in a rich mosaic of financial transactions. They are frequently small scale lenders and borrowers at the same time, making loans to friends or relatives while taking a loan from a trader. They build up borrowing capacity through voluntary savings, through participation in traditional social groups and through linking themselves with others who borrow from formal institutions — landlords, traders, input suppliers and richer entrepreneurs. They value and preserve these relationships because they need the insurance of being able to borrow in cases of emergency or unusual opportunity. To preserve good relations with informal lenders, they repay them first when they experience cash constraints.

There are, of course, important differences between the two types of enterprises. It is a well-known fact that the relative importance of agriculture declines with economic growth while the industrial and service sectors increase. Therefore many small farmers will eventually disappear but the number of small nonfarm enterprises will rise. Farmers produce largely homogeneous goods and cannot easily differentiate their products. Nonfarm enterprises often thrive precisely because they successfully develop a product that finds a market niche. Farm enterprises suffer the risk of natural disasters, weather, disease and pests, while nonfarm enterprises are exposed to risks such as interrupted supplies of water, electricity, and other production inputs. They also risk the heavy hand of government if they are discovered operating without an appropriate licence, disobeying labour laws or stealing electricity.

Although small scale enterprises face innumerable obstacles that threaten their survival, policymakers especially notice their few formal loans, their lack of long-term loans and their high interest rates for informal loans and immediately conclude that credit is a real bottleneck (or at least one problem policymakers think they can do something about in the short term). Furthermore, existing financial institutions, especially banks, are considered 'bad'. They are perceived as being overly cautious, averse to risk and unimaginative with respect to lending to small enterprises. Instead, they prefer to lend to their friends in larger enterprises, industry, commerce and trade. Little appreciation exists for the value that banks provide in supplying safe, dependable deposit and savings services. The 'need' of small enterprises is mostly thought to be cheap loans.

Supply-leading finance

The perception of unsatisfied demand for loans and inadequate supply of funds from the banking system has led policymakers, often in conjunction with donors, to develop a strategy in which increasing the supply of loans was expected to 'lead' economic activities. The following summary characterizes many of the policies and programmes designed for agricultural credit and many of these features are also found in small or microenterprise programmes.

1 Increase the supply of funds available for lending to the priority sector (small farm or nonfarm enterprises) through:
(a) portfolio quotas or targets for existing lenders,
(b) the creation of specialized financial institutions to service the priority sector(s),
(c) grants and subsidies for non-financial institutions (ministries, departments, institutes, NGOs, PVOs),
(d) central bank rediscount programmes, often funded by donors,
(e) mandatory placement of bank and/or public sector deposits in specialized lending institutions, and
(f) nationalization of banks that fail to meet social objectives;
2 reduce the interest rate on loans made to the priority sector through:
(a) interest rate ceilings on loans with the lowest rates set for the smallest/poorest borrowers,
(b) low interest rates charged by central bank on refinance funds,
(c) encouraging banks to cross-subsidize by charging higher rates to non-priority borrowers in compensation for lower rates to priority borrowers, and
(d) direct government interest subsidies to lenders;
3 reduce lending risks and costs through:
(a) detailed targeting of loans including requirements about production practices and input use required of borrowers,
(b) crop and loan guarantee programmes,
(c) creation of joint liability through lending to groups of borrowers, and
(d) technical assistance to lenders to help improve institutional efficiency.

These financial measures are often taken in conjunction with programmes to provide technical assistance, modern inputs, marketing, business management support and other services. These services are directly linked to finance when extension agents must authorize farm loans made by banks.

Alternatively, these inputs and services are provided in an integrated package by a government agency or an NGO.

The supply-leading financial strategy has succeeded in expanding lending, at least temporarily, to target groups in some countries. Some financial institutions have gained experience in lending to a new clientele, and some have introduced innovations to more efficiently serve their customers. The failures of the strategy are more numerous, however. They have been extensively documented elsewhere and will only be summarized here.

1   lenders ignore or evade lending quotas and targets through creative loan documentation and multiple small loans to large borrowers;
2   lenders employ the alternatives offered to increased lending such as investing in low interest government securities;
3   cheap rediscount funds discourage rural deposit mobilization by financial institutions;
4   interest rate controls result in non-interest credit rationing that raises borrower transaction costs and concentrates loans among wealthy borrowers;
5   cheap loans are diverted from targeted purposes into higher return uses of funds and borrowed funds substitute for own capital;
6   heavy reporting and documentation costs create high lender transaction costs;
7   political intervention directs subsidized loans to favoured clients and protects delinquent borrowers;
8   lenders experience high loan delinquency and default;
9   the viability of lending institutions is undermined becaue of their failure to cover costs, mobilize deposits and recover loans;
10 lenders are unreliable sources of funds for their customers because they are prisoners to the ebbs and flows in government and donor funding.

In summary, because of these policies and programmes, a few select borrowers have enjoyed a one-shot increase in liquidity but viable institutions have not been built. A viable rural financial institution is one that is self-sustaining, that covers its costs, that provides services valued by rural households and businesses, that serves an ever increasing number of customers, that is dynamic in providing new financial products and services, and that actively searches for ways to reduce transaction costs for itself and/or its customers. By implication, it operates over a long time horizon and becomes a reliable rural institution for its clientele.

Programmes or markets?

The negative experience of small farmer credit provides insights into the alternative strategies for developing financial services for microenterprises. At one end of the continuum of possibilities is the 'financial markets approach' which has the objective of developing viable financial institutions that compete to serve a large number of customers with a variety of financial products. At the other end is the 'programme approach' which has the objective of meeting credit needs of a specific target population usually with subsidies for the borrower and the lending institution. The institutional form in the first case is usually a financial institution, frequently some type of bank. Although many credit programmes are implemented through banks, the emphasis in the second case is on a wide variety of nonbank institutions whose primary or exclusive role is to provide loans: government agencies, institutes, associations, NGOs and PVOs. A comparative analysis of the alternatives of programmes versus market follows.

Access

The 'need' for credit is widely debated,[1] but it is probably true that loans draw clients to small enterprise projects.[2] Our fundamental concern should be the number of small enterprises that have access to financial services. The market approach is criticized because banks do not serve enough target clients, yet frequently bank programmes serve many more low-income customers than nonbank programmes. Some of the biggest programmes are found in Asia. Timberg reports that the Indian IRDP (Interest Rate Differential Programme) reached over 15 million families in the period 1980-85.[3] Indonesia has several bank programmes, and the BKK (Badan Kredit Kecamatan) programme from 1972-1983 provided 2.7 million loans totalling over $55 million (Goldmark and Rosengard). Likewise, the Bangladesh Grameen Bank currently reports about 70,000 groups with 350,000 members operating in over 7,500 villages. Furthermore, it is likely that bank statistics underestimate total small enterprise access because they usually do not count the number of small, but untargeted, loans provided out of regular bank funds. By comparison, many nonbank programmes operate in only one or a handful of locations and access is limited to several dozen or a few hundred participants. One NGO programme I recently visited in the Philippines had eight loans! Moreover, it is not the case that bank programmes cannot reach the poorest with the smallest loans. Many of the bank loans made in India, Indonesia and Bangladesh are quite small.

Access is directly related to proximity. Banks with a widespread branch network or a nationwide system of unit banks reduce borrower transaction costs through their proximity to entrepreneurs. A PVO or a cooperative working in just a few villages or a government programme with only one office located in the capital city cannot provide access to many people, particularly for small loans where noninterest costs (including travel time and expense) represent a large share of total borrowing costs.

Interest rates also have an important impact on access. A policy of charging interest rates high enough to cover costs is frequently rejected by those who advocate lending to the poor. Yet the choice may be serving fewer people with lower-cost loans as against serving more with unsubsidized loans.

Subsidized programmes deny their services to nonparticipants when they fail to recover costs through interest income from participants. Furthermore, interest rate ceilings on banks are self-defeating and raise the cost of credit to the very sector that the government intends to support. Banks perceive that transaction costs and the risk of lending to small enterprises is greater than making larger loans to other sectors, so they either will not lend to the small scale sector or will pass on to borrowers a greater share of the risks and costs through noninterest chages.[4] Low interest ceilings and fixed interest spreads have tended to benefit larger borrowers with collateral in Asia at the expense of smaller borrowers with little collateral but profitable projects.[5]

Low loan rates also imply low rates paid on deposits; this thwarts an institution's ability to mobilize deposits. Without deposits, a lender is dependent on donor and/or government funds. These sources have proven to be quite uncertain; at times, the institution has funds to expand lending while at other times it does not.

Inflation erodes the real value of a loan portfolio. If interest rates are too low to cover inflation, the real value of new loans made will decline even if the institution achieves 100 per cent loan recovery. Repeat borrowers get smaller loans and there are no funds for new customers.

There are obvious limits to the level of interest rates that borrowers can pay. If little capital is used in an enterprise, the implication is that the marginal return on its use must be high and the marginal return from borrowing should also be high, at least for small, incremental loans. Small entrepreneurs frequently complain about lack of credit, but not about high interest rates. They put higher priority on speed of loan disbursement, availability of second loans and simplicity of procedures.[2] The large amount of lending to the poor that occurs in the Indonesian BKK programme with rates of 5–10 per cent per month, in the Grameen Bank with effective rates approaching 25 per cent per year and in a Bangladesh Rural Finance Experimental Project with rates up to 36 per cent per year support this observation.

Credit guarantee schemes have been used in several cases to overcome lender resistance to small enterprise lending. These schemes aim to encourage financial institutions to lend to small businesses that have viable projects, but are unable to provide adequate collateral or prove they are creditworthy. These schemes have frequently not lived up to expectations because they are costly, complex to design and manage, and it is doubtful that they really contribute to much additionality in lending.[5,6]

Viability

Institutional viability is closely related to access. If a financial institution cannot achieve viability and support itself, the expansion of its services to participants will be limited by the amount of subsidies it can extract from government and donors. By definition, poor countries cannot afford large subsidies, yet since the poor are so numerous, large subsidies are required if many are to receive financial services. Donors cannot continuously be relied upon to provide new resources to finance an institution's expansion.

The level of interest charged and the spread between lending rate and the cost of funds is crucial to determining institutional viability. Although interest expense is usually a small component of a borrower's total operating expense, interest income is the most important source of revenue for a bank and may also be important for a nonbank programme. Interest rate regulations must be relaxed so the operating spread is more favourable. Cheap government and donor funds are not necessarily a substitute because of the costs of reporting and documenting their use and impact. For example, Cuevas and Graham found that transaction costs for lending through a government-owned and a privately-owned bank in Honduras far exceeded the 3–4 per cent margin allowed with donor funds.[7] Lending costs for the private bank using donor funds were nearly five times the cost of lending its own money for farmers. Likewise, Ahmed and Adams found that the Agricultural Bank of Sudan was limited to charging 7–9 per cent per year on loans when its administration costs average 10–15 per cent of the value of loans.[8]

The subsidization of costs can have an insidious impact on nonbanking institutions, especially NGOs that function in a relatively resource rich environment. When resources are abundant, survival becomes unlinked from performance and self-evaluation is not a priority.[9] Administration is lax, costs are not controlled, and there is relative indifference to loan recovery. Commercial organizations working in a competitive environment face relatively greater pressure to perform, therefore giving them an entirely different orientation to lending and perhaps increasing their chances of long-term survival. This observation is relevant for many, but not all, banking operations. Nationalized banks are often a key exception.

Subsidies also invite political intervention and corruption. Subsidized interest rates create an excess demand for funds, so implicit rationing must occur. Political connections influence those who are the lucky few to get a loan. Rent-seeking employees of the financial institutions exploit their opportunity to extract gifts or 'tea money' for granting subsidized loans. Leaders of cooperatives and credit unions use their positions to gain disproportionate access to loans. Borrowers with political leverage can avoid loan repayment while borrowers who 'bought' their loans see little reason to repay. High loan delinquency is a logical outcome in these situations and it can severely weaken an institution. Incentives to repay decline even more when borrowers perceive that an institution is weak and they may not get a new loan after repaying a current one.

Multiple financial services

Entrepreneurs need financial services, not just loans. A programme that offers only loans forces a borrower to obtain deposit, savings and chequing services elsewhere. A bank can offer these services in addition to the loan, along with other services such as the international transfer of funds important in labour exporting countries. Furthermore, depositors reveal important aspects about their financial management abilities by the way they conduct their deposit and savings operations and this information is useful when lenders process loan applications. Banks recognize the value of this information and often require that an enterprise maintain an account for several months before considering a loan.[10] The Grameen Bank requires an established record of weekly savings before a group is considered for a loan,[11] and other programmes have similar requirements.

Accepting deposits also imposes discipline on an institution's lending because management realizes that to keep itself credible it must have funds to meet depositor demand. By using its own funds for lending rather than relying solely on government-targeted programmes, an institution can escape some political intervention over deciding who gets a loan and who must reapply. There may also be a salutary effect on repayment when borrowers recognize they are stealing their neighbour's rather than the government's money when they default on loans. It is frequent in the Philippines, for example, to hear that a 'dole-out' mentality affects repayment on government projects.[12] Cooperatives and credit unions performed well in Latin America in the 1960s but many deteriorated in the 1970s when they began to accept external funds.[13]

Graduation

Many special programmes propose to graduate participants once they can obtain loans from regular financial institutions. The rationale for this idea recognizes that, as enterprises grow, they pass through different stages of financial sophistication and the financing options widen as they build up their assets and their reputation.[10] It has also been recognized that programmes should disburse small amounts as a first loan to a client. This will test repayment ability, but it will also avoid overburdening the business with more money that it can invest wisely.[14] Traditional agricultural lenders have been criticized for being inflexible in determining amounts to be lent and have encouraged borrowers to accept more than was really needed.[15]

Data on graduation rates are sparse, however, and most programme evaluations, if they mention the concept at all, fail to provide much evidence. The lack of data suggests it may not really be that important a performance indicator in actual practice. Clearly there are real disincentives for both programmes and borrower to graduate. If the loan is highly subsidized, a borrower will face higher costs when graduating to another source. The increase in the size of loan obtained must be large if the cost differences are large. For the programme, graduation implies losing an established good performing participant and substituting another with all the costs and learning that implies. It may be far better and cheaper if funds are tight to extend another loan to the established client.

The graduation problem suggests that a better approach may be for the programme not to lend directly but to become an advocate to help the participant obtain loans from financial institutions. Graduation to larger loans will then occur naturally as repeat loans are made to valued customers. Important performance incentives can be given to the programme by providing operating subsidies in direct proportion to the number of participants it successfully helps obtain loans. The programmes are also relieved of the costs of developing expertise to efficiently manage loan accounts and can concentrate resources instead on providing those nonfinancial services they can best provide.

Conclusions

Supply-leading rural finance has been an integral part of development policy in many developing countries during the past two decades. It has also been a mechanism through which donors have pumped billions of dollars of foreign assistance into developing countries. In general, the results have been disappointing. Although there have been temporary increases in loans for a few lucky borrowers, financial systems have not been created to provide self-sustaining financial services. The funds available to the rural sector, and especially small farm and nonfarm enterprises, has actually shrunk in many countries in the past few years after rising during the 1970s.

The emphasis of the supply-leading strategy has been misplaced. Policymakers have addressed the supposed need for cheap loans by low income entrepreneurs and have ignored the fact that the policies and programmes they created undermined the viability of the financial institutions induced or created to make the loans. Evidence of the failure of the strategy can be seen by the multitude of failed and struggling banks and dependent NGOs and PVOs that survive only through government and donor aid. Non-viable institutions cannot hope to meet the financial needs of small enterprises. They can assist a few participants up to the limits of their subsidies, but they cannot hope to expand their services to a broader number of equally deserving clients. This issue frequently boils down to serving fewer clients with lower cost loans as against reaching many through unsubsidized loans.

Finance is important: a sound financial system is necessary for economic development. The development challenge is to create competitive, viable rural financial markets in which entrepreneurs of all income levels with appropriate projects will find loans and all entrepreneurs and households will find suppliers for their chequing, deposit and savings needs. Subsidizing a few entrepreneurs with cheap loans contributes little to developing a viable financial market.

Strong financial institutions find it hard to operate in the unfavourable economic environment that exists in many developing countries. Likewise, entrepreneurs cannot prosper in such an environment and a few subsidized loans will not resolve their fundamental problems. As we struggle to find ways to assist the development of microenterprises, we must be alert to the fact that by tinkering with financial policies, we may just be addressing symptoms of the problem, not the problem itself.

Banking on the Informal Sector

HENRY R. JACKELEN

Introduction

The following paper discusses how programmes and projects that provide financial services to microenterprises can function as 'specialized intermediaries' and provide a bridge to the formal-sector financial institutions of developing countries. The paper argues that it is preferable to use these FIs rather than to create a new bank or quasi-bank for every programme that assists microenterprises. The paper proposes that banks can be used to leverage guarantee funds by as much as ten to one on a graduated risk basis.

Brazil and Bangladesh are used to illustrate several points. These two countries have been chosen to demonstrate cross-cutting informal-sector issues that affect the 'richest' as well as the poorest developing countries in regard to access to credit.

The importance of access to capital

It might be said that there is a point on which Karl Marx and Adam Smith are in agreement: the need to 'democratize' access to (or power over) capital. Smith, in the 'level playing field' of perfect market economics, envisioned a society in which entrepreneurs with ability, creativity and drive would have equitable access to the factors that would enable them to create new and dynamic enterprises. Marx's critique focused on the monopoly power of capital in the nineteenth century as the means by which the accumulation of wealth (and power) was segregated to a small, self-perpetuating class.

During this century the evolution of the economies in the developed world has largely been the story of pragmatic reform and greater respect for competition and market forces. These conditions have allowed for the explosion of technological growth and innovation. Within this evolution, the mechanisms that govern access to capital have undergone the most fundamental change imaginable: financial institutions in these societies have brought services to market segments previously considered unbankable and high-risk. Venture capital-type mechanisms have evolved which allow ideas to be transformed into multi-billion-dollar industries.

HENRY R. JACKELEN, of USA and Brazil, is a consultant working in the field of microenterprise development. In April 1989 he joined the United Nations Capital Development Fund in New York as a Senior Adviser.

Access to capital in the developed world may still be far from 'level,' but it certainly bears no resemblance to the absolute monopoly that was the hallmark of Marx's era.

While capital is not the only factor that allows for the growth or creation of enterprises, it is the most vital, for without it creativity, drive and innovation cannot be transformed into material actions.

In the developing world in general, formal-sector financial institutions show no signs of mimicking their counterparts in the developed world. On the contrary, these institutions appear to be evolving into entities which bear little resemblance to a bank.

Banking in the developing world

The formal-sector mechanisms which control access to capital in the developing world are on the whole far worse than anything that existed at the time of Marx or probably even Smith. In general the financial institutions in developing countries are dominated by the public sector and all too often this results in a costly and inefficient system best described as 'bureaucratic' banking. This system does not maximize returns or efficiently mediate between the owners and the users of capital but instead allocates resources based on bureaucratic, often political and usually uneconomic considerations. In many developing societies, the operation of these institutions has the pernicious effect of taking rural-based savings from the many and diverting them to urban-based economies for the few, at subsidized rates of interest.

The greatest contrast between these institutions and their developed country counterparts is that, in much of the developing world, the fundamental concept of banking has been distorted by subsidies on the one hand and low recovery rates on the other. Thus there exist such anomalies as the banking system of Bangladesh, where paper profits mask recovery rates more appropriate to grant-giving institutions than to lending estabishments.

At the other end of the spectrum, the banking system in Brazil illustrates how the mechanisms of access of capital can be manipulated by the few even when the system mandates lending to the many. Until recently, Brazil's multi-billion-dollar lending facility, though created to subsidize millions of small farmers, was profitably used by a few thousand large farmers to borrow and invest the proceeds in the financial markets at a comfortable spread (plus ten per cent). Brazil has also mandated that its banks lend a fixed percentage of deposits to small and microenterprises, but this effort seems to be proving as ineffectual as the loans to small farmers.

Banking systems such as those in Bangladesh and Brazil are kept afloat by massive government interventions, the funding drawn from scarce resources gathered most often through value-added taxes (of which the poor bear an unfair proportion) or from the considerable funds provided through the over $40 bn pa development industry. Paradoxically these banking systems are characterized by continual growth and fairly high liquidity, due to the constant inflow of funds.

Notable exceptions to this state of affairs are the multi-national and some privately owned banks, whose survival is dependent on their own acumen.

Finally, in surveying the deficiencies of formal-sector financial institutions in developing countries, it should be noted that small- and medium-scale enterprises ($500,000 in assets), which are far more 'bankable' than microenterprises and have good prospects, generally suffer from an equal lack of access to capital.

In this context, credit programmes to assist microenterprises tend, with good reason, to ignore the existing formal sector institutions. However, this bypassing normally leads to the creation of quasi-banks or even full-fledged banking institutions, adding several layers of complexity and risk to a project. Further, these programmes usually become wholly dependent on external sources of heavily subsidized development capital, sources which can prove unreliable over the long term.

The 'unbankability' of microenterprises

The reasons for the incompatibility between microenterprises and formal-sector financial institutions are well-known. Even in the most efficient and dynamic banking system, several factors would account for the unwillingness of the banks to finance microenterprises.

First, microenterprises do not normally have sufficient collateral to satisfy banking requirements, nor do they maintain financial records that allow for reasoned financial analysis.

Two other equally important but generally less understood reasons for incompatibility are the transaction costs and the 'client treatment' associated with microenterprises. Formal sector institutions are structured to handle much larger individual transactions or loans than those required by microenterprises. Even at the most efficient bank, this type of lending is prohibitively expensive because of overhead costs too high to be adequately compensated by 'spreads' on the small loans of these enterprises. Finally, the 'client treatment' given to those microenterprises that venture into a formal-sector institution is inevitably marked by abuse and hostility. Microentrepreneurs are especially vulnerable to paying bribes and to the necessity of numerous, costly journeys to transact their business.

Given the general state of formal-sector financial institutions in the developing world, it is unrealistic to expect the massive reforms that would enable and encourage them to lend to microenterprises. Nor would such an expansion of purview be advisable; these institutions have enough to do in carrying out their functions properly in the formal sector.

Putting microenterprises in perspective

In recent years informal sector entrepreneurs have been endowed by their admirers with a certain aura, a mystique that inspires great expectations regarding growth potential and eventual graduation to the formal sector. Those who base projects on these optimistic assumptions thereby justify even the costliest of programmes offering a series of services to microenterprises. But how realistic are the greater expectations which these economic units are inspiring in the burgeoning informal sector?

Brazil is perhaps one of the most extreme examples of the accelerated growth of the informal sector. While it claims the distinction of being the eighth largest economy in the world, a substantial majority of its work force survives from income earned through informal sector activities. Statistics show that, from a predominantly (60 per cent) rural population in the 1950s, Brazil has become urbanized to such a degree that a vast majority (more than 70 per cent) live in cities. In the same period, the population has more than doubled. The net result is a threefold growth of urban-based populations, while the rural-based population has remained static in absolute terms. This mass of urban humanity far surpasses the formal sector's ability to absorb it as a labour force, and these people survive, for the most part, through self-employment.

At the other end of the spectrum, the burgeoning of the informal sector in Bangladesh has less to do with urbanization than with the landlessness of more and more people. This densely populated country continues to be predominantly rural (80 per cent). However, small subsistence farmers constitute a minority in the rural population; the majority of the landless poor survive by selling their labour or through self-employment.

In both countries, the term 'self-employment' is best understood to embrace the economic survival stategies pursued by most if not all non-infant members of poor families, through a multiplicity of marginal activities.

These countries represent dramatically different levels of development, but in both, the poor, whether urban or rural-based, subsist on the fruits of their ingenuity and their ability to pursue marginal economic activities. The ingenuity of some individuals translates into a level of entrepreneurship that can be nurtured into larger enterprises, but the vast majority of these entrepreneurs have limited prospects for growth.

However, despite their limited prospects, microenterprises are not inherently unbankable. They can even be commercially viable clients.

Microenterprises as bankable clients: successes and failures

The 400,000 borrowers who meet weekly to pay loans and deposit savings at the Grameen Bank in Bangladesh are challenging the conventional wisdom on poverty and the informal sector. These borrowers, arguably the poorest of the poor in one of the poorest countries in the world, are proving themselves to be commercially viable clients for a banking institution. They are also, to the surprise of many, proving their ability to save, as witnessed by an accumulated savings of over $7,000,000 (which, in rural areas, averages out to more than one month of wages per borrower). Grameen demonstrates the powerful impact on the economic lives of the poor that guaranteed, equitable and dependable access to capital can have. Economists may find fault in the possible displacement effects and the marginal nature of the economic activities pursued by Grameen borrowers, but these myopic criticisms ignore or underestimate the importance of establishing a self-sustaining mechanism that provides access to capital for the most unbankable segment of the population. In accord with Adam Smith's vision, such mechanisms as the Grameen Bank open the 'level playing field' to those individuals (supported by the guarantee of peers) whose ingenuity can be rewarded with financial gain. They also break, or at least dilute, the monopoly control of capital by such age-old institutions as moneylenders.

There is one question that inevitably arises concerning Grameen: is it the exception that proves the rule, or is it a new rule that demands to be adhered to? Beyond the question of replication is the question of whether Grameen represents a sound strategy in a development industry whose attempts to bring a myriad of services to intended beneficiaries are prone to be integrated, unwieldy and costly.

That Grameen should be increasingly considered the rule rather than the exception is evidenced by a number of other experiences in the developing world. Besides the lesser known and studied Badan Kredit Kecamatan (BKK) of Indonesia, which may have as many borrowers as Grameen, and a number of examples in India, there are a number of initiatives, particularly in Latin America, which merit notice. Four years prior to the experiment in Jobra, Bangladesh, which gave rise to the Grameen Bank, Action International (AITEC) was starting its first programme to assist informal-sector entrepreneurs in Recife, Brazil, where the term 'microempresa' was first used. While AITEC's programmes in 11 countries in Latin America have not led to a single programme demonstrating the sustained, exponential growth of a Grameen, the more than 30,000 borrowers currently enrolled in these programmes are proving their viability as bankable clients. More importantly, these AITEC programmes use the basic element of the Grameen 'model': non-collateralized lending based on five-person group guarantees (Grupo Solidario). As stated by AITEC itself, the adoption of the group-guarantee method was a change directly influenced by Grameen and by the Working Women's Forum of Madras. As such, AITEC's programmes represent an important first step in proving the replicability of the Grameen approach in the vastly different social and economic context of Latin America.

There are many other efforts occurring in Latin America, some claiming as many as 40,000 borrowers. And in Asia and Africa, some 14 countries are replicating the Grameen model.

Still, other than Grameen, a few cases in India and possibly BKK, none of these efforts has had an impact on a scale that, once and for all, could end all scepticism about the credit worthiness and commercial viability of lending to the microenterprises.

One reason why so few programmes have achieved high levels of impact is that, to the tasks of selecting, supervising and (often) training microentrepreneurs, most add the complex task of establishing a bank. Throughout the developing world, between bilateral, multilateral and NGO efforts, hundreds, if not thousands, of attempts to reach grassroots borrowers or microenterprises fail or have to be evaluated on non-recovery grounds. Many, perhaps most, of these projects share the following characteristics:

1 they lack accounting infrastructures capable of providing the type of management information system (MIS) needed for even the most rudimentary banking effort. Without early warning of non-payment or, at the least, timely reporting of payment due dates, meaningful supervision is almost impossible. This deficiency becomes acute as programmes grow into thousands of borrowers;

2 any attempt to reach microenterprises is, almost by definition, a labour-intensive proposition. A tremendous amount of legwork is required to identify, properly select, approve, appraise and, above all, supervise borrowers. Projects which fail to achieve high recovery rates often have not properly dimensioned the field staff requirements. If the MIS is inadequate, the ability of the programme to detect these problems is considerably hindered;

3 the lack of proper supervision via an adequate MIS rapidly translates into a perception on the part of field staff and borrowers that repayment is flexible and ultimately not important;

4 finally, and perhaps most important, when programmes set up their own banks, it is extremely easy to accept and justify inadequate recovery rates. The 'soft' funding allocated to credit provides an unrealistic subsidy (independent of interest rates charged), since it does not sustain the rigorous discipline on which existing informal-sector credit mechanisms such as moneylenders depend.

A number of the programmes that failed in terms of recovery, along with others that, although successful, were unable to expand significantly, might have had dramatically different outcomes if they could have concentrated exclusively on developing a methodology for efficiently reaching microenterprises. Instead, because they must build banks as well as mount outreach efforts, these programmes are somewhat schizophrenic.

The complex task of establishing the outreach capacity (or delivery mechanism) and extending services to microenterprises is quite separate from the equally complex task of setting up a bank. Often, in fact, the two objectives will be in conflict: the outreach function requires a sympathetic approach, but successful banks are unrelenting in collecting what is due them.

Building a bridge between the formal and informal sectors: the role of specialized intermediaries

Any programme, organization or bank that specializes in one particular type of market or client can be described as a Specialized Intermediary (SI). An SI develops a particular know-how (or methodology) for bringing services to a market segment that is not attractive to the general providers of these services. Thus in the developed world there are numerous examples of SIs that arrange mortgages, insurance, consumer financing and business loans for clients who otherwise could not obtain these services. These SIs can be extremely profitable and earn their 'spread' based on a fee schedule scaled above the normal cost of these services. Often they are able to build middleman relationships with established providers of financial services. Some of these SIs even grow large enough to become attractive investment prospects for the large service providers.

Key to the long-term success, growth and profitability of a SI in the developed world is its ability, within a particular market segment, to aggregate exponentially-growing numbers of clients who pay for the services rendered to them. In risk-related services such as credit or venture capital, these SIs will often start relatively small, then build their client portfolios in a methodical, step-by-step fashion based on performance. Thus, as they grow, they can carefully verify and fine-tune their methods of analysis, promotion and approval to ensure that the risks (losses) are adequately covered by the level of fee income. Once a successful formula is found, these SIs often grow exponentially.

Among the better examples of this type of self-monitored growth are some of the large insurance companies which originated in the US in the 1940s to develop the life insurance market among low-income immigrant populations in urban areas. A network of salesmen paid monthly calls on the insured, collecting as little as 25 cents per policy. Life insurance in this market essentially meant burial insurance, and the service was specifically geared to the needs and traditional practices of the targeted market segment. These practices bear a remarkable resemblance to a common informal-sector savings practice throughout the developing world: burial societies. Like the latter, these American insurance companies built a bridge between the informal practices of a selected group and formal-sector savings institutions.

There are also examples of SIs that abuse their intended markets. In Brazil, with the rapid proliferation of television, an enterprising European immigrant founded a multi-million-dollar empire on a simple strategy that targeted a very specific market segment: domestic servants. During an all-day

Sunday television programme, the day off for millions of domestics, most of whom are unable to travel to their distant homes, this entrepreneur would raffle off houses, cars and a wide range of consumer items. To enter the raffle, the participant had to open a 'savings' account requiring monthly deposits. The catch was that the 'savings' did not earn interest and could only be used to purchase items in the stores owned by the entrepreneur. Eventually, several years after the enterprise began, the government did require that these accounts be paid interest, but even so, in an inflationary society, the deposits generated immense profits for the showman/entrepreneur who held them. The few houses and cars raffled each week fuelled the fantasies of the poor, and millions sent in their monthly deposits religiously.

Microenterprise programmes as specialized intermediaries

Most microenterprise programmes are attempting to bring financial services to a market segment or niche that is not covered by the established service providers. It is conceivable that they can become commercially viable SIs. Aside from lack of access to domestic capital, what usually prevents these SIs from evolving into self-sustaining entities is that many are established as social programmes with extremely high overheads, depending on the range of services intended. However, those programmes which specialize in providing a single service, credit, extremely well have every chance of becoming self-sustaining if domestic capital is available to finance their growth. SIs that achieve wide market penetration with high recovery rates should be able to attract loan funds from formal-sector institutions.

Instead of the much hoped-for but rarely achieved goal of 'graduating' microenterprises into the formal-sector financial institutions, it would be more practical to graduate those programmes or projects that achieve high levels of market penetration and recovery. The portfolio of clients developed by a microenterprise programme is an asset whose quality can be objectively measured by recovery performance. Based on this asset, a long-term pragmatic relationship can be negotiated with a bank.

For example, an SI that is able to generate $15,000,000 in loans to 40,000 borrowers in a year at high recovery rates can be considered an 'excellent' potential client for a bank as long as the risk considerations and administrative costs are reasonable. It is also possible to build a long-term, contractually binding commercial relationship between an SI and a bank based on mutually agreed upon performance criteria and safeguards.

An advantage to the bank is that such an arrangement would bring in an important new group of clients with potential for growth. These clients are businesses which — due to risk considerations and, more important, the high transaction costs required to properly carry out this type of lending — are not presently bankable in the commercial system. The SI would assume responsibility for all the selection, appraisal, approval, monitoring and supervision of these clients at no cost to the bank. For its services, the SI would charge a fee to its clients based on a fixed percentage of loans granted.

Problems with using banks for microenterprise lending

Previous unsuccessful attempts to use formal-sector financial institutions merit mention because these failures have influenced the proposed strategy.

The most significant example of both success and failure in using formal-sector financial institutions is Grameen. From its early project days in 1976 to the establishment of a formal bank in late 1983, Grameen functioned as a Specialized Intermediary between the banking system in Bangladesh and the intended target group. The first close to 60,000 borrowers in the programme were actually borrowing from some six Nationalized Commercial Banks. An evaluation conducted by the Bangladesh Institute of Development Studies (BIDS) concluded that programme overheads at that time were 15.6 per cent per annum on funds lent. Most important, the evaluation showed that the high overheads were because the cost to the bank was *equal* to Grameen's, even though Grameen was responsible for the bulk of the work. The high cost to the banks was due to the total redundancy of accounting systems, the high volume of transactions (weekly payments, deposits and disbursements) and, most significantly, the extremely low productivity of bank staff. This situation, along with ongoing operational difficulties, were major factors in the decision to create a new full-fledged bank.

In Recife, Brazil, the UNO programme was dependent on the local state bank, which often took 100 days or more to process loans. This caused a major bottleneck in the programme that threatened its viability. After some 6 years, the bank in question streamlined its procedures and was processing loans in ten days. One of the key problems eliminated by the streamlining was that previously the bank had insisted on approving each loan; under revised procedures, the bank approved all loans submitted by UNO, vetoing only those whose applicants had bad records.

In both Brazil and Bangladesh, state-controlled banking systems were accessed through SI with mixed to negative results. While the Brazilian bank did finally improve its performance, whether the overheads of the bank made this type of lending viable is open to question. These are examples of bureaucratic banking. Although banks doing business in such a system can be mandated or ordered to lend, the Grameen and UNO projects raise questions about costs and efficiency.

There are also, throughout Latin America, many examples of microenterprise lending that involve private commercial banks. Typically what occurs is that the senior management or ownership of these banks will, for altruistic or political reasons, accept to lend to microenterprises selected by a SI. Usually a substantial liquid guarantee is required from the SIs. A frequent problem is that branch managers, many of whom are evaluated according to the profitability and loan losses of their operations, are unsympathetic to microenterprise lending and tend to create obstacles.

Finally, the various guarantee programmes established by governments throughout the world constitute a separate category of attempts to involve formal-sector financial institutions in lending to small and microenterprises. These are not considered in this paper because they do not rely on SIs. Nor have they been very successful.

Microenterprise programmes as a bridge between banks and borrowers

Whether private or public, efficient or technically bankrupt, banks can be among the best suppliers of loan capital to microenterprises if a pragmatic and realistic long-term agreement is carefully negotiated with SIs to cover cost and risk considerations and to provide enforceable safeguards for the bank. The advantage to the SI is that, without becoming a bank, the SI can gain constant and growing access to loan capital, with the discipline that recovery performance will require. The disadvantage is that the cost to the borrower will increase because the extension of loans must be based on the cost of funds to the bank plus a spread to cover administrative costs. Also, the SI will have to charge a service fee, which on the long-term will allow it to be self-sufficient, once a 'critical mass' of clients and lending is achieved.

For borrowers, the cost implications of this strategy are that they will pay 5–10 per cent more for loans than the 'best risk' clients with access to formal-sector financial institutions. But this premium should be accepted as realistic and justified, because in fact it costs substantially more to lend to microenterprises than to large clients. The premium must also be analysed in relation to what access and at what cost microenterprises borrow in the informal sector. While in a moral sense it may seem extremely unfair to charge less to the rich and more to the poor, in a commercial sense it is logical, and ultimately, if it dramatically expands the access to capital in a society, it is also fair.

In the simplest sense, the proposed strategy is that the formal-sector banks be used solely as administrative entities providing automatic access to loan funds for programmes that perform to an agreed level, and cutting off programmes that do not. These banks should have no role in the selection or approval of microenterprises, and for this reason the strategy is based on a 'graduated risk', whereby initially a time deposit (or similar liquid guarantee) is used to establish an ironclad, 100 per cent guarantee of the principal and interest due to participating bank(s) from borrowers selected and approved by the SI. However, this guarantee will only be provided if the bank accepts, on the long term, to decrease the guarantee requirement based on mutually agreed levels of performance. In this fashion, guarantee funds would be leveraged 10 times by bank lending in a period of 5–6 years — *if* the

SI is able to maintain the high standards of performance agreed to formally.

One of the important conditions of the funds used to guarantee the participating bank is that, in order to ensure maximum leveraging of bank funds, the guarantee is always at 'first risk'; ie bank losses would occur only if all guarantee funds had been expended. In this manner, the banks are in no position to argue that they are being asked to bear any significant risk.

The main risk incurred by the participating bank in this situation is in allowing an intermediary to, in effect, act in its name, since the intermediary has all powers of selection and approval. Even though compensation for any losses is fully, or at least adequately, guaranteed, there is still the risk that if questionable borrowers or poor risks have been selected by the intermediary, the image of the bank could be adversely affected in the communities where these loans were made. To minimize this risk, any arrangement made with a bank would have an escape clause whereby, if the recovery rate for the portfolio should fall below an agreed level (for example, 80 per cent), the bank would have the right to suspend all lending activities for the programme regardless of the level of guarantee. In other words, even if the guarantee were 100 per cent of principal and interest and the volume of lending far less than the guarantee coverage, the bank would still have the right to refuse to process any additional loans *until* an acceptable performance level for the portfolio (for example, 90 per cent) had been achieved. This provision is critical to the overall success of the proposed strategy because it establishes a rigid, uncompromising discipline for all levels of SI staff. It will also identify problems early enough to allow for programme modifications that could lead to its long-term success.

Resolving the risk considerations of participating banks is far simpler than solving the administrative problems. The Achilles heel of the proposed strategy is the difficulty that banks in developing countries have encountered in their efforts to track the performance of loan portfolios. But tracking has become far more viable in the 1990s than it was in the 1970s due to the rapid proliferation of micro computer hardware and software, which, when properly implemented, can significantly improve reporting systems. Computers are not a panacea, but with their increased capacity and lower prices, they offer realistic alternatives for the banks of developing countries.

Latin American banks have few problems providing needed reports since the level of computerization is high in practically all countries. Even in Africa, in many urban areas, banks can be found that are sufficiently computerized to handle what is a relatively simple reporting requirement. But where appropriate levels of computerization exist, the banks are still required to make minor modifications in their reporting systems. These modifications would make sense to the bank only if the long-term objective of the microenterprise programme promises to reach significant numbers of borrowers, a precondition which should have a positive effect on how programmes are designed.

Administrative problems are more serious in areas like South Asia, where the banking system is hampered by centuries-old bookkeeping practices incompatible with the reporting required by the proposed strategy. Here and in similar areas, it may be advisable for donors to subsidize a modernization of the banks, to make them capable of reporting at the required level. A significant benefit would accrue to these banks from the experience they would gain by using a small part of their lending operations to modernize reporting systems that could bring about improvements in their overall management information systems.

To summarize, the proposed strategy requires that a participating bank have the means to accurately monitor the performance of the overall portfolio, in order to ensure compliance by the SI with the minimum performance standards agreed to. This will entail certain administrative cost considerations (in particular, the capabilities of extant computerized systems), which would need to be carefully detailed. Over time, the interest rate structure agreed to should compensate for any additional administrative costs incurred by the bank.

In the end, the bank would track and service (but only in terms of administration) a portfolio of loans generated by the SI. The performance of this portfolio would determine the 'bankability' of the SI as a viable conduit between the formal banking system and microenterprises.

Summary of negotiation points with banks

Principal required conditions for successful negotiation

1 The interest and spread, as agreed to by both parties, should not be subsidized and should reflect the costs and risks borne by the bank;
2 the graduated risk (leveraging to ten times the amount of guarantees provided over time — 5–6 years — based on mutually agreed to performance standards) should be considered reasonable by the bank;
3 the bank must accede to the SI's authority in the selection and approval of borrowers, under carefully negotiated guidelines; the loans would be granted by the bank directly to the individual borrowers;
4 once proper documentation had been sent to the SI and the borrower, guarantees provided under the agreement would allow immediate and automatic debiting for any loan (principal and interest) past due for ninety days or more.

Other key points for negotiation

If a bank is agreeable to further negotiation, with a view to the signing of an agreement, the following points would require in-depth discussion:

1 what will be the means of accurately tracking the performance of the loan portfolio as envisioned?

2   what would be the minimum loan size acceptable from an administrative point of view?
3   what are the terms and conditions of loans that might affect administrative considerations (length, payment periods, collateral, etc)?
4   what are the overall policies and procedures for the programme?
5   what will be the method of calculating recovery rates (on time, for the period, overall, etc), and when would they be calculated?
6   what time period would be required, and at what level of disbursement, to prove the portfolio's performance to the satisfaction of the bank, so that the bank could leverage additional funds into the scheme with the same amount of guarantees?

Grameen Bank: Organization and Operation

MUHAMMAD YUNUS

Introduction

Grameen started out as a small personal project in 1976 in a village next to Chittagong University campus. It struggled through several years to grow into a bank owned by the poor (75 per cent of the shares are owned by the landless borrowers, the remaining 25 per cent by the Government of Bangladesh) for the poor. Today it has 400,000 borrowers, 82 per cent of whom are women. Grameen Bank lends out more than US$2.5 m each month in tiny loans averaging US$67. Its recovery rate is 98 per cent. Now it has over 400 branches working in 8000 villages (out of 68,000) of Bangladesh. Borrowers have accumulated over US$7.0 million in their savings funds.

In this paper we shall discuss the basic features of Grameen Bank, its future expansion plan and the question of its replicability and present some extracts from the evaluation reports.

Basic features of Grameen Bank

Close relationship

The close relationship that is developed between the bank and the borrowers, and among the borrowers themselves is a very important feature of Grameen Bank.

Peer pressure and peer support

The formation of small five-member groups of the members' own choosing, and federating the groups into centres, helps to create the right kind of peer pressure at times when a member tries wilfully to violate Grameen rules, and peer support at times when a member falls into any difficulty in pursuing his economic aims.

Grameen tries to reach the poorest

We feel that mixing the poor and the non-poor is a sure path to failure. Grameen makes entry into a group by an individual quite an elaborate process. It puts so many checks in the way that it would be quite a tough job

---

Professor MUHAMMAD YUNUS is Managing Director of The Grameen Bank in Dhaka, Bangladesh.

for 'a non-poor' to get in. Again within the eligible poor, Grameen tries to reach the people at the bottom. One strategy which Grameen finds helpful in reaching the poorest is to start its operation initially with only women groups. In a Muslim society like Bangladesh it is almost an impossible situation to attract a women's group. With the opposition from the religious leaders, and frightening rumours floating around the village regarding what will happen to a woman if she takes a loan from Grameen, it is only the desperate women who finally push their way through to form the first group. These groups gradually set the level of economic conditions of the future members. Better-off people are kept away because they do not enjoy being classed with these destitutes.

Process of group formation
The process of group formation itself contributes to the strength of Grameen. Usually it takes some time for the members to identify each other and consult each other before they make an announcement that they wish to form a group. Many times members screen each other out before they arrive at the final five. Some drop out because of fear instilled in them by relatives and neighbours. Before even beginning negotiation with the bank, the members have already gone through a process of understanding and mutual confidence-building. By the time the bank confers on a group the much sought-after recognition, a member has got to know the bank quite well, the bank knows her well, and the rules and procedures of the bank come quite easily to her. She has come to know her other partners in the group and in the centre. It is a long period of suspense and learning. It gives her a great thrill when she receives the final recognition: it is a great moment for her, and she knows she has earned it by herself. It gives her the first important lift in building self-confidence. Now she feels she can do it.

Whenever Grameen starts functioning at any new location it creates an impression that it is in no hurry to do anything
It allows the process to take its time. It offers the following explanation: 'Why hurry? If poor people have survived without Grameen for all these years now, they will survive without it for some more years to come.'

A branch gets into operation in a slow and easy manner. The manager, usually accompanied by someone with the title of associate manager, will arrive in a village where Grameen has decided to set up a branch. (An associate manager is someone who will be given the responsibility to set up a new branch, maybe within two months.) They will have no office, no place to stay, no one to get in touch with. Their first assignment is to understand and document everything about the area which may come under the coverage of the proposed branch.

The manager is free to decide whether he should go ahead and start the process of setting up the branch, or whether he should abort the process. He recommends the general location of the future office. While making up his mind, he draws a map of the area, writes reports on history, culture, economy and the poverty situation of the area.

After he decides to continue with the process of setting up a branch, he talks to the people, explaining the rules, procedures and objectives of Grameen. About four weeks later he organizes a public meeting to give maximum exposure to these rules, procedures and objectives. He invites everybody to this meeting, particularly the village leaders, religious leaders, teachers, government officials, etc. Some high-ranking Grameen officials will address the meeting explaining everything in detail and giving everybody an option either to accept Grameen with all its rules and procedures or tell them within a specified time to leave the village.

No one has ever asked Grameen to leave a village, but giving the option helps. It is made clear that there is no compulsion on either side.

The manager and his associate walk for miles every day to talk to people and to answer questions. They explain the procedures for forming a group. They insist that they will accept only women's groups from the villages which are located farthest away from the proposed location of the branch. Usually when the manager and his associates start talking to the women, trouble with religious leaders begins. The situation quickly gets very tense, and both sides get ready for a showdown. Frightening rumours are floated against Grameen and the women who want to become members. The desperate women defy every threat and declare their solemn resolution to join Grameen. Women who have been abandoned by their husbands leaving children with them, and who have no place to turn to, who feel that they have nothing to lose, stand solidly together against all odds. Sometimes religious leaders will ask the manager not to enter their village. If he does, he is told he will do so at his own risk: they cannot guarantee him any safety for his person. The manager tells the potential members that he is not coming to the village any longer. If they have to go through the orientation meetings they will have to see him in the neighbouring village. The women are ready to do anything to form the group. They are more determined than ever.

When the women ultimately receive a loan from the bank, many more women want to form Grameen groups. They ask the manager to come to their village. The manager insists that, since some people in the village have asked him not to enter, he should not. Only if the same persons come and request him to enter the village will he do so. Sooner or later pressure on the people who prohibited the manager from entering the village will become so strong that some of them will come and ask him to forget about what they said.

All this moves in a slow manner, but Grameen is in no hurry. It knows that ultimately everything will work out in its favour.

Managers create an environment of respect towards Grameen

Only two persons, with modest belongings, arrive in a village to set up a Grameen branch. Everybody looks at them with disbelief. They look like two helpless persons. They don't know where they can spend the night, where they are going to eat. This is very much unlike government officials who arrive in a village creating an aura of tremendous importance around them, and who take it for granted that the village leaders will make all arrangements for them and that they will find delicious meals and snacks waiting for them at the rich person's house.

Grameen managers usually find a shelter at some abandoned house, school hostel or local council office. They decline offers of food from the well-to-do people, explaining that this is against the rules of Grameen. They usually cook their own food.

People come to learn that both of them have masters degrees from the university and are highly educated people. School teachers are usually the first ones to recognize their educational status. When they learn about Grameen, the teachers extend their moral support to the bank. Teachers find it only natural for them to show respect for education, because they themselves are trying to inculcate a sense of respect for education in everybody. None of these teachers ever made it to the university — they may have aspired to it, but circumstances did not allow them to succeed.

They cannot believe that after completing university education anybody would ever come back to work in the village and to work with poor people, walking several miles every day — no big chair, big table, big office — no glamour.

Grameen managers never fail to give a mild shock to everybody by their having good university degrees and deciding to work in the village. From their activities everybody gets the impression that not only they have decided to work in the village, they have done so quite willingly and they are enjoying the work they are doing. We have never had any experience where the villagers did not notice this aspect of Grameen and fail to come up with genuine admiration for the young managers.

When the manager gets into action, gradually some of his respectability wears off. He becomes the subject of rumours and allegations. Interested people, particularly money-lenders and religious leaders, will help spread strange rumours. Here are some examples:

1   the manager will run away with the money he collects as group savings;
2   he has no intention of giving any money — if he represents any bank, why does he not have any office or staff?
3   if he is a manager of a bank, why does he live like a peon, cooking for himself — and has anybody ever heard of an MA cooking his own meal?
4   why does he run after women? He must have some evil design. He is connected with a big international smuggling ring which smuggles girls to the Middle East;

5 he is working for the Christian missionaries to destroy our religion by bringing our women out of purdah;
6 if he is a high official like a bank manager, why doesn't he tell the Union Parishad (Local Council) chairman to do the things needed to be done? Why does he have to walk for miles to do these?

The Grameen manager quietly goes on with his work. As time goes by people see how hard he works. In rain or shine he never stops walking and working. He never tries to take short-cuts by appointing some of the villagers as his agents. They soon find out that even on religious issues his understanding and knowledge is deeper than that of most of the people in the village. His explanation of Grameen rules and procedures sounds very convincing.

Ultimately, it is not his word, but his hard work, which softens the attitude of the people in the village. Even if you don't like his ideas, his ways of doing things, you are convinced it is helping the poor people, you are convinced that he is not doing all this work to reap some personal benefits, but to improve the condition of the poor. The attitude of the people gradually turns in his favour.

Organizational structure of Grameen

We usually describe Grameen as a highly decentralized organization, as decentralized as a franchise business. Grameen's organizational structure. may perhaps be better described by saying that this is organized on the principle of having circles within circles. Each circle is complete, but it is located within a bigger circle. The biggest circle is the head office, the smallest circle is the group. Groups belong to the bigger circle of a centre, which belongs to the still bigger circle of the branch, branch to the area office, area office to the zonal office, zonal office to the head office. Each bigger circle tries to pass on the responsibilities to the immediately next smaller circles within itself, while keeping close watch on what goes in each constituent smaller circle. In case of emergency the higher circle takes up the responsibility more directly to bail out the lower circle.

Grameen is a group of multi-layered federations of constituent units. Each bigger circle is a federation of immediately smaller circles. In management decisions the spirit of federalism is widely visible. Each federating unit is trying to protect its own autonomy by doing things right without being told what to do. Branches try to do their thing without any intervention from area office. Area office tries to do their thing without being pushed by the zone. The zone enjoys its own autonomy; it won't be happy if head office steps in to direct it in its routine work.

In order to retain autonomy each unit has to work hard. Any lapses or shortcoming will invite intervention from the higher authority. The federal body tends to take up the role of a control tower in relation to the aeroplanes flying in the sky under its guidance. Federating units may be viewed as the flying aeroplanes. The control tower supplies all the necessary intelligence to the pilot to fly the plane safely, but it does not attempt to assume the role of the pilot itself. But in an exceptional situation when the pilot fails to fly the plane properly, the control tower takes over a very active role in flying the plane to safety.

In Grameen we try to make it very clear to our 'pilots' what their responsibilities are. One of our pilots can grumble about his co-pilot, his navigator, his flight engineer, even his whole crew, but he knows that the total responsibility remains squarely with him alone.

Responsibilities are clearly marked out. To give an illustration: for a special achievement in a branch congratulations will go to the branch manager, not to his boss, the area manager, who will only receive a copy of the letter. But if something bad happens in a branch, the person who draws the fire from the top is the area manager, not the branch manager.

Supervisory offices (area office, zonal office and head office) are there to make sure a minimum qualitative level is maintained in all the units under its supervision. Continuous monitoring of events in the lower units becomes the most crucial function of the supervisory offices. Access to information automatically reduces the necessity for day-to-day administrative control. The more information is available on a regular basis, the more easy it becomes to dispense with regulatory administrative measures. Self-regulation in one's own self-interest is the most effective form of regulation.

Participatory decision-making process

Like any organization, Grameen has to come up with new decisions which effect the work and life of many people. Being a new and fast-expanding organization, Grameen needs to modify old decisions and introduce new decisions quite regularly and frequently. In coming up with new decisions Grameen management always tries to assess the views of the people whose work and life would be affected by these decisions.

When Grameen was a small organization it was easy to keep in personal touch with others in Grameen, but now it is a big and widely spread out organization. With a work-force of nearly 8,000 it is not easy to have person-to-person contact.

Head office still avoids taking unilateral decisions. If it has to frame new policies or rules or regulations, it will make a draft and circulate the draft among departmental heads and zonal managers for comments and modifications. If the subject covered by the draft is of greater importance, copies of the draft will go to the area manager. Depending on the seriousness of the matter, those who receive the draft may send their comments in writing, or each recipient may hold his internal meetings to debate the issues and come up with reactions. After all the opinions and reactions are received by the head office they are sent to a standing committee, the 'drafting committee', which reviews all opinions and suggestions and prepares the second draft. This is again circulated to generate opinions. If everybody seems generally satisfied with the second draft it is officially adopted and circulated as official policy. If the second draft generates another wave of reactions, the drafting committee again goes back to the drawing board.

If no satisfactory draft emerges in several rounds of drafting it is referred to the zonal managers' conference which is generally held twice a year. There the issues would be debated and a decision would be arrived at.

In Grameen the zonal managers' conference plays a very important role in the decision-making process and also in the general administration. It is a three-day intensive affair. In head office, each department prepares its agenda items, papers for circulation, a report on the activities of the department, future plans, etc. Head office consolidates all departmental agenda items to prepare a single head office agenda.

The zonal managers (ZMs) prepare their own agenda, a review of the zone's activities, successes and failures, future plans, papers for circulation, reports on innovative activities of the zone and a report on the problems they are facing: trend analysis, profit-loss analysis and many such things. Each ZM may bring an aide to assist him during the conference — an area manager usually comes as an aide.

All through the conference all departmental heads in the head office, along with their aides, remain present in the conference, and the managing director presides.

Customarily, during the conference head office representatives are not allowed to make accusations, or express displeasure for anything done by the ZMs or for any failure to follow any instructions by any zones. This conference, as you would expect from its name, is looked at as one where the ZMs speak out and complain against the head office. Head office can only defend itself by explaining the circumstances, clarifying the situation, and coming up with new arrangements with ZMs to expedite matters.

ZMs are encouraged to criticize each other's performance and find gaps in their reports. They ask piercing questions of each other and try to establish that one zone is run better than another.

Departments in head office bring out figures showing the performance of each zone and each area, compared to the others. Discussions are initiated as to why a certain area or zone is lagging behind. Corrective measures are discussed, not by head office telling the zone what to do, but by giving ideas for the consideration of the ZM. The ZM is free to accept or turn a deaf ear to any suggestion, although since he himself is worried about a particular problem, he is on the look-out for a pragmatic solution. If he finds one he grabs it.

The Monitoring and Evaluation Department of Grameen presents bundles of comparative pictures to bring out the strong and weak points in each zone. The M and E Department itself gets corrected if there is any error in the information it circulated earlier, or circulated during the conference. Mutually, all try to find ways to improve the quality of information and quality of analysis.

ZMs arrive one day ahead of the conference and they are expected to stay in Dhaka for another two days after the conference. This gives them time to resolve many of the pending administrative problems and make arrangements for future trouble-free support from the head office for implementing their plans.

At the conclusion of each ZMs' conference I am always amazed to find how much has been achieved in such a short time. Every participant in the conference goes back to his work with new vigour and life. Many have nicknamed this conference the 'battery recharging conference.' One feels quite filled with enthusiasm and becomes eager to go back to the zone to build a still better Grameen in his zone.

Encouraged by the results achieved from the ZMs' conference, ZMs organize the Area Managers' Conference in their own zones following the same format.

By opening doors for everybody to participate in the decision-making process a large amount of misunderstanding and tension in the organization has been avoided. Now everybody knows what the decisions are, and why these decisions were taken. Inadvertent mistakes through careless use of words are avoided because somebody has already pointed them out at the draft stage. This type of decision-making creates support for the decisions taken. Everybody knows what is coming his way and if he does not like it, he can try to stop it, or at least modify it.

Creativity and innovation

Grameen tries to build a problem-solving attitude among its people. Statements similar to the ones listed below will be heard around the training classes and office rooms of Grameen quite frequently. In the context of a real situation one sentence, correctly chosen from among the following, may give you encouragement to find a solution. It even guides you towards a solution. The relationship between a problem and its solution is usually stated in the following variations:

1 every problem has a simple solution. A problem and its solution are two sides of the same coin, they are always together;
2 a problem is only half the truth. A problem and its solution makes up the whole truth. Discover the whole truth;
3 if you don't find the solution to a problem it is because you don't understand the problem;
4 if you can comprehend the problem properly you are half-way to the solution;

5   the solution is born in the womb of the problem. Artificial solutions do not last long;
6   a solution cannot be found away from the problem itself;
7   you must immerse yourself totally into the problem before you can start touching the surface of the solution;
8   as you go deep into the problem you come close to the solution. This is the sure route to the solution;
9   neither can I solve *your* problem, nor can *you* solve *mine*. If it appears that I have solved your problem, it was possible only because I made your problem mine;
10   look for the solution where the problem is. It is intermeshed with the problem itself;
11   each problem may have many solutions, but there is one which is the best. Keep trying to get the best;
12   a problem is a state of a particular configuration of events.

Grameen trainees will hear these statements many times during their training period. Grameen tries to make them believe that they can find solutions to all the problems they'll face and also to feel that facing a problem is fun — you get a chance to test your wits.

There is emphasis on creativity and innovation all around. One of the statements usually displayed at the training institute, and in many branches, reads as follows: 'We have to be creative. In order to be creative we must observe everything carefully and think about what we see.'

When young men and women enter Grameen as trainees the first thing they are asked is to give their opinions and suggestions for improvements in Grameen procedures, even before they have had a chance to find out what Grameen does and how. They are very surprised; they came to learn, now they are asked to teach. They are sent out to observe Grameen operations in different branches, one in each branch. They realize that they have to first find out what Grameen does, before they can suggest alternatives. They pay a lot more attention to Grameen procedures to find out its faults than they would have if they were sent out to learn them.

It is made very clear to the trainees that Grameen objectives are much more important than the rules and procedures. Anyone in Grameen can suggest major changes in Grameen rules and procedures provided the objectives are not adversely effected. Anyone can do this either during the training period or at any time afterwards. Trainees are told about changes that came about in Grameen rules and procedures in the past through the suggestions of bank workers and branch managers. Many new aspects were added to Grameen not by people in the head office, but people who work in the field. It is made very clear to everybody that Grameen's commitment is to the people, not to the rules and procedures.

Grameen's training programme always tries to avoid producing Grameen workers cast in a single mould, looking alike, thinking alike, reacting alike. Grameen tries to retain diversity. It feels that diversity brings strength. In a time of crisis, an organization where everybody's thinking and acting is patterned in a standard way has a greater chance of collapsing than an organization where many opinions and minds can interact. Grameen wishes to produce good Grameen workers, each having respect for the other while still preserving their individuality. Grameen trainees come from a wide variety of socioeconomic backgrounds, with a wide range of political and religious beliefs. Grameen does not try to change these affiliations. Grameen trusts in their ability to analyse the objective reality and come to their own conclusions. Grameen encourages them to be politically and socially aware.

Grameen brings its workers face-to-face with the reality of poverty. Poverty is nothing new to them, but they have known it in a different context. That is why it looked different. Some of them knew poverty from such a safe distance that they had to imagine things for themselves to make up stories of poverty.

Grameen brings them eyeball to eyeball with raw poverty and makes them look at it as a soldier looks at the enemy. Grameen gives them some organizational and financial tools and tells them: fight. They develop the instinct to fight and a will to win. They get into a fight. They win. The more they fight and the more they win, the more they get excited.

Grameen tells its workers that Grameen is not the only way to fight poverty. There must be many other known and unknown ways of fighting poverty. They must keep up the search for better methods. While the search goes on, the fight must go on. There may be improvement in the Grameen methods, there may be an entirely different method available to replace the Grameen method, there may be some supplementary methods to support Grameen methods. The search must go on.

Grameen's expansion programme

By the end of 1988 there were 500 Grameen branches in Bangladesh. Together they will serve 500,000 borrowers in 10,000 villages. In terms of the number of branches Grameen ended 1988 with 100 new additions to its previous year's total. By modestly increasing the number of additional branches in each successive year, Grameen tries to find out whether it is straining itself too much in the process of expansion.

Annual figures for branch expansion are only tentative. Pressures are never mounted on the zonal and area offices to fulfil any particular quota. Some zonal and area offices exceed their tentative numbers, while others fall short of these numbers. The entire expansion programme depends on how the zonal and area managers feel about it, how quickly or slowly they want to take their steps. That is why the year-end final count of branches is always an exciting affair. Everybody waits to see at which number we have closed the year.

If everything works out well, how many more branches should Grameen add during the current four-year period? Our present dream is that it will add another 500 branches. If by the end of 1992 Grameen can reach an optimistic figure of 1,000, it would be ready to make an addition of 700 more branches within 1993–95. Arriving at a total figure of 1,700 by 1995 sounds like a plausible dream. This will make Grameen's presence a nationwide one.

The question of replicability

Can Grameen be replicated outside Bangladesh? By way of a first guess one can stipulate that in countries similar to Bangladesh, in terms of socio-economic conditions, there should not be any difficulty in organizing Grameen-type credit programmes and Grameen-type institutions. SAARC countries fall into this category. There are many similarities among the poor people in these countries. There are formidable differences also. Some people argue that in India a Grameen-type operation will be impossible to organize because of the strong caste system. People from one caste will never form groups with people from another caste. Similarly, it would be difficult to organize centres, because each caste would try to have their own centres.

Religion in Pakistan and the high literacy rate in Sri Lanka are pointed out as possible factors negatively affecting a Grameen-type operation. But they may not be negative factors. Nepal is already involved in the Small Farmers' Development Programme (SFDP) which has many similarities with Grameen. The Women's Development Programme of the Panchayet Ministry of Nepal has sent their workers to visit Grameen to gather experience in running a credit programme for poor women. The Governor of Nepal Rashtra Bank visited Grameen to discuss the possibility of setting up rural banks in Nepal. The Governor of the Central Bank of Sri Lanka also visited Grameen Bank. High-ranking government officials and NGO representatives from SAARC countries visit Grameen regularly.

Other Asian and Pacific countries
ESCAP organized a seminar in 1984, entitled 'Study Tour of Grameen Bank'. Many representatives from the governments of the ESCAP region, bankers and women programme leaders participated in the seminar. Grameen has received official mission members from Indonesia studying Grameen to work out a programme for Indonesia. A three-member team visited Grameen from the Area Development Project of West Pasaman, Indonesia, to learn about the rules and operational procedures of Grameen. This project in Indonesia is funded by GTZ of Germany. Delegations from Agricultural Bank of China (ABC), the Philippines and Malaysia visited Grameen.

Malaysia formulated a project to experiment with Grameen-type credit for the poor in Selangor State. Selangor State Government, the Science University of Malaysia and APDC are collaborating in this project, which started during the second half of 1986. This is the first serious replication attempt of Grameen outside Bangladesh that we know of. The experience of this Grameen project in Malaysia has been excellent, and it is being expanded to cover more states. The Governor of the Central Bank of the Solomon Islands also visited Grameen to explore the possibilities of adopting its features in their own banking system.

Africa
Grameen has attracted several visits from Kenya, Tanzania, Rwanda, Malawi, Egypt. Malawi, Burkina Faso, Mali and Egypt are getting ready to launch Grameen look-alike projects in their countries.

USA and Canada
Surprisingly, serious preparations are afoot in Arkansas and Chicago in the USA to have a Grameen-type credit operation. Grameen came into contact with two Chicago bankers, Mr Ronald Grinzinwski and Ms Mary Houghton, who visited Grameen as Ford Foundation consultants, and later as member of the IFAD Appraisal Mission for Grameen. They found Grameen to be a very effective banking programme. They spread the word in Chicago and Arkansas, and later, during the visits of the Managing Director of Grameen to Arkansas and Chicago during February and October 1986, ideas crystallized. In Arkansas, Grameen Microenterprise Programme will be a programme under a newly set up bank called Southern Development Bank Corporation which is funded by the Rockefeller Foundation ($3 m), the Ford Foundation ($2 m) and individual investors ($3 m). Governor Bill Clinton is personally taking an interest in the Grameen programme. The Chicago programme will be offered by the Neighborhood Development Corporation and operated through local community groups. In Oklahoma, the Cherokee people are getting ready to have their own Grameen programme.

In Canada, Calmeadow Foundation, Toronto, is taking a serious interest in Grameen for replication in Canada and Africa. They want to initiate the programme in Canada on the Indian reservations.

Grameen has attracted attention from all directions, from the poor countries to the richest countries, for good reasons. Wherever there is the problem of poverty, Grameen appears like a possible solution. If the poor can improve their condition with the availability of mere credit, why not try it? On the surface, it appears to be too simplistic to be true, but in Bangladesh it gives some hope. Maybe it will work in other countries too. If the US can attract welfare recipients to take loans and improve their condition to the extent that they might not be on welfare any longer, this would be a great economic idea to try.

Unemployment problems worry many of the industrialized nations: they cannot keep the economy moving all the time at the pace which will ensure everybody a job. A Grameen-type credit programme opens up the door for limitless self-employment, and it can effectively do it in a pocket of poverty amidst prosperity, or in a massive poverty situation. This potential of the Grameen system makes it equally attractive to both the South and the North.

Steps for replication

It is obvious that any organization whose primary business is to deal with human beings cannot be replicated by following a 'do-it-yourself' manual. It would need a thorough understanding of the philosophy and procedures which make the organization tick. This can be achieved by going through an intensive dialogue and exposure programme in the existing units. Anyone who would be responsible for implementing a programme to replicate Grameen must go through this dialogue and exposure programme. In any country, whenever a replication of Grameen is to be seriously undertaken, we recommend that it should be initiated in several widely separated areas — five would be a good number. The advantage of trying it out in several places is that this way one can eliminate local and personal factors, competition is generated among the branch managers, one can pick up varieties of problems at one go, varieties of solutions are produced and non-problems do not have a serious chance of confusing people for long.

At the end of the first round of trials, one can sort out the features which worked well and leave behind the features which did not show much prospect. Out of the five trials, it is likely that one would show the greatest promise and one would be falling behind everybody else. It is good to study all five and determine the next strategy. In round two, that is the second year, another five branches should be started in another five locations based on the experience gathered in the first round. It is always a good idea to give flexibility to the branch managers in suggesting rules and procedures, but someone away from the responsibility of running the day-to-day affairs of the branch should have the sole authority to decide what suggestions to accept.

In replicating Grameen one must remember right from the beginning that, if the recovery is not near 100 per cent, no matter how good it looks, it is no Grameen. All the strength of Grameen comes from its recovery performance. It is not merely the money which is reflected through the recovery rate, it is the discipline which speaks loud and clear through the rate.

The second thing which must be remembered clearly is that Grameen works with the poorest men and women, with emphasis on women. In any experimental situation one would be well-advised to start the experimentation with the poorest women, say, the bottom 20 per cent of the total population. If one compromises on this issue, replication may not proceed in the right direction.

The third advice to someone who wants to replicate Grameen would be to pick up fresh young people to run the programme. Persons having no job experience of any kind would be best suited for Grameen. To have previous experience of any kind always distracts people from the Grameen-type work.

The fourth advice is: always start in a very low key and small way. Go as slow as you can. The slower one proceeds, the better start one makes. One can pick up speed only when everything looks perfectly in order.

At the beginning everything looks as though it is perfectly in order. One can detect faults only after the first two years have gone by. When a branch receives the full repayment of the first one hundred loans it advanced without the slightest hitch, then one can feel that things are moving in the right direction. Before that, one can only hope for the best and try one's hardest.

Evaluations

Grameen is perhaps one of the most studied institutions. Because of the unorthodox ways it works, and the unconventional concepts it promotes, it has created interest among researchers both from within and outside the country. Widely circulated works are the following:

1   Hossain, Mahbub *Credit for the Rural Poor, the Grameen Bank of Bangladesh,* Bangladesh Institute of Development Studies, Dhaka, 1984.
2   ———— *Credit for Alleviation of Rural Poverty: The Experience of Grameen Bank*, BIDS, Dhaka, 1986.
3   Ghai, Dharam *An Evaluation of the Impact of the Grameen Bank Project,* IFAD, March, 1984.
4   Siddiqui, Kamal *An Evaluation of the Grameen Bank Operation*, National Institute of Local Government, Dhaka, July 1984.
5   Ahmed, Mahbub *Status, Perception, Awareness and Marital Adjustment of Rural Women: The Role of Grameen Bank*, Dhaka University, 1985.
6   Ray, Jayanta Kumar *To Chase a Miracle — A Study of the Grameen Bank of Bangladesh*, University Press, Dhaka, 1987.
7   Fuglesang, Andreas and Chandler, Dale *Participation as a Process. What We Can Learn from Grameen Bank of Bangladesh*, NORAD, 1986.
8   ———— *The Paradigm of Communication in Development, from Knowledge Transfer to Community Participation. Lessons from Grameen Bank, Bangladesh*, FAO Development Communication Case Study, 1986.
9   Rahman, Atiur *Demand and Marketing Aspects of Grameen Bank. A Closer Look*, University Press, Dhaka, 1986.
10   ———— *Impact of GRAMEEN Bank Intervention on the Rural Power Structure*, BIDS, July 1986.
11   ————*Consciousness Raising Efforts of Grameen Bank*, BIDS, July 1986.
12   ———— *Impact of Grameen Intervention on the Food Availability and the Nutritional Status of Its Members*, BIDS, June 1987.

13 Rahman, Rushidan Islam *Impact of Grameen Bank on the Situation of Poor Rural Women*, BIDS, Dhaka, July 1986.
14 Ack, Bradley, Prince, Paul and Robinson, Rand *The Grameen Bank: Reaching The Landless Poor in Bangladesh: A Project Analysis* USA, May 1986.

On the success of Grameen

Here are some quotations from these documents on the success of Grameen:

'We consider Grameen Bank to be an exciting success, even more so when viewed against a landscape littered with failed development projects. The reasons for the Bank's successes provide many useful lessons for development managers.'[14]

'... the loanee women on the average worked 4.2 hours a day in their Grameen loan financed activity ... Housewives in non-loanee groups worked on average of 15 to 58 hours a month on such productive work. This comes to 0.44 hours to 0.66 hours a day.'[13]

'The usual scene of a poor rural woman is that under a long veil she bows down and eyes are fixed on the ground and she talks in a shy and timid manner. She never looks straight to the eyes of an unknown urban visitor (male or female). When one talks to a Grameen loanee woman the difference is striking and very obvious. They will stand confidently and speak out as an equal partner in a conversation. Though they have veils on the head and a baby on the lap, they do not bow down but reflect the spirit that now they are being valued by the society. The spirit is more apparent among those women loanees who have been members for a longer period. The new ones are proceeding step by step.

'We do not want to overemphasize the progress. But when an outsider goes to a group of female loanees he/she is likely to be moved to see that those poor rural women who were simply ignored, have risen to establish themselves as independent entities.'[13]

'Within a short span of its existence Grameen Bank has already made profound impacts in terms of significant improvements in household output, income and consumption. Most of the Grameen credit is going to the desired target groups ... the rural poor people. 78 per cent of our sample loanee households owned no cultivated land.
'... In terms of value of non-land assets, the situation has improved significantly over time.
'... Grameen operations have contributed to a significant improvement in incomes. The average per capita income of loanees (as reported by them) has increased in real terms from Tk 1762 (1982) to Tk 2697 (1985 in 1982 price) a relative increase of 53 per cent.'[9]

'Not only the food intake, the intake of nutrients also is better for Grameen loanees. Though they have not been able to meet fully the calorie requirement, but their intake is relatively better than their counterparts in the target control group of the same period.'[12]

'Groups and Centres of Grameen loanees are working as focal points of solidarity and cooperation amongst the loanees. The group spirit is emerging in concrete terms, and Grameen through its various special programmes is making relentless efforts to consolidate this spirit of cooperation. Poor women have been the greatest beneficiaries of the Grameen efforts. Rural poor women are becoming income earners with the help of Grameen loans and subsequently are asserting their rights on their male counterparts and the society at large. They have become quite confident of their own ability and can easily stand against social injustice.'[11]

'a. There has been an increase of socioeconomic status of the female clients of Grameen Bank when measured in terms of occupational, income and class mobility (ie ownership of land).
b. There has been a great degree of increase in the perceived socio-economic status of the respondents.
c. Husbands' perception of their wives has improved a great deal; at least in the economic sense; a notion of compatibility is persistent.
d. There is a high degree of awareness on the issues of women's rights except on the notion of gender equality.
e. Overall, there is a high degree of marital adjustment of the loanee couples.'[15]

'Grameen is a remarkable rural development experiment in a poverty stricken country like Bangladesh. Perhaps, its significance will one day overshadow even that of Comilla experience of the 60s. It will have far-reaching implications, despite its immediate outcome. Its internal logic is generally sound and consistent, and as this evaluation attempts to establish, it is really the externalities within which Grameen must operate, which are in the dock. It would thus be no exaggeration to suggest that the importance of Grameen as a credit disbursement model for poverty focused rural development will perhaps be better comprehended once the basic structural changes in the society have been completed.'[4]

'Finally, we turn to the question of lessons that may be drawn from the experience of the Grameen for the planning and implementation of rural development activities. The first lesson to be drawn is that it is possible to devise projects which directly and immediately benefit the poorest strata of rural society — landless men and women. This may appear a banal conclusion, but considering the extremely high rate of failure among rural development projects and their almost universal tendency to confer benefit on the powerful and the affluent, the experience of Grameen Bank holds out a glimmer of hope for an alternative development pattern based on low cost, self-reliant and participatory programme.'[3]

'To observers of Grameen Bank it is striking how the management and staff members communicate and work creatively together, comporting themselves with openness, perceptiveness and self-confidence. It is an atmosphere very different from that in a typical hierarchical bureaucracy with the stagnancy derived from prevailing factors such as fear of authority, inefficiency and corruption. The driving force in Grameen Bank's progress for the benefit of the poorest is undoubtedly person-to-person communication.'[8]

'Although it is very often argued that Grameen pursues "economic" by concentrating on the credit, its efforts at humanizing at every stage clearly indicates that it sees the interest of the poor in the long run. It is creating sound economic base for the rural poor so that they themselves can one day take up the responsibility of political mobilization and ensure their participation in development.'[10]

Grameen Bank: Cumulative progress over years (Amount in Taka m)

(Exchange rate US$ 1.00: Tk. 31.00, 22 March 1988)

Particulars	1976	1977	1978	1979	1980	1981	1982	1983	1984	1985	1986	1987
1 Disbursement												
A General loan	0.0075	0.081	0.341	3.053	20.147	53.673	94.558	191.288	470.697	877.366	1,411.613	2,206.650
B Collective loan							1.019	3.631	28.581	50.362	57.848	72.837
C Housing loan									3.62	20.772	26.515	167.248
Total	0.0075	0.081	0.341	3.053	20.147	53.673	95.577	194.919	502.898	948.500	1,495.976	2,446.735
2 No of members												
A Male	8	60	220	1,297	10,175	14,772	18,631	31,782	53,006	59,260	60,458	63,556
B Female	2	10	70	903	4,665	9,356	11,785	26,538	68,045	112,362	173,885	275,600
Total	10	70	290	2,200	14,830	24,128	30,416	58,320	121,051	171,622	234,343	339,156
3 Total no of branches	1	1	2	7	25	25	54	86	152	226	295	396
4 Savings												
A Special savings									7.678	21.290	33.257	51.143
B General savings									1.865	16.771	57.402	146.616
C Current account savings										9.076	15.705	126.593
D Education fund savings									0.002	0.456	2.898	9.458
Total									9.545	47.593	109.262	333.810
5 No of housing loan									317	1,581	2,042	23,408
7 Group fund savings			0.037	0.235	1.565	4.434	8.142	15.984	37.937	71.423	114.536	186.300
8 Emergency fund savings					0.029	0.331	1.436	3.370	6.245	12.658	22.336	34.661
9 Total of permanent employees	1	1	6	41	140	208	401	824	1,338	2,827	3,665	4,687
10 Rate of repayment	99.00	99.00	99.00	99.00	99.00	99.00	99.00	99.00	98.92	97.22	97.13	98.14
11 No of villages	1	2	4	17	363	433	745	1,249	2,268	3,666	5,170	7,502
12 Profit/loss								-3.064	4.896	0.463	0.359	0.438

PART IV

Technical Services for Microenterprises

Institutional Aspects of Microenterprise Promotion

MARILYN CARR

Introduction

The process of microenterprise support is highly complex, a consequence for the main part of the nature of the microenterprises themselves.

The sector is vast and varied, covering a multitude of trades and incorporating unknown numbers of people from all segments of society. As most microenterprises operate in the informal sector without being officially registered, documenting their numbers, needs and constraints is a virtually impossible task. What we do know is that they tend to be very small, often consisting only of family members. The people involved are usually very poor indeed — often being landless and assetless and turning to petty manufacturing or trade as the only way of scraping a living. In most countries, women account for a high proportion of the owners and workers in the sector: most of these women come from the poorest households which are dependent on the women's earnings for survival.

Microenterprises are widely dispersed and are often mobile or located within the household. Especially in rural areas and especially when the proprietor is a woman, they are usually not operated on a full-time basis. Generally, they are sparing in their use of capital, draw heavily on local skills and resources and produce basic consumer and producer goods demanded by the bulk of the rural and urban population. Tools and techniques utilized tend to be less complex than in larger enterprises and access to improved technologies and techniques is limited. They have little, if any, contact with formal training, credit or technology institutes and they tend to survive in spite of rather than with the help of government policy measures.

Given the difficulty and magnitude of the task in hand, it is hardly surprising that the attention of assistance agencies has, until recently, been focused on relatively easier target groups such as modern small-scale industry and small farmers and even those agencies which have attempted to start working with microenterprises have tended to concentrate on the relatively easier segments within it. Thus, they tend to be biased towards urban rather than rural enterprises, retail and service rather than maunfacturing

---

MARILYN CARR is now Adviser on Technology and Small Enterprise Development for the United Nations Development Fund for Women (UNIFEM) in Harare, Zimbabwe. Formerly she was with the Intermediate Technology Development Group in the UK.

enterprises, better off clients rather than poorer and male entrepreneurs rather then women.

Exactly what sort of assistance or support microenterprises need is an issue of some considerable debate. Methods of assistance range from the provision of a full package consisting of credit, business and technical training, production and technology advice and assistance, social promotion and political lobbying, to the provision of a single input such as credit or training.

The single input approach is obviously the simpler one to contemplate, and there is now considerable evidence to suggest that valuable assistance can be delivered relatively quickly in situations where a group of microentrepreneurs have a common, identified problem which can be addressed by an external assistance agency. By contrast, assistance programmes which seek to provide a whole package of inputs to a diversity of enterprises tend to be costly and incapable of reaching large numbers of people.

Of course, direct assistance programmes do not operate in a vacuum — the policy environment is also of great importance. Generally, government economic policy discriminates in favour of large-scale enterprise and policies such as artificially low interest rate ceilings, overvalued exchange rates and extensive regulation of business tend to make it harder to assist microenterprises. Other factors which have an impact on the effectiveness of assistance programmes include the presence or absence of a tradition of entrepreneurship in society and the general state of the local and national economy.

Whatever the nature of the assistance programme and whatever the nature of the policy and socioeconomic environment within which it is delivered, the remaining issue to be addressed is that of the institution or institutions which are best qualified to give effective support to microenterprises. Here, two questions need to be asked:

1   what type of institutions can assist/support microenterprises and what are the strengths and weaknesses of each;
2   what institutional arrangements can be made to combine the strengths of some or all of these institutions in the service of the microenterprise sector.

Simply put, who is best at doing what and how can they all be brought together?

Obviously, there can be no blueprint for a successful institutional framework since different types of institutions are more or less useful in different combinations depending on the type of microentrepreneur being assisted, the type of assistance programme needed, the nature of the external environment within which the programme is operating and the stage of the programme's life cycle.

Generally, a whole range of institutions would need to be involved in some way, at some time during an assistance programme. They include: microentrepreneurs' own organizations and cooperatives; local NGOs; research institutions, training institutions and technology centres; large commercial companies and business associations; commercial banks and other financing institutions; government departments and agencies; international NGOs; bilateral and multilateral donor agencies.

It is impossible here to go into the relative strengths and weaknesses of each of these in any great detail, but some of the more relevant points and issues can be summarized.

Microentrepreneurs themselves have much knowledge and skills to contribute to their own development. All too often, however, they have not been consulted or enabled to participate because of the top-down methods of many implementing agencies and because of factors (such as lack of transport or inability of male extension workers to reach women entrepreneurs) which inhibit effective communication. One way of drawing on this otherwise wasted resource is to assist microentrepreneurs to form their own organizations which provide a channel between their members and assistance agencies seeking to help them. Such organizations include the Self-employed Women's Association and the Working Women's Forum in India which have a membership of thousands of rural and urban women who rely on them for a range of technical and financial services and indirect support.

NGOs also have an important role to play. Many are based in the rural and urban slum areas where most microenterprises are located and they usually have a dedicated staff who have lived and worked for many years with the people they seek to assist. As such, they have a capacity to understand the needs of microentrepreneurs and to induce trust and cooperation. They also tend to be flexible, willing to take risks and are less subject to political controls and intervention than public development institutions. They do, of course, have their problems. Their 'community development' orientation often means that their generalist staff lack the necessary understanding of technology or business management to give effective advice and assistance to microentrepreneurs and, generally, they are too small to have an impact on large numbers of people through direct intervention. Many wish to remain small so that they do not become subject to government interference. A wish to remain invisible also means they often have little interest in influencing the policy environment.

There are many types of research and training institutions and technology centres ranging from those in the formal sector with no interest in or capacity to do anything about microenterprise, to those which have been established by government, universities or NGOs with the specific purpose of working with such sectors. Generally, they tend to be distanced from the clients they are supposed to be assisting. Thus training is done in a centre rather than on-the-job and often involves the use of inappropriate equipment or materials. Technologies are designed in a vacuum without the necessary involvement of the microentrepreneurs who are supposed to use them.

Commercial companies and financing institutions can play a number of roles in microenterprise development including research and development, subcontracting to microenterprise, and provision of credit. Obviously, such institutions only become involved if they can see some financial advantage in doing so and there is usually the need for an NGO or public sector agency to work as a catalyst in bringing this situation into being.

Government agencies are important at a number of levels. First, they can set up special agencies which give support to the microenterprise sector. Generally, however, government support agencies have related to registered small industries rather than reaching the unregistered informal sector (which in any case is nervous of dealing with government). Secondly, it can help other agencies to assist microenterprises through removing direct constraints such as harassment of illegally located businesses. Thirdly, they can set up committees or units to assess the effect of goverment economic policies on microenterprise and introduce macro policy reforms which support the sector. Evidence suggests that government agencies can be more effective in giving indirect support rather than direct support to microentrepreneurs.

Finally, bilateral and multilateral donor agencies can help by earmarking loan funds specifically for support of microenterprises, and through providing funds for the replication of programmes developed on a small scale by NGOs.

A successful support system for microenterprise involves bringing together the strengths of all these various agencies, helping to overcome their weaknesses, and establishing institutional relationships when necessary. Factors which need to be considered in this process include:

1   criteria for choosing a focus agency which can coordinate all the various inputs and methods by which this coordination can be achieved;
2   methods for implementing a truly collaborative approach to development, whereby knowledge travels up from the microentrepreneurs to the assistance agencies and the international agencies learn from and listen to the local agencies, as well as the other way round.

These points are not unrelated since the choice of focus agency will, by and large, determine the extent to which a trickle up approach to microenterprise development is likely to occur.

Generally speaking, while government institutions have tended to be the focus agency for small industry promotion, evidence suggests that they are less well-suited to playing a lead role in offering direct support services to microenterprises. NGOs, starting with their understanding of and commitment to poor communities, are much more likely to be able to coordinate effective support programmes in this sector, providing they can be persuaded to move away from their normal resource-intensive, comprehensive approach to assistance and start acting more as a catalyst and lobbying force.

In the following section, some specific experiences in microenterprise support are summarized in an attempt to illustrate some of the above points and to emphasize the importance of getting the institutional framework right.

Particular attention is given to the process of transferring improved technologies and techniques to microenterprises since of all the types of assistance which microentrepreneurs are offered, this is the one which has received the least attention.

Experiences in microenterprise promotion

Micro-hydro in Nepal

This programme began with the efforts of two agencies — the United Missions to Nepal (UMN) and a Swiss government supported engineering company (BYS) within the Department of Industrial Development. Both were interested in finding an appropriate way of driving grain mills in remote areas based on abundant supplies of water power.

From small beginnings in the mid-1970s, there are now 450 turbines (with associated milling equipment) installed in rural areas and a total of nine companies producing, installing and providing after-sales service to entrepreneurs investing in these. Uptake of the technology has been facilitated by the decision taken by the Agricultural Development Bank of Nepal (ABDN) to switch its loans from diesel mills to watermills and successful operation has been ensured by the care taken by the Bank and the two original (and still the major) producers of turbines to ensure proper selection of entrepreneurs and sites, along with adequate training of owners/operators and after-sales follow-up. Given the success of the project so far, the ABDN has negotiated a loan from the Asian Development Bank to facilitate the installation of a further 450 turbines and mills, and there are thought to be over 700 sites identified by ABDN and the manufacturers as suitable for installations.

In addition, the government of Nepal's policy support has been essential to the success of the programme. It has decreed that no licence is required to generate and sell electricity below 100 Kw, which has permitted local mill owners to join the UMN electrification programme.

Recently, the government has made a subsidy of up to Rs 1 lakh for the purchase of electrification equipment. Basically, the government has decided to support the independent, private sector approach to rural electrification as the most viable option for small, remote village applications and has used legal and other policy measures to provide incentives for increased activity by UMN and its collaborators in this area.

The benefits of this project are numerous. Income and employment have been generated in the manufacture of turbines. Farmers (and particularly female members of farm households) have benefited from the availability of a processing technology which is cheaper and more flexible than diesel mills and more efficient than traditional processing techniques (including traditional water mills). A more profitable source of investment has opened up for village entrepreneurs. Indigenous technical capacity has been greatly increased with technical skills being passed on from expatriates to Nepalis within the original agencies and from Nepalis within these agencies to outside companies as well as to mill owners/operators and extension workers.

Fishing boats in South India

This project is run by a number of closely linked non-government organizations which have spent a great many years working with the artisanal fishing communities of Kerala and Tamil Nadu. The lead agency, the South India Federation of Fishermen's Societies (SIFFS), is, as its name suggests, the apex organization of a number of District Federations which are run by and for local fishworkers. Its major function is to assist its members to run viable businesses through the provision of technical advice and assistance.

The fishing boat project started in the mid-1970s in response to the needs of the fishermen for alternative boat-building materials and designs which could help them cope with the problem of replacing their traditional craft in the face of declining resources of timber. Over the years, the local organizations (drawing on technical assistance from international agencies when necessary) have worked with the fishermen themselves to come up with a range of improved boat designs (made from marine plywood) which meet the varying needs and preferences of communities along different parts of the coast.

There are now over 400 of these plywood boats in use and the three village-based boatyards which produce them have far more orders than they can cope with. The boatyards, which are owned by fishermen's societies, are well on their way to being self-financing even though an attempt is made to keep boat prices as low as possible. Together they provide employment for nearly 70 village youths.

Superimposed on the problem of decreasing timber supplies is that of declining yields of fish along the coast. This is ascribed largely to the introduction of the inappropriate techniques of mechanized bottom trawling and purse-seining. In response to this problem, many artisan fishermen have turned to the use of outboard motors on their boats to enable them to cover greater distances and fish in deeper waters. The new plywood boats are better suited to the use of engines than the traditional craft and this has increased their popularity amongst the fishermen. This means increased business for the boatyards, and although it presents artisanal fishermen with a way of competing with trawlers, the long term effect of even this lesser level of mechanization on the fishing communities needs careful consideration. In the meantime, SIFFS is responding to the fishermen's needs for training in use and maintenance of motors and is engaged in a programme of training village youths in engine maintenance and repair — in part to provide an alternative source of income (along with building and repair of boats) to the next generation.

SIFFS has tended to rely on external agencies for specialist expertise and for small but timely sums of money in implementing this project. Results so far have led to more substantial funds being acquired from central government — initially for training relating to the use and maintenance of outboard motors. News of the project has also led to fishermen's organizations in other parts of South India requesting SIFFS' assistance in responding to fishing communities' needs for design and decentralized production of improved boats.

Stovemakers in Kenya

This is a joint Government of Kenya/indigenous non-governmental agency (KENGO) project which was started in 1981 as part of the Ministry of Energy's programme for combating the adverse effects of the woodfuel problem. It has received external assistance from a variety of external agencies including USAID, ATI, ITDG and CARE and has drawn on the resources of several Kenyan agencies to assist in various stages of implementation. KENGO has tended to take the lead in this project since the government had no mechanism for dealing with the informal artisan sector on which it is based.

Starting with the traditional metal jiko (already popular for use with charcoal in the urban areas), project staff worked with artisans and prospective users to come up with an improved stove design incorporating a ceramic liner. Although more expensive to buy (currently Ksh 55–Ksh 120 as opposed to Ksh 20–Ksh 55 for a traditional jiko) this stove offered substantial savings to households in terms of charcoal consumption (estimated savings of Ksh 60 per household per month).

Through a series of carefully planned activities designed to address constraints relating to both supply (training and credit for producers) and demand (demonstrations, TV, radio), the project had exceeded its original target of producing 5,000 stoves by late 1983, and by the end of 1985 it was estimated that 180,000 stoves had been sold and were in use in 52,000 households (mainly urban) representing the capture of 10 per cent of the traditional jiko stove market.

Adopters of the improved stoves are obviously benefiting from this project — a benefit which is likely to increase as prices fall with increased production. At the national level, savings on fuel costs are estimated at US$ 2 m pa, representing an equivalent of 1.5 m tonnes of cut trees — a saving which, when combined with the complementary reforestation programmes, is thought to more than compensate for any adverse effect in terms of substitution of efficient charcoal stoves for wood-burning stoves.

Artisan metalworkers have also been able to benefit through accruing substantial profits in the short term and a number of new and existing urban-based ceramic factories and rural-based groups of women potters have found a new and profitable source of income in the production of ceramic liners. More importantly, the involvement of artisans in the project has led the government to recognize the importance of the informal sector in the development process and has resulted in a series of policy pronouncements and changes which promise to give it all necessary support.

Given the substantial reliance on existing production and marketing systems, penetration of the market is likely to proceed even without further external funding. However, external assistance will help to speed up the diffusion process within Kenya and is already proving useful in helping to replicate the project in other countries in the region.

Pappad rollers in India

Shri Makila Gricha Udyog Lijjat Pappad is a women's food processing cooperative with over 6,000 active, earning members. During 1978–79, the organization manufactured and sold Lijjat Pappad, worth Rs 3 crores, through its 21 branches, throughout India. This was a remarkable achievement for the seven lower-income group women who first thought up the idea in 1959.

The originators borrowed Rs 80 to get started and paid this back with interest within 6 months. The institution opted for the goal of self-reliance and self-growth from the start and as a matter of principle no monetary help or donation was to be sought from any source. As such, the work started on a sound commercial footing as a small scale venture. This, together with the principle of maintaining a very high quality product, has contributed to the organization's success.

Lijjat is unique as an organizational model. It is a women's organization, a public trust, a registered society and a cooperative. It is a commercial enterprise which manufacturers and sells selected goods. Legally, Lijjat is registered simultaneously under the Societies Registration Act and the Public Trust Act in Bombay, but functionally, it has incorporated all the features of a cooperative society. Operationally, it has organized its business activity in a manner generally associated with commercial enterprises.

For women who are still not able to leave their homes for long hours and thus prefer work which can be done at home, Lijjat offers a way of doing this without the women having to endure exploitation or domination. In Lijjat, all the intermediaries are women and all are members. All workers are partners rather than employees.

The day for a Lijjat centre begins very early in the morning. The supervisor, normally risen from the ranks of the pappad rollers, has already prepared flour and spices the day before. At about 4 am, the women engaged in the preparation of the dough arrive at the centre and start work. Most centres have their own mini-buses which collect staff from home. By 6 am the dough is ready for distribution to members, who bring with them the pappads they have prepared at home the day before. The pappads are weighed. The receivers tally the quantity of dough taken in the previous morning. Quality control checks are very thorough and very strict; if the pappads are not clean, white and completely dried, they are rejected. They are then sent to the packing section for packing in polyethylene bags and labelling. Members are paid according to quantity and quality and given the next consignment of dough. This will be rolled out at home in the afternoon, after the women have done their household tasks and when the sun is very hot, so that the pappads dry quickly. On an average, payment amounts to about Rs 7.20 for 6 kg of pappad with Rs 1.20 deposited in the compulsory savings account. A woman can earn anything between Rs 4 and Rs 40 per day.

Production is never carried out on the cooperative premises. In the case of rural centres, this necessitates some positive adaptation of the system since members' homes did not have the space or are not clean enough for food processing. Here, the organization provides the women with sheds to work in. It is also considering extending into products such as matches, agarbattis (incense sticks) and leather goods to overcome this constraint and enable rural groups to set up more centres, thus creating more jobs in these areas.

In a pragmatic departure from the accepted practice of cooperative endeavours, which rely on official marketing outlets (eg Khadi Village Industry Commission (KVIC), or on other semi-official organizations), Lijjat adopted a strictly commercial marketing technique from the very beginning. It appointed agents on a commission basis ensuring that only those who had previously enjoyed a reputation for successful business dealings were selected. By offering a commission per packet sold, the Lijjat organizers involved the agents directly in the sale of pappads and created conditions in which maximum sales would be ensured. This deliberate choice of a commercial marketing network reflects the instinctive commercial orientation of the Lohana community which founded the Lijjat enterprise.

Informal sector in Ghana and India

This is a comparative account of two autonomous university-based R&D centres, both of which have impressive support programmes for small and microenterprises. The Technology Consultancy Centre (TCC) at the University of Kumasi in Ghana has tended to work with existing microentrepreneurs. By contrast, the Small Industry Research and Training Organization (SIRTDO) at the Birla Institute of Technology in Ranchi, has worked in an area in which there is no tradition of entrepreneurship and has tried to assist the landless to establish microenterprises.

Established in 1972, TCC was intended primarily as a research and development facility for outreach to Ghana's ailing industrial sector. From the start, attention was focused on Kumasi's large informal sector (with about 20,000 artisan units) — initially through the establishment of campus-based experimental training and production units for the manufacture of nuts and bolts, soap making equipment and other light engineering processes, and later through the establishment of off-campus Intermediate Technology Transfer Units (ITTUs) sited within the informal industrial areas themselves. TCC relied on small amounts of funds and technical assistance from external agencies (primarily NGOs) during its early years and has gradually built up the amount of core funding it receives from the government (near 60 per cent) and its own earnings (sale of products, consultancy fees etc). With the advent of the ITTUs however very large sums of money were required to meet capital costs. This was beyond the means of NGOs and bilateral donors were approached. Although the government has directly supported the work of the TCC, many of its policies over the years have hindered the process of transferring appropriate technology to the informal sector.

TCC has undertaken most support activities itself given the absence of other suitable agencies in Ghana which are able and willing to work with the informal sector. Despite this 'direct' approach, it is able to deal with about 1,000 clients per year.

It would be difficult to quantify the benefits of TCC's work: since its clients are involved in the production of machinery, the multiplier effects in terms of output, employment and income in other industries are enormous. Of greatest importance is the fact that some of TCC's clients are now mini-TCCs themselves, developing products, testing practicability and viability in the market place and then putting them into production. This represents the beginnings of the informal sector's ability to carry out its own technology development and diffusing rather than relying on a research institute to perform this task for it.

SIRTDO is a joint venture of the Birla Institute of Technology (BIT), the Birla Institute of Scientific Research and the State Government of Bihar. Established originally to assist BIT's engineering graduates to set up modern small-scale industries, it later turned its attention to reaching a wider and less well-off clientele through helping the landless poor to establish rural microenterprises.

In 1983, a special rural programme was established in a poor rural area to provide technical and managerial/business training to landless men and women and to help them establish their own businesses. At the first training centre to be established in the area, courses of 3 to 6 months were given in a variety of trades including leather working, radio and TV assembly, brick making and food processing. Although technical skills have been successfully transferred, graduates have failed to proceed to establish businesses owing to a lack of confidence in their own ability. As a consequence, the centre has been reorganized to cater for trainees to stay on in production units until they feel confident enough to leave.

There are plans to establish four more centres, each of which will produce 300 prospective entrepreneurs each year.

Both TCC and SIRTDO have shown a willingness to move away from a limited concentration on technology development to a wider technology diffusion approach. They have both also moved away from a campus orientation to work with and in the midst of their clients. The major difference is that TCC has insisted on working with existing entrepreneurs, whereas SIRTDO has set itself the more difficult task of trying to create them.

Lessons learned

The experiences described in the previous sector illustrate that quite substantial numbers of existing or potential microenterprises can be given valuable assistance through properly designed support programmes. Together, they allow a number of conclusions to be drawn about the elements which lead to success or failure.

First, the experiences support the view that private organizations make good lead agencies in microenterprise support programmes. All those mentioned have provided some assistance directly but have also acted as a catalyst in bringing the resources of other agencies to benefit microenterprises when they themselves could not help. They have coped well with the business and technology aspects of microenterprise and have also actively forged links with government and public institutions as a way of securing funds for replication or of affecting policy change.

Second, it does seem that the most effective programmes are those which concentrate on a single sector (metal workers, fishworkers etc) and which seek to provide varying degress of assistance to existing entrepreneurs who have clearly identifiable problems.

Third, an important aspect of most of the programmes is the fact that funds have been invested in developing a technology which is appropriate to local conditions, rather than simply relying on commercially available alternatives. Significant amounts of funding from government and development agencies have been used to undertake research into improved stoves, improved boat designs, micro-hydro plants and light engineering process. Without this funding local NGOs and technology centres such as KENGO, SIFFS, UMN and TCC would be unable to do the necessary research — and obviously microenterprises are not able to invest resources themselves in undertaking R&D work. An equally important point, however, is the way in which the microentrepreneurs have been fully involved in the technology development process.

Fourth, the programmes show a good understanding of the nature and location of training needed to support microenterprise. In the Kenya stoves programme, great care was given to choosing and providing the most appropriate type of training for artisanal producers, this being given on the spot through a mobile training unit. In the South India boats programme, provision is made for training of village youths in boatmaking and engine maintenance and repair, as well as training of fishermen in use and preventative care of engines. Again training is given at the village level. In the micro-hydro programme in Nepal, extensive formal and informal training is available for owners and operators of turbine-powered mills as well as for agency and bank personnel involved in site selection and mill installation. In Ghana,

TCC provides on-the-job training in its campus production units to the workers to be employed by entrepreneurs adopting its technologies. These are all thought to have contributed to the success of the programmes concerned.

Fifth, the programmes show evidence of having built up an indigenous technological capability within the microenterprise sector which will allow it to adapt to changing circumstances without continued dependence on external advice and assistance. For example, the artisan boat yards in South India are producing variations on the original improved boat design to meet the varying needs and circumstances of fishermen along different parts of the coast. Small commercial companies in Nepal have sprung up in response to the market for water-powered devices and are devising and producing a range of technologies to suit varying circumstances. Many of the microenterprises assisted by the TCC in Ghana have now become product design, testing and diffusion agents in their own right. In all these cases, the transfer of technical skills from expatriates to nationals within projects and then to nationals outside projects has been quite remarkable.

Sixth, the programmes demonstrate that while credit is a crucial component of microenterprise support, it is often quite unnecessary to set up special credit institutions or schemes, since programme implementors can successfully gear up existing credit mechanisms to provide the needed loans. Often, the technical assistance agency is used by commercial or goverment banks to provide technical and financial assessments of loan applications from their clients.

Seventh, the experiences show how important it is to think in terms of integrated systems of support which rely on a range of different agencies for a range of different purposes. At the micro level, more thought needs to be given to ways in which these various agencies can be enabled and encouraged to collaborate on support programmes. Proper attention also needs to be given to the fact that a high proportion of people involved in the sector are women and that they usually face even more constraints than men in running enterprises. Evidence suggests that agencies with significant numbers of women extension staff are best able to reach women microentrepreneurs. At the macro level, strategies are needed which encourage and enable governments and donors to introduce policies which make it easier rather than more difficult to assist microenterprises.

Training and Technical Assistance for Microenterprise

MALCOLM HARPER

Introduction

Much development assistance to smaller enterprises is intended to fill gaps; the availability of jobs may lag behind the availability of trained people, or there may be a need for people who have been trained in specific skills, so that there is a bottleneck which constrains development. People may have the necessary skills, but lack capital, they may have the skills and the capital, but lack markets, or premises, and the role of aid is to identify the gaps and to attempt to fill them.

As in other areas such as health, education or agriculture, the uneasy progress towards 'development' or 'industrialization' thus proceeds by fits and starts; as each bottleneck or gap becomes evident, it is filled, generally through people's own efforts, which are sometimes supplemented by assistance from their governments or foreign donors.

We are concerned with microenterprises, which belong to what is still called the informal sector. It is easy to spend time on definitions in order to avoid facing substantive issues; when faced with a given enterprise, however, most observers would probably be agreed as to whether or not it was a microenterprise, and most enterprises which were agreed to be micro would also be said to be in the informal sector. There might be disagreement at the margins, but if unanimity is possible for the majority of cases, we should rest content with the terms we have.

This sector, therefore, however defined, is rather different from the more traditional areas of development in that it is both a symptom and an internally generated and hopefully interim remedy for under-development, rather than a condition which development assistance projects should help people to attain, except in special cases. It is not a discrete or clearly delineated part of the economy, but it is, for the most part, self-contained and balanced, in that there are informal mechanisms for providing finance, for marketing and supply, for premises and for training. They may not be ideal, but they do exist and expand or contract in response to demand, because this sector of the economy has, at least until recently, been forced to rely on its own resources. Such official interventions as there have been were mainly intended to discourage and limit the scope of microenterprises and many still are.

MALCOLM HARPER is Professor of Enterprise Development at Cranfield School of Management, Cranfield, UK.

Existing services

Microenterprises have therefore developed a more or less self-contained network of support services, and they might be said, as a sector, not to suffer from the same bottlenecks and problems of imbalance as do the far smaller number of larger modern sector enterprises whose owners are trying to operate in an under-developed environment businesses of a type which originates from industrialized societies.

These support services and their equivalents in the modern or formal sector can be summarized as:

Service	Microenterprise sector	Industrialized sector
Credit	Moneylenders and supplier/customer credit	Banks
Training	Family links, apprenticeships	Training schools
On-demand Advice	Informal contacts, observation	Consultancy and extension services
Information	Informal networks	Data banks, circulars, newsletters
Marketing and Supplies	Traders	Marketing corporations, cooperatives
Premises	Squatting, pavements, home locations	Industrial estates

The services listed under microenterprises are often themselves microenterprises, and they all match the informality and small scale of the enterprises they serve. Some are illegal, all are flexible, they are unplanned and they are above all immediately responsive to the needs of those who make use of them. Networks are used when they are needed, and involve no expense when they are not, traders go out of business very quickly if they cannot buy or sell what people have and want to purchase, and young men and women only enter into apprenticeship arrangements, or other forms of on-the-job training, if they believe it will be to their benefit. There are no stipends or subsidies and nothing can outlive its usefulness.

The formal, modern sector services are totally different; they are operated by salaried staff whose jobs and rewards rarely depend on the short term, and often not even on the long term, value of their services to their clients, they are planned and systematic, they are often subsidized, and they are usually provided by and almost always authorized by governments. In general, in fact, they are about as different and 'distant' from microenterprises as it is possible to be; such officially provided services often fail to satisfy the needs of larger more modern enterprises, but they can very rarely be of any use to microenterprises, except to those at the margin of informality, which are striving to formalize.

If well-meaning governments or foreign assistance agencies attempt to provide services of this sort to microenterprises, they may do no more than fail harmlessly to do anything, and thus waste the funds that they spend on them. Given the record of aid projects, this is not too unsatisfactory an outcome, but such programmes can actually harm their clients, or other microenterprises.

One or two examples of the types of programmes which fail may serve to remind us that technical assistance which is not properly designed to address the needs of its clients, or is not effectively 'marketed' to them, can be worse than useless.

In many countries, numbers of people who are variously known as business consultants, counsellors, advisors, or extension staff are employed to go round local small enterprises, to provide business advice to the owners of microenterprises such as village shops, laundries, tinsmiths, carpenters, mechanics or pig farmers. They are in no position to offer any technical advice which is specific to the types of business, they have no business experience or management expertise as such and they are unable to help with privileged market or supply information or contacts.

They owe their credibility solely to the fact that they are employed by small business lending institutions. The only advice they can really offer is on bookkeeping; they tell their clients how to keep records, but cannot tell them how to use them, and the business people go through the motions of keeping books, either because they wish to remain in the good graces of the lending institution or because they erroneously believe that their businesses will somehow benefit from records which they themselves have no idea how to use.

The credit supervision function could far more economically and effectively be carried out in a different way, but these advisors also mislead some of their clients into thinking that management of a small enterprise is mainly a matter of bookkeeping; those who cannot keep books, perhaps because of limited literacy, lose confidence, and some of those who can keep books believe that this ability should guarantee their success.

A not dissimilar situation was revealed by investigations of the financial performance of a large sample of rural shopkeepers. Analysis of the data came up with the apparently strange finding that the shops whose owners kept records were in most cases earning a significantly lower rate of return on total capital employed than those which had no records. The explanation was that business owners who had been to courses, where they had been taught to keep records, had often also achieved the goal for which they went to the course, namely, to get a loan. Their management ability had been in no way improved by the course, and their profits had therefore remained static; the rate of return on investment was therefore reduced.

In most poor countries, large numbers of people are forced to be entrepreneurial because there is no other way for them to survive. They are motivated by the need to achieve, that is, to survive, and they display all the traditional characteristics of entrepreneurs, by grasping opportunities, working persistently and delaying gratification in order to accumulate and preserve the modest capital they need.

Numerous agencies offer 'entrepreneurship development programmes' which are based on learning methods originally designed to enhance or reveal entrepreneurial qualities in people who had never set up in business for themselves. Some of the microentrepreneurs attend these courses, attracted by stipends, the hope of loans or other associated assistance or by the belief that the courses can actually help them.

The participants enjoy themselves enormously, playing a variety of games, and everyone expresses great satisfaction and high intentions at the end. The actual results are often less encouraging; some participants have higher expectations, which are unfulfilled when they fail to obtain improved access to markets, cheaper credit or whatever other service they really needed, and the final effect can be damaging.

Many rural training courses are designed to enable people to start their own small handicraft businesses. The participants are trained in sewing, weaving or other skills, and they also receive some instruction in simple management techniques and in achievement motivation.

After the courses, it may be possible for participants to obtain a loan to buy a sewing machine or a loom, but they often discover that it is almost impossible to purchase raw materials or to sell their products from their villages. Some give up and fail to repay their loans, thus disqualifying themselves from further credit for any other purposes. A few of the more enterprising trainees use their new skills to escape from rural poverty and go to the city, usually to find a job. This latter may not be an altogether unsatisfactory outcome, but it is quite different from what was intended by the course organizers.

The above is only a very small sample of programmes which have been designed to assist microenterprises but have actually helped them very little or not at all; a tool and raw material supply project for small producer cooperatives in Burma has the effect of further concentrating attention on a favoured few units in the Rangoon area, and exacerbating official neglect of the vast numbers of more needy and more deserving units elsewhere. Projects to provide street vendors with permanent stalls and other facilities in Malaysia, India and other countries have give municipal authorities a pretext to expel the vast majority of microtraders for whom official places cannot be provided, thus depriving them of a livelihood and their customers of convenient sources of whatever they used to sell.

Other 'projects', in many different parts of the world, have had similar effects: they have either assisted a few at the expense of many, or have even damaged the few they have tried to help, often by bringing them into the formal sector, but not to the extent necessary to enable the benefits to outweigh the costs of formality. There are probably very few programmes which can really be said to have been a success, in that the additional earnings of the beneficiaries exceeded the costs of the programme, including foreign donor costs; the linkages, if damage to non-beneficiaries can be so called, would make the equation still less favourable.

Entrepreneurship development programmes, with a substantial component devoted to training which has the objective of developing entrepreneurial motivation or behaviour, are often the least valuable form of assistance, in that their participants have clearly demonstrated whatever qualities are required by their survival in the microenterprise sector. Academics and others responsible for this type of programme often bewail the lack of entrepreneurs in their countries while their cars are beset by enterprising vendors at every street junction from which government has not succeeded in excluding them.

Other policy makers sponsor courses to create proper manufacturing entrepreneurs where the policy environment creates conditions such that short term and usually illegal trading is the obvious outlet for entrepreneurial skills. Training and otherwise assisting people to do things which they cannot do, or which are not in their long term interest, is, fortunately, bound to fail.

What can be done?

It might in fact be argued that the only genuine bottleneck in the microenterprise sector is the lack of credit; since microenterprise is the resort of those who are too poor or otherwise disadvantaged to obtain other employment, or to farm their own land because they have none, it is not unreasonable to assume that money is what they lack. Informal sources of capital are well known for their monopolistic and extortionate behaviour; experience in a number of countries, as documented by the PISCES studies and others, shows that modest interventions in capital supply, with a minimum of associated assistance or supervision, can achieve remarkable results and can even eventually become self-sustaining enterprises in their own right.

If there are resources available which are for some reason tied to technical assistance, rather than to credit, it may be that the most effective way to use them is to provide imaginative and intensive training for government officials, at every level, in order further to accelerate the growing trend towards tolerance of microenterprise. Much has already been achieved in this area, as a result of many different influences. It has in many countries become increasingly difficult in a physical sense to continue with a policy of oppression, and popular opinion has some effect, even on undemocratic regimes.

Public utterances and clauses in development plans are not always matched by actions, however, and much remains to be done. It is easy to over-simplify the issues, and effective training can play a part in identifying and resolving the various dilemmas that face any official, at any level, who wants to make a practical contribution to liberalization; since most owners of micro-enterprises agree that their main need is to be left alone to make their living as they can, the best way of satisfying this need may be to train and otherwise assist the authorities who can make this possible.

Three types of objectives

The terms 'formal' and 'informal' are notoriously contentious and sometimes even misleading, but it may be useful to apply such a framework to the enterprise sector and those who participate in it, as a way of classifying the objectives of assistance programmes. The hierarchy of sectors and types of programmes may, very simplistically, be illustrated as follows:

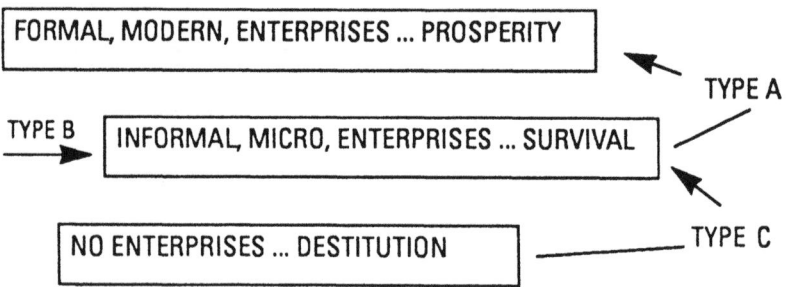

The objectives of training and assistance programmes for people in micro-enterprises may then loosely be classified as follows:

A those programmes which aim to enable their participants to move 'up' from the informal, micro sector to the modern sector;
B those programmes which aim to enable their participants to operate more effectively and profitably within the informal, micro sector, but not actually to become formalized;
C those programes aimed at participants who are at the 'bottom' of the informal sector, or are dependent on charity or other forms of non-earned income, and which attempt to 'lift' them into the informal sector.

Type A programmes
These typically include topics such as the following:

1   training in bookkeeping and accounts, both for better management and also to satisfy taxation authorities and credit institutions;
2   information about product and workplace standards;
3   information about procedures for employing others in a formalized way;
4   training and assistance in obtaining credit from banks and other financial institutions;
5   introductions to larger formal marketing outlets and suppliers;

6   training in the selection and use of modern equipment;
7   access to better premises, training in modern methods of sales promotion and marketing.

Such programmes, which are fundamentally designed to help people operate more effectively in a modern commercial environment, may or may not be effective; they are, however, better described as a form of release from the informal, micro sector rather than a way in which people can be helped to operate better within it. They are mainly oriented towards skills and information, and are relatively easy for formal institutions to provide, since they cover formal aspects of business and involve no more than simpler versions of traditional programmes which are already offered to modern sector trainees.

Such assistance programmes usually include a range of services, with privileged access to scarce resources such as subsidized credit, premises or raw materials. They can, therefore, only be offered to a small proportion of the vast numbers of people who might want to formalize their businesses, and their timing and location often mean that microenterprise operators are effectively debarred from participation in any case.

Many such programmes are targeted at particular groups which are felt, for political or other reasons, to be unusually deserving, such as the educated unemployed, or retiring civil servants or military personnel; they should, perhaps, not really be included in any consideration of assistance for microenterprise, since they are designed to help people graduate from microenterprise, rather than to help them be more successful within the same general scale of activity.

Type B programmes
Programmes of the second type, which are designed to help people do better within the informal or micro sector, are less common, less easy to design and less likely to succeed. Outsiders, from the formal world of government, official assistance agencies and voluntary organizations are, or should be, humbled by the ingenuity and persistence of the operators of microenterprises. Management has been defined as 'making the best use of scarce resources'; it would be difficult to find a better way of describing the day-to-day activities of microbusiness people, who often turn their capital over once a day or more, who make raw materials out of what others have discarded, who find market niches in the most obscure corners and construct machinery and tools of amazing ingenuity and economy.

An assistance programme of this type, other than one providing credit, would have to include topics such as:

1   new ideas for using unfamiliar scrap materials;
2   improved methods of working capital management;
3   better ways of avoiding regulations and finding more profitable locations;
4   methods of identifying consumer needs and satisfying them.

It is hard to see how assistance which would achieve these and similar objectives could possibly be provided, particularly by a formal assistance agency; it would probably not achieve the objectives, and even if it did, it is doubtful that any external agency could provide such help as effectively, or as economically, as the informal networks on which microentrepreneurs rely.

The ultimate measure of evaluation for any assistance project should perhaps be the question, 'would the money spent on the project have been of greater benefit to the "beneficiaries" if they had been given the money, and allowed to spend it as they chose?' Microentrepreneurs are above all good at making the best use of their resources, and it is difficult to see how any outsider could make better decisions than they could. External intervention may be necessary to help them get themselves out of the informal sector, to a 'higher' level, but if the objective is to improve their lot within it, they are the best judge of how this might be done.

Credit is of course the way by which people can be helped to improve their lot by using money as they see fit; the most successful credit programmes for microenterprise are not those which are heavily supported by training and supervision, and which demand extensive feasibility studies which often deprive borrowers of the flexibility that is one of their main advantages. Technical assistance of this type is usually expensive and counterproductive; a minimalist approach to credit, such as that adopted in the ACORD programme in Port Sudan, the Rural Enterprise Assistance programme in Kaolack, Senegal, or the revolving loan fund in Kalingalinga, Lusaka, may be less attractive to trainers and consultants, because of its simplicity, but is more likely to be effective and economical.

If technical assistance to help people rise above microenterprise is not really assistance for microenterprise itself at all, and assistance other than minimalist credit is of little value to those within the sector, is there any role for technical assistance in relation to microenterprise, except as a small adjunct to credit?

Type C programmes

There only remain programmes with objectives of type C, which are designed to help people enter the world of microenterprise, rather than to do better within it, or to leave it. Given the fact that the informal sector is in a sense the last resort, for those who cannot find formal employment and cannot live off the land, it might be thought that there were very few people who were so unfortunate as to be below the lowest; if microentrepreneurship is the refuge of desperation for the marginal, are there any potential beneficiaries for technical assistance with type C objectives?

There are in fact large numbers of such people, who might be called submarginal and who are at the fringes of the informal sector, or not even part of it at all. They are, in most cases, genuinely 'the poorest of the poor', towards whom assistance agencies are repeatedly exhorted to direct their activities.

They are difficult to reach, and to help once they are reached, but the humanitarian and sometimes political reasons for trying to help them mean that the benefit side of the cost benefit calculation may be less rigorously estimated than for people who are already in the mainstream, even of the informal sector.

These people include refugees, the disabled, ex-offenders, women (in some societies) and minority or occasionally majority communities who have for some reason been excluded from the economic mainstream. The informal sector has been described as the marginal sector, but the term may be misleading when those who are said to be marginal in fact far outnumber those who are central. Possibly the informal sector is the centre, numerically at any rate, and the real marginals are these disadvantaged groups.

Unlike people who are already well integrated into the informal sector, members of these disadvantaged groups would be unlikely to be able to make effective use of money alone to become self-sufficient. They lack the connections, the skills and sometimes the self-confidence and it is sometimes possible for technical assistance to fill the gaps. It is clearly better to try to help these sub-marginal groups to enter the informal sector, rather than encouraging them to leapfrog this sector, and go straight into formal business. Attempts of this sort usually end up as agency-run projects, nominally run by the refugees, disabled or other target groups, but actually owned and managed by the assistance agency. This may be as far as some people can ever go, particularly the severely disabled, but there are many examples of programmes which have helped very disadvantaged people to become genuinely independent microentrepreneurs, holding their own in the informal sector.

These usually succeed because they are based on a clear understanding of what it is that is stopping members of the particular group from starting and successfully maintaining their own enterprises. Successful programmes do not scratch where it does not itch; they provide the help that is needed, and allow their participants to do the things they can do without help. There are in fact many programmes which have successfully helped apparently helpless people to become self-sufficient.

The physically handicapped need above all the skill to practise a trade. A number of physical rehabilitation centres and orthopaedic hospitals, in India, the Philippines and elsewhere, provide basic training in skills such as watchmaking, sewing or carpentry to cured leprosy patients, polio victims or others who through disease, accident or congenital disability are less physically able than the majority of the population. Some such people are able to start their own microenterprise with this assistance alone. In India, such institutions do not usually need to provide finance, since there are many specialized lending institutions; all that is needed is introductions and access. Elsewhere, the rehabilitation institution itself may have to provide finance.

Some handicapped people, particularly those who have suffered from birth, have become accustomed to being treated as perpetual dependents, or even as objects of family shame. In these cases, it may be necessary to provide the sort of psychological rebuilding treatment which is often, generally unnecessarily, included in entrepreneurship development programmes for the able-bodied. Such treatment is generally better provided on an individual basis, through sensitive counselling and extensive post-training support, to ease the shock of entry into the 'real world'.

Refugees are another sadly very numerous group who are submarginal, and who may need more than money to enable them to get on to the bottom rung of the enterprise ladder. Some need technical skills, since they may have been nomads and must now settle in a fixed urban or rural location in their new homes, and others may need language training. The majority, unless they have migrated across artificial frontiers and are re-settled in the same ethnic community from which they have come, need some substitute for the informal networks which are the means whereby microentrepreneurs gain access to markets, supplies, premises and so on. Such links are very difficult for an external assistance agency to provide, but there have been some successes.

In Somalia, local business people were paid by an assistance project to train refugees in appropriate local skills. This not only ensured that the skills and the training were in fact relevant to the local resources, but it also provided a means whereby the trainee refugees could start to make contacts in the business where they were being trained, in preparation for starting on their own, rather than being protected within a training institution. It was remarkable how willing the Somali business people were to offer this type of training, although they were helping to create large numbers of new competitors.

It is obviously in society's interest to try to help ex-offenders to find alternative, legal ways of earning a living. They are often disqualified by their past records from obtaining formal employment, even if jobs are available, and their ability to recognize and grasp opportunities is a good basis for self-employment in the informal sector. Their existing skills may or may not be appropriate for legal enterprise, and they almost certainly lack access to the networks of marketing, supply, premises and so on.

The Don Bosco self-employment programme in Liluah, Calcutta, has had some success with young men who have been rescued from the community of several hundred people who eke out a living at Howrah station by begging, stealing, unofficial portering and so on. Many of them have been there since they were six or seven years old, many are addicted to a variety of drugs and they are probably as genuinely marginal a group as could be found anywhere.

The Don Bosco programme puts them through a skills training course, and then some of them graduate to a converted house where they start individual one machine businesses. They remain in this 'nursery', paying a share of their incomes as rent, until they have repaid their equipment loans; one of the rooms in the house is given rent free to a middleman, who is a local trader who finds the orders, arranges for finance, maintains quality control and generally plays the intermediary role. This role is often neglected by assistance programmes, because the traditional middleman is seen as exploitative and unnecessary. The lack of this type of connection is perhaps the most serious gap for these trainees, once they have acquired the necessary technical skills and the Don Bosco Fathers have appreciated this fact, and filled the gap.

Minority or even majority communities who are not felt to be properly represented in the economies of their countries are another group who may need technical assistance, not only capital, to enable them to start their own businesses. They may in fact have land or other assets which could be used to obtain capital; they may lack skills and connections to the network of enterprise, and their own and other people's view of their role in society may make it very difficult for them to succeed in business without extensive assistance.

There are often strong political reasons for helping these people to play a greater part in the economy, even if they are not suffering physical poverty as a result of their virtual exclusion from the non-farm economy, or, as with many tribal groups, they may be living in dire poverty, on marginal land, so that microenterprise provides a route to survival as well as self-respect.

There are many programmes to help such people; some offer a total package of support, and thus create the impression that the target population are quite incapable of doing business on their own. Others, where there is no political need to be seen to be offering generous assistance, but only the humanitarian motive to assist people as economically as possible, offer only what is needed and are both successful and economical.

Self-confidence and access to networks are here again the most important components, together with technical training, and many voluntary agencies, particularly those of local origin, operating on a community level, are themselves close to the informal sector and are able to help people to become integrated into it. Some forms of behavioural training may have a role to play for such marginal communities, although it is difficult to distingish the impact of such types of training from the rest of the programmes.

Conclusion

Technical assistance, as opposed to credit, has a limited role to play in the microenterprise sector. Programmes which are intended to help people rise above the sector are not really our concern, and are in any case likely to be limited in their impact on those who remain in it.

Technical assistance for those who are already operating microenterprises, except for marginal groups on the bottom fringes, are also of limited value. There is very little that outsiders from a formal environment can do for those who are in the informal sector, and the numbers are so vast that even if it was possible to run a cost-effective programme, it would only reach a very small proportion of the potential target group. Most people who operate microenterprises are already managing their limited resources rather well and it is difficult for any programme to achieve better results than could be achieved by the microentrepreneurs themselves, if they were to be given the resources used by the programme and allowed to use them as they wished.

There is a need to train government officials and others who so often harass microenterprise, and possibly to study in some depth the reasons why officials do this and to devise ways in which they can be motivated to act otherwise. This may be difficult and is certainly less dramatic than trying to work for microenterprises themselves, but will probably be of more lasting benefit to them.

Many microentrepreneurs do need credit, with as few strings as possible, and technical assistance has a very limited role in such credit programmes. Staff must be trained to operate efficiently and quickly, to recognize the merits of rigorous management and to respect the ability and self-respect of their clients. Effective evaluation systems must be designed and used, but these must not be sophisticated, since the long or even medium term goal must be for the lending programme to operate as a self-sustaining business enterprise itself; the main role of technical assistance, in fact, is to render itself redundant as rapidly as possible.

Members of sub-marginal groups such as refugees, the disabled or communities who have been excluded from the economic mainstream may need assistance not to rise above microenterprise, or to be more successful as existing microentrepreneurs, but simply to start microenterprises. These people may need technical skills training, which is probably best provided within existing microenterprise, linkages to informal networks, self-confidence and other support.

Technical assistance of this sort is very difficult to deliver, but can play a major part in alleviating suffering and giving genuinely poor people some chance to become independent. Small, locally funded and rigorously managed voluntary agencies appear to have the best chance of offering successful programmes of this type.

In general, technical assistance can do little for microenterprises, except for the sadly large numbers who wish to start some modest economic activity. Apart from these groups, the main need is to allow microentrepreneurs to operate with a minimum of interference, to provide them with access to credit on economic but not extortionate terms and to structure the economy so that as many microentrepreneurs as possible will be able and willing to formalize their operations, because the legitimate growth of economic enterprises is attractive for individuals and beneficial for society as a whole.

The Role of Technology in Microenterprise Development

MATTHEW GAMSER and FRANK ALMOND

Problems in promoting micro-producers

The important role of microenterprises in developing country economies is increasingly being recognized by government and donor agencies. In particular, micro-scale production operations are key players in these economies, providing significant employment and income to poorer groups, and providing essential goods and services to poorer communities. Enterprises employing fewer than 50 workers account for the majority of jobs in the manufacturing sector in most developing nations (with the exception of the Newly Industrializing countries of Asia and Latin America) and small manufacturers generate a significant proportion of manufacturing GDP in many countries.[1] Most of these small firms employ fewer than five persons, are located in rural areas, and, in many countries, are run by women.

As a result of this new awareness of the importance of micro-producers to national economies, many developing country governments recently have implemented radical policy changes to 'legitimize' them. In Kenya, for example, the *jua kali* (literally 'outside in the hot sun') artisans now operate on land provided by the government, and in some cases enjoy workshops and power provided for their convenience — while two years ago they lived in constant fear of government officers evicting them from their squatter sites. Such support and recognition is not always seen as an unmixed blessing by informal sector entrepreneurs, as it brings increasing contact with officialdom to businesses working outside, or on the blind side, of legality. Recent years have seen a proliferation of government and non-government programmes to provide special incentives for small enterprises. The heart of most of these programmes consists of some form of special credit provisions for small entrepreneurs.

However, despite the appreciation of the importance of small producers, this group does not appear to have been the major beneficiary of this new assistance effort. Trade-based microenterprises, and not micro-producers, absorb by far the greater part of available credit. A recent Ford Foundation evaluation of the small enterprise credit programmes it has supported notes that, although lending to manufacturers may lead to greater employment and

---

FRANK ALMOND is Chief Executive and MATTHEW GAMSER the Policy Economist of the Intermediate Technology Development Group in the UK.

income impacts, trade credit is far easier for new banking operations. Its four 'good performers' in microenterprise credit (the Grameen Bank, the Self-Employed Women's Association of Ahmedabad, the Working Women's Forum of Madras, and the Annapurna Caterers of Bombay) all have clients who borrowed more for trade than for manufacturing.[2]

Micro-producers, finding the doors barred at most government and commercial lending institutions, must raise their capital through personal and family savings. A recent Michigan State University survey of small-scale industries found that government and commercial funds accounted for less than one per cent of their start-up capital. Informal financial sources such as money lenders also appear to shun small producers, providing less than one per cent of initial capital.[1]

Those micro-producers that do receive loans are often involved in only a limited number of technology areas. In southern Africa and the Caribbean, for example, a large proportion of micro-producer funds tend to go to grain milling operations. While milling clearly is an essential post-harvest processing activity, in many of these countries the proliferation of micro-mills has led to a saturation of the market for this service, with the end result being the inability of many of the mills to operate profitably. Tailoring is another micro-production operation in danger of being proliferated excessively through credit programmes. (Indeed, it can be argued that such activities as milling and tailoring have more of the characteristics of service-type industries than true producers.) At the same time, needs and market opportunities for other goods and services go unfulfilled or have to be satisfied by more expensive outputs from large producers or importers.

A major factor behind the failure of many microenterprise support programmes to develop new production-based operations, and behind the economically counterproductive clustering of the producers they do support in relatively few production sectors, is the absence of a technological component to their promotion efforts. Whereas the importance of technology is widely appreciated at larger-scale enterprise levels, the technological concerns of micro-producers have been largely neglected. Microenterprises have great potential, but also pose great technological problems, which finance alone rarely can resolve.

Technological constraints to micro-producers

Although they operate on a smaller scale, micro-producers' problems are neither simpler nor less expensive to resolve than those of the large manufacturer. Three main factors increase the difficulty of resolving technological problems on a micro-producer level:

1 the limited availability of tried and tested production systems for small-scale, decentralized operations;

2 the need to work with uncertainty and variation in raw materials and equipment supply;
3 the frequent presence of government policies that restrict the producers' abilities to use even those limited materials and techniques at their disposal.

Micro-producers' limited technology choice

While larger producers often have a selection of technology packages to choose from, micro-producers rarely can draw upon 'off-shelf' products and processes to meet their needs. A striking example of the absence of technology choice is found in Zambia's experience in searching for machinery to manufacture egg cartons. The market for eggs was severely constrained by problems in transporting them from production sites to stores and homes. Several overseas firms were located that could supply egg carton manufacturing plants — the problem was that even the smallest of these plants could meet the nation's annual requirements in less than one month's work. Developing a technology that could support production on the scale needed required considerable time and effort to identify expertise to attack the down-sizing problem, and to apply that expertise with local manufacturing and entrepreneurial know-how in designing and introducing a new paper pulp packaging system.[3] It is inconceivable that this small-scale production problem would have been addressed, much less resolved, without technological support as a supplement to more conventional enterprise assistance.

A large manufacturer of lime can select from a number of kiln designs and manufacturers to fit local raw material and market conditions. Small lime producers generally must design and build their own kilns. Like all engineering designs, lime kilns reflect the dictates of a number of design criteria. In the case of modern-sector, large scale plant the need to produce continuously large quantities of lime to exacting chemical standards and with minimum operational costs has led to the adoption of high capacity rotary or shaft kilns. This technology involves a high degree of automation and uses easily controlled gas and liquid fuels. Different criteria apply at a smaller scale, where simplicity of construction, use of available fuels (including the possible lack of electrical power), and ease of operation without instrumentation or automation become the major considerations. In this case, as in many others, down-scaling is simply not the answer, and a different technology must be used. Fortunately, small masonry-built natural draft vertical shaft kilns, using timber or coal fuels, satisfy these conditions and are inherently fuel-efficient. Most indigenous artisanal designs are not of this type, and therefore considerable technological support is needed to facilitate their introduction.[4,5]

Small bakeries face similar problems. Larger operations, which tend to be located in urban centres, can draw upon a wide range of commercial oven designs. They can use solid fuel (wood or coal), petroleum, or electricity as the basis of their energy supply. A variety of electronic control systems also are available to assist in maintaining an even production quality and in minimizing operating costs and losses.

The micro-baker has none of these technological facilities at his/her command. The micro-bakery oven is built by the baker, for even if funds were available to purchase commercial systems, none are small enough to operate economically for the tiny markets he/she serves. The oven must rely on biomass fuels, for even if fuel alternatives are available, it is unlikely that their use and storage would be economically feasible for this level of production. Production control will depend upon human skills and actions, not upon purchased control systems, for these are not likely to be affordable or sustainable. Yet, the micro-bakery needs to produce bread and other products that compare with larger bakeries' on both a quality and a cost basis, or else the baker will lose his/her local market to deliveries from the larger competitor.

Credit alone cannot solve the micro-baker's problems. Help is also needed to assess available raw materials and skills, and to utilize these in developing ovens that provide the level of supply required, and that can be operated and maintained efficiently by local staff and artisans.

Not only is the choice of technology more limited at the smaller scale, but its availability is also restricted. There are many powerful reasons why equipment manufacturers do not service this end of the market; not only is small scale production equipment inherently likely to be low in capital cost per unit of output, but there are strong economies of scale in equipment manufacture and sale. This lack of interaction with the industry in wider terms brings many invisible penalties to the small producer. Access is cut off to design and operating experience, training, after sales support and service and many other facilities offered by equipment supplies. All this leaves the small operator very isolated. This constitutes a double penalty, since most small operators have to play a large role in designing and constructing their own plant or equipment.

Production materials and techniques constraints

Another common problem confronting micro-producers is the lack of sufficient technique to exploit local opportunities. The producer may be well aware that certain commonly used articles and implements can be locally manufactured, but does not know how to alter his/her operation to meet local consumer requirements. This is not because the micro-producer lacks skill, but because he/she works in a more difficult environment than a larger manufacturer, in which materials choice is limited, and in which basic services such as power, transport, and water are absent or in unreliable supply. Technological support is needed to identify ways of operating within this environment while maintaining levels of production and quality required to capture local markets.

In many countries rural blacksmiths would like to play a greater part in the provision of agricultural implements and other essential tools, but face stiff competition from urban suppliers or importers. Often these blacksmiths are severely constrained by raw material availability and by inefficient forges and handling tools. Advice on upgrading available metal scrap through simple tempering procedures can greatly increase the range and the durability of products they can fabricate. Help in adapting forges to increase temperatures and to reduce fuel consumption can reduce the blacksmiths' operating costs and raise production levels and quality. In a detailed study of artisanal production in the Mulange South District of Malawi, ITDG has determined that improved forges will sufficiently reduce fuel and overall operating costs to enable rural blacksmiths to produce knives, axes, and maize mill hammers that can compete with supplies from larger urban producers. More details can be obtained, upon request, from the Blantyre and Lilongwe Agricultural Development Division, Government of Malawi.

As small producers are encouraged to address wider and more diverse markets, the importance of product standards and consistency increases. It may be that the product has to compete on equal terms with the output of large scale manufacturers or there may be industrial or national standards to be met.

For example mini-cement factories in India are required to produce Portland cement to Indian Standard 267 (British Standard 12), despite the fact that much of their production is used in rural areas for low-rise housing or other low-stength applications. China, however, with its ability to control the market, is able to direct part of the output of small producers to such non-critical applications, and therefore supports a wider range of less stringent standards. Similarly, small scale sugar factories need to produce fine white crystal sugar and cottage spinners need to produce mill-quality yarn if their market is not to be restricted. This does increase the technical demands on small producers in sometimes not altogether obvious ways. For instance, a large cement factory will be sited on a large, uniform limestone deposit and will also be able to blend its raw materials in the stockyard; a mini-plant will probably make use of a small and geologically much more variable deposit, and because of its small throughput will not easily be able to blend out fluctuations in raw material composition.

The technological needs of micro-producers involve more than just advice on materials selection and process technologies. In post-harvest processing operations, which have become a major concern of goverment and NGO enterprise promotion efforts, special attention must be paid to the health and safety aspects of food product preparation. For example, canning operations present microbiological problems, most of which are unlikely to be within the capacity of micro-producers to control. On the other hand, many drying, smoking, and acid preservation operations (jam, chutney, and pickle production, for example) can be carried out on a micro-scale in ways that are inherently less risky.

Both micro-producers and government authorities involved in these operations need to be aware of the potential hazards and how these can be detected and avoided, however. Large producers have the means to employ food technologists to supervise processing operations, and governments usually have the resources to monitor the health standards of larger, usually urban firms. Micro-producers, however, cannot afford to employ such specialist staff. Nor can most developing country governments hope to monitor the outputs of small, decentralized food processing operations. For this reason, both the micro-producers and the agencies that support them need to acquire an understanding of both the health and safety aspects of post-harvest processing and the means to enforce quality control. The United Nations Development Fund for Women (UNIFEM) is greatly assisting in this public education process by supporting the publication of technical manuals covering many aspects of small-scale food processing. These are presented in Marilyn Carr's *Women and the Food Cycle*[6].

Technological aspects of public policy constraints

Sometimes the major constraint to the development of smaller-scale production operations is not the producers' lack of technological know-how, but government regulatory agencies' lack of knowledge of the technological options for economic development in a particular sector. In such cases policies are put in place (or left in place) that restrict or prohibit micro-producer activities.

These sorts of policy constraints are common in the building materials and construction sector. While almost all developing countries possess deposits of limestone and pozzolanic materials which could be extracted in small mining operations and used as cements in many types of buildings, most still maintain building codes that require the use of Portland cement in all construction. These codes, for the most part, are remnants from the colonial era, and are usually copied verbatim from European building regulations. These are concerned with maintaining safety standards in large urban conurbations, in which building size and structure bear little resemblance to most construction in developing nations. Alternative local building materials are perfectly suitable for most domestic housing and many institutional needs there, and their use, in addition to providing employment and income generation opportunities for small producers, would also reduce many countries' foreign exchange requirements for building materials. The problems posed by the absence of appropriate standards for building materials were discussed in a recent international workshop in Nairobi.[7,8]

Similarly, the development of new microenterprises producing construction materials from local resources is often hindered by the absence of national standards covering their quality and use. For example, roofing tiles made from fibre-reinforced concrete can be produced and installed by micro-producers, while competitive materials such as galvanized iron sheeting and clay tiles require larger, more centralized production facilities. The former material, in addition to providing work for microentrepreneurs, can be produced at a lower cost than the others in countries where cement is readily available. However, until it acquires an official national standard, it cannot be used in any public works projects. This bars it from the most lucrative building materials market, and discourages both microentrepreneurs and credit agencies from investing in new production facilities.[9]

Apart from removing obstacles, positive government support for emergent microenterprises demands a level of cross-departmental cooperation not readily found in most state bureaucracies. Kenya is typical of many countries in having numerous small mineral deposits which can serve the raw material needs of its growing industrial sector, much of which is currently imported. Pilot projects have shown the need to coordinate action between the Department of Mines and Geology, which has extensive knowledge of mineral resources, and the Trade and Industry departments and parastatals that know of industry requirements and standards.

In the above cases, the major issue is not producer technological know-how, but government technology awareness and the application of this in policy reforms. It is unreasonable to expect decision-makers to change regulations or approve new standards without first increasing their own understanding of the principles upon which established codes and standards are based, and thereby increasing their appreciation of why reforms are necessary in order to create policies more appropriate for local living conditions. Technological inputs, such as materials testing and comparative evaluation, demonstration building construction, and technical education for key government officials are needed to prepare the way for policy changes.

Institutional issues

Accepting the need for technological support on the microenterprise level represents only a small step towards resolving some of the technological problems faced by micro-producers. Delivering this support on a sustained basis poses considerable difficulties. Finding an institutional home that provides both technological competence and strong links with widely dispersed entrepreneurs is essential for a producer support programme, but few established government or non-goverment agencies offer all these resources. Whatever institutional home is selected, finding ways to offer technological assistance in a manner affordable both to the producers and the support organization presents a structural as well as a financial challenge.

Homes for micro-producer support agencies
Determining the means through which technological assistance can best serve to promote micro-production operations raises an entirely new set of

issues. There are a number of institutional channels through which technological support can be delivered in supplement to financial and other assistance. In the past most of the research and development surrounding small enterprise production technologies has come from specialist technology centres. Most of these institutions were based in university or government ministry environments. Some of these, such as the Technology Consultancy Centre in Ghana, have succeeded in generating numerous micro-production innovations, and in becoming an inspiration for small entrepreneurs. Unfortunately, many others have failed to establish strong relationships with microproducers, with the result that few if any of their ideas and inventions have led to new microenterprise successes.[10]

Perhaps it is the recognition of the problems of many of these academically-based institutions that is the reason behind the recent trend towards siting small enterprise technology support units within new institutional homes, such as financial institutions and business development agencies. Examples of the provision of technological 'legs' to the former can be found in the work of the Industrial Development Bank of India and the Agricultural Development Bank of Nepal. Micro-producer oriented technology units within business development organizations can be found in the Small Enterprise Development Organization of Malawi, the Small Enterprise Development Corporation in Zimbabwe, and the Kenya Industrial Estates programme, among others.

The advantage of a financial or business development agency home for technological assistance work is that it provides a more direct link to microentrepreneurs, who already exist on the agencies' client lists. These institutions are far more frequently visited by micro-producers than are universities and research centres, and many have a network of field agents that pay regular visits to producer workplaces. This closer contact with microenterprises should provide a better sense of their problems and aspirations, and could lead to a more needs-responsive technological assistance effort.

On the other hand, such agencies do not possess the reserves of scientific and technological knowledge nor the equipment and facilities of dedicated research centres. In theory they can still draw upon such resources from other sources, but in practice this is rarely the case. Financial and business development organizations also find it difficult to attract top scientific and technological personnel into their programmes (perhaps due to the above lack of resources), and as a result often lack sufficient internal know-how to respond to the broad range of problems and enquiries presented by microentrepreneurs. With targets primarily based upon levels of loan issuance and repayment, staff from such institutions can find themselves pressured into seeking quick and dirty production solutions in order to achieve work goals, which can place an intolerable burden upon technological investigations, regardless of the quality and experience of the persons involved.

All things considered, the physical home of a micro-producer technological support unit is less important than the relationship it establishes with its clients in the field. In-house technical expertise is of little use without an understanding of the practical needs and constraints of small, often remote production operations. At the same time, regular contact with micro-producers will not identify key technological problems or opportunities if the extension officers making contact do not sufficiently understand the production systems they encounter. Both field presence and technological credibility are required to attract producer interest and involvement in the work of microenterprise support units.

Affording technological support for micro-producers
Unlike academic institutions, financial and business development organizations usually are expected to pay their own way. While programmes of technological advice to larger producers can provide returns through consulting fees, royalties, and other channels, it is unlikely that microproducers are prepared to offer sufficient compensation for such services (many of them do not even pay taxes). The costs of providing technological support to a generally more numerous and dispersed micro-entrepreneur clientele, moreover, is likely to be greater than that for larger firms. A technological unit within a financial body may be restricted in the development of its relations with micro-producers by requirements to demand immediate compensation for services rendered, whereas one operating within an academic environment may have more freedom to explore various means and schedules for securing returns from clients.

That said, alternative methods of financial assistance may offer more promising avenues for the development of self-financing technological support units within banks and business development agencies. The Industrial Development Bank of India, in cooperation with Appropriate Technology International, is exploring the potential of venture capital as an alternative to conventional credit and consulting measures. Venture finance, in which the finance organization takes an equity stake in the microenterprise, may provide greater flexibility for the micro-producer to explore new technology directions by not requiring fixed term repayments for capital or technical assistance provided.

However, microenterprises involved in new technology research and development efforts will require at least as much time as their larger producer counterparts to turn promise into profit. Venture finance organizations aimed at smaller producers will need sufficient capital reserves to maintain their liquidity during these developmental stages; even though the individual investments they make may be small, their start-up funding requirements will not be, and it will take some time before the dividends from their micro-producer partners begin to make a significant contribution to their reserves.

Whatever institutional channels and finance mechanisms are employed, the provision of technological support to micro-producers will be a costly exercise. The absence of substantial research and production experience at smaller levels of output means that few producer enquiries can be responded to quickly and cheaply. Although the producers' outputs may be low, the technical problems they present require high levels of skill and effort to resolve. Given the small margins and risk aversiveness that characterize the microenterprise sector, producer support units must be equipped to shoulder much of the initial R&D burden in order to attract entrepreneurs to new production opportunities.

Technical assistance and microenterprise development

There are considerable institutional obstacles facing micro-producer support, but there also are considerable institutional resources which can be devoted to this effort. Developing country governments and donor agencies can help to make small-enterprise support institutions more technologically capable. Private companies also can assist in the transfer of knowledge and capability to micro-producers, but this assistance generally cannot be offered in the same manner as it has been for larger manufacturers.

Government and donor contributions

Donor agencies and developing country governments have key roles to play in insuring that the institutions established to promote microenterprises can provide for the needs of production as well as trade-based concerns. The inclusion of technological components within these institutions can provide a means for reducing the costs and risks to micro-producers in investigating and developing new opportunities, whether these involve creating new production systems or refining existing systems and skills to acquire shares in local markets. Without technological support to supplement credit and other assistance it is likely that the present pattern of a few opportunities being overly developed and saturated, and numerous others being unexplored will continue.

Once donors and governments have made a commitment to investigate the technological aspects of micro-enterprise development, the major obstacle they must overcome will be ignorance of the technological bases of existing small production operations. Many countries presently have business development or extension staff in place even in the most remote areas, but few of these people possess sufficient technology awareness to recognize either problems or opportunities. Providing facilities for research or training in various production areas is a relatively simple task, but providing information about what sorts of facilities, training, and technological support are most needed is impossible without the presence of more informed staff in the field.

Developing a cadre of technologically aware staff within microenterprise organizations requires new training approaches. It is not practical to attempt to produce a corps of master carpenters, blacksmiths, bakers, builders, etc, large enough to serve the needs of the widely dispersed network of micro-producers. Each technological support unit will need a core of expertise in certain key producer areas; but it also will need a larger group of more generally trained field officers who can understand and function within workshop environments. These field officers must be able to communicate on a technological level with micro-producers, in order to identify problems and potential for the experts to investigate.

One of the major challenges facing microenterprise promotion is the creation of technology awareness training that, without the vast time and effort required to produce skilled artisans, can produce technologically-sensitive generalists, a sort of barefoot production consultant. While these generalists may not be able to forge an adze or plaster a wall to the standards of the entrepreneurs they visit, they would understand enough about what is involved in the manufacture of a given product or the execution of a given technique to guide more expert staff to the most critical areas for technological support.

While several small enterprise development agencies and technology centres have developed technical training courses for their clients, the authors know of no agency to date that has organized general technological training for its field or extension staff. Because of this deficiency, agency staff that spend the most time in direct contact with micro-producers usually possess insufficient understanding of the producers' trades, and as a result cannot properly communicate with producers about problems and opportunities.

Linkages with overseas firms

Overseas firms have a key role to play in technological support for micro-producers, but this role will be more indirect than that played in their interactions with larger developing country enterprises. Microentrepreneurs do not possess the time or resources to undertake the administrative and other requirements of direct twinning relationships. Most would be unwilling even to become substantially involved in overseas supply or licensing arrangements, as these would include government reporting and other requirements that micro-producers often prefer to avoid. Also, many micro-producers place a strong value on the independence of their operations, and shun any formal linkages with other entities as a matter of principle. From the overseas firms' point of view, the prospect of having to negotiate and collaborate with several small, often remote producers cannot seem very attractive.

These reservations on the part of microentrepreneurs and overseas firms make it generally necessary to channel overseas company involvement in technological support through an intermediary organization. The intermediary handles importing, licensing, and other 'official' matters. It coordinates the overseas firm's provision of advice and other assistance so that as many small producers as possible can benefit, and at the same time collects any compensation from them for these services that has been agreed upon. It undertakes those matters which the firm or micro-producer would find awkward or impractical, enabling the two parties to concentrate on problem solving, training, and promotion.

The value of such an intermediary is seen in the work of the United Mission for Nepal (UMN), a non-government agency consisting of a consortium of Protestant missionary organizations, in coordinating the inputs from both overseas and national firms and aid agencies in the development of the highly successful Small Turbine and Mill Project.[11]

The project to date has resulted in the installation of over 600 small turbine mills for agricultural processing and electricity production in rural areas of Nepal, and the formation of 13 Nepali microenterprises for the provision of the machinery and services required to design, construct, operate and maintain these micro-hydro systems. It involves the participation of government departments and financial institutions, non-government agencies, and private overseas companies.

The project has faced formidable technological problems. One of the major obstacles was the lack of turbines suited to the small power output requirements and limited financial resources of rural mill owners. The UMN linked Swiss engineers with local manufacturers in the development of cross-flow turbines which greatly reduced hydro-system costs.

When the demand arose to add electricity generation to the outputs of the mills, the UMN and ITDG arranged for a British company, GP Electronics, to collaborate in the development of an electronic load control device (ELC). This device was less expensive than the mechanical governors used in larger hydroelectric systems, and did not require a highly skilled operator. GPE provided ELC kits which were assembled by Nepali companies, and provided training in their manufacture and servicing. All its assistance was arranged and coordinated through UMN. Without UMN to act as a liaison between the British company and the micro-producers GPE would not have considered becoming involved in the project.

The ELCs enabled mill owners located several days' walk from the nearest road to provide electricity to their villages. They also provided a new production opportunity for the Nepali microenterprises involved in the hydro sector. These producers now wish to develop the capacity to manufacture ELCs for smaller hydro-systems in-house, and the UMN will assist in negotiations with GP Electronics for further training, licensing, and other arrangements necessary to complete this transfer of capability. At the same time, the UMN is negotiating on the producers' behalf with Norwegian engineering firms for assistance in the development of new turbine designs for larger village electrification schemes now demanded by clients encouraged by the project's success in converting small mills into electricity producers.

The presence of the UMN makes it possible for Nepali microenterprises to take advantage of the technical resources of companies and research bodies from overseas, and for overseas firms interested in helping developing countries to gain sufficient understanding of local needs and production constraints to be able to contribute to problem solving at the microenterprise level. It also has played a critical role in attracting financial support for mill construction and upgrading through the Agricultural Development Bank of Nepal, and in clearing a major policy obstacle to mill electrification by helping to persuade the Nepal Electricity Authority to lift restrictions on private electricity generation for installations of less than 100 kilowatts capacity. The UMN has served as a catalyst for the development of a strong partnership between public and private sector assistance and microproducers.

Conclusion

Although production-oriented microenterprises face considerable technological obstacles, they have a vast potential to generate employment and income, particularly in rural areas. This potential can be realized only if these micro-producers are given access to resources to address their technological problems. Providing this access represents a challenge to established technical and financial support structures. More attention needs to be paid to small-scale production issues, particularly to issues faced by systems working with variable raw material and fuels. New modes of capital provision need to be explored that can accommodate the time and effort required to introduce new technologies to make better use of micro-producer skills and resources. Just as the growth of high-tech industries such as micro-electronics and biotechnology has required the development of new approaches to the management and support of research and development, the growth of microproduction in developing countries will necessitate corresponding changes to the work of governments, NGOs, and donor agencies involved in small enterprise support.

Microenterprise as a Social Investment

JAIME CARVAJAL

Introduction

To talk of the informal sector in Latin America is to speak about the way of life of most Latin Americans. There is a formal industrial sector, with varying degrees of state-of-the-art technology, competition and dependency on imported inputs and growth. Surrounding this formal sector is a marginal disorganized throng of small-scale intermediary and productive activities, verging on bankruptcy, relying on rudimentary technology but, nevertheless, creating more employment than in any other sector of the economy and generating income for over half the labour force.

Thus, the answer to the question of whether it is socially necessary to promote the organization and development of these informal activities is that it is, in fact, the region's most urgent social need.

Moreover, experience has shown that it is in the informal sector that social investment has the highest returns, that entrepreneurial activities are pursued most ardently and that more people are, in its various enterprises, put to work.

After the family, the small micro-business, whether it be a repair shop, a small-scale manufacturing industry or a neighbourhood convenience store, is one of the most common Latin American institutions.

Without much support and, clearly, with much less aid than has been channelled into the development of the industrial sector, the informal sector has absorbed a large share of the huge supply of labour produced by the population explosion.

Workers in Latin America's informal sector suffer low wages and little job security, but the fact remains that they do have some form of income and employment, which is what distinguishes them, almost as a privileged class, from the ranks of the unemployed.

Thus, the goal of turning these microenterprises into efficient units and enabling them to expand in terms of their size, organization and ambitions can produce highly positive economic, social and political results by helping to reduce unemployment, increase household income and strengthen democratic institutions.

JAIME CARVAJAL is Chairman of the Board, the Carvajal Foundation in Cali, Colombia, a local NGO assisting microenterprises.

The Carvajal Foundation Programme

What distinguishes the Carvajal Foundation programme operating in Cali, Colombia, is its focus on business administration. In my opinion, this approach has been a decisive factor in its success and has led 12 private foundations to extend the programme to 26 intermediate cities and 15 smaller towns and villages (with less than 50,000 inhabitants) throughout Colombia, with the invaluable assistance of the Inter-American Development Bank.

The explanation for this approach goes back to the very beginnings of the Carvajal Foundation. Created in 1961 in an effort to help integrate the growing numbers of poor in depressed areas of Cali into the social mainstream, it began by offering educational and health services, but it was not long before we realized that it was more important for these people to have jobs and a means of earning at least enough to survive, through various forms of productive activities.

Dismissing further academic investigation, we concluded that finding a means of generating employment through the organization of such efforts was the most effective and least costly means of pursuing our goal of social integration.

And so it is. The average cost of creating a job in the microenterprise sector is $1,000, a figure which can be compared only in theory with the much higher cost of creating employment in the manufacturing sector, since the latter has failed to generate any measurable amount of employment in Colombia for the past decade.

In academic terms, what we did was to create a business administration curriculum addressed at participants with little formal education managing small-scale enterprises — in other words, the opposite type of training to that offered in university programmes of study oriented to big business management. The training programme, developed over the course of 11 years of work, consists of 10 courses in accounting, costs, marketing and sales, investment projects, production, financial analysis, personnel management, quality control, principles of business administration and business law.

Slightly over 30,000 microenterprise owners throughout the country have been trained under the programme, of whom 8,542 have received a total of $10,000,000 in loan funds. Although part of the programme cost is presently subsidized, there is a sizeable income from the 12 per cent IDB interest earmarked for training, as well as from tuition fees collected from microenterprise owners.

Training is complemented by follow-up advisory services for microenterprise owners to enable them to apply successfully the general concepts taught in the training courses to the management of their respective businesses.

If necessary, both these activities are reinforced by credit programmes operated by an outside agency, or a financial intermediary.

Practical lessons from the Colombian experience

I would like to follow up my brief description of our programme of work with a few comments which I believe might be of use to foundations interested in supporting microenterprise development programmes.

1 It's easy to get the impression that the greatest need of microenterprise is that of access to credit. Microenterprise owners believe this to be the case and, when considering the technological constraints and the shortage of working capital hindering their growth and development, it is easy to be convinced of the validity of this argument.

However, experience has shown that, while credit is often necessary, it should come at a later stage, after the microenterprise owners are first trained to manage their businesses properly.

Owners of microenterprises generally know their trade, but know nothing about running a business. As soon as they set up an accounting system, more than half realize that they had been heading straight for bankruptcy. Certain owners convinced of their need for credit get on without it after completing their training. At the same time, owners benefiting from management training who do take out loans prove to be excellent credit risks, meeting all their payment obligations. According to our experience in Colombia, losses from loan defaults in well-run programmes are virtually nil.

2 You cannot teach business administration solely through training courses, but must also provide follow-up assistance at the field level to teach business owners how to apply the skills and knowledge acquired in the classroom to their own specific context.

Thus far, virtually all advisory services have relied on field visits to microenterprise owners at their place of business, which is not only costly, but also relatively inefficient, since the advisory session is being constantly interrupted by the innumerable incidents arising in the course of the day's work which claim the owner's attention.

We are therefore currently testing a new approach with a fair amount of success, under which such sessions are being conducted at the Foundation's advisory services office. Naturally, from time to time, the advisor must still visit the microenterprise owner at his place of work to familiarize himself with the business itself. But 80–90 per cent of such sessions can easily be held at Foundation headquarters, with microenterprise owners coming duly prepared for their appointment, armed with their accounting ledgers.

This new approach means sizeable savings for the training programmes per se and, most probably, more efficient advisory services as well, since the microenterprise owner is not distracted by other concerns and is in an atmosphere more conducive to assimilating the advice received at such sessions than at his place of business.

3 Although we talk about the need for self-sustaining programmes, this goal is feasible only for programmes focusing exclusively on the provision of credit. Programmes providing training could cover the cost of their courses, but it is impossible for microenterprise owners to pay the cost of corresponding advisory services, which is extremely high in the light of the large amount of time devoted to each individual.

We need only consider how education is subsidized in every country in the world to realize how impossible it is for training and advisory programmes to ever be self-sufficient, particularly when we consider how these services are targeted at persons of humble means.

In Colombia, for example, while all programmes collect some sort of fee from microenterprise owners, they generally start out charging very little and may gradually raise their fees as they become more popular. Their cost is spread among different sources, namely tuition fees collected from microenterprise owners, government subsidies and the one per cent monthly interest earmarked by the IDB for the use of foundations in subsidizing training and advisory services.

Fortunately, the interest aroused by microenterprise throughout the country has generated sufficient private support, often supplemented by official grants, to sustain subsidized microenterprise development programmes. However, it is not always sufficient to ensure consistent programme quality. In any event, there has always been enough funding to operate both programme components, namely formal training courses and follow-up advisory services, although the latter have had to be cut back severely when adequate funds have not been forthcoming.

Thus, these programmes must invariably be subsidized to remain in existence, which fact underlines the importance of a forum like the present conference attended by the very donors financing small enterprise development.

4 The informal sector is, by definition, a sector marginalized not only in relation to social benefits, but from society itself. Thus, it lies beyond the scope of legal formality, not out of any desire to break the law, but rather because it is unable to obey the law. Laws simply weren't made for the informal sector. The cloak of legality just does not fit. Commercial law is concerned with governing the operations of large-scale enterprises capable of complying with complex regulatory codes.

There is no legislation made specifically for microenterprises, nor are they accorded any special treatment at the initial stages of their development. Nor, in general, do microenterprise owners benefit from any form of government support.

Logic dictates creating special regulations for microenterprises, which would gradually begin to comply with legal formalities as they develop. In other words, businesses under a given minimal size, employing less than a given minimum number of workers or, even better yet, with under a given minimum sales volume or turnover, should be exempt from observing certain regulations until reaching and/or surpassing the statutory limits making compliance mandatory.

This has never been tried and the little I know about foreign legislation leads me to believe that nothing particularly promising has been accomplished in this area. Colombia has done virtually nothing in this direction, despite the fact that the government is firmly convinced of the need to support microenterprise and despite the existence of a national plan for microenterprise administered by the National Planning Department, a government agency which has been performing an extremely important if limited task in coordinating the country's various microenterprise programmes run by private voluntary organizations, or PVOs.

The best argument for special legislation for small-scale enterprises is that microenterprise owners themselves are very keen to legalize their activities and become a legitimate type of national institution — which is precisely what does happen when they find themselves in a position to do so.

The importance of aid

Thus, our experience has convinced me that the reason microenterprise owners enrol in personal training and business development programmes is because such programmes promote their entrepreneurial spirit, because this kind of progress is not something being handed them, but rather something they are doing for themselves through hard work and effort. Through these programmes, microenterprise owners are made to feel that the community appreciates their enormous social value as productive members of society.

The cost of the educational process furthered by training and follow-up advisory services, through which microenterprise owners gradually attain this feeling of self-worth, is only a fraction of the cost of a university education or of formal technical training.

Just as formal education is largely subsidized and such subsidy is viewed as a positive and enduring social investment, the preparation of microenterprise owners should also be subsidized and with even greater reason in view of its impact on much larger numbers of individuals.

Thus, all of us involved in these programmes are duty-bound to encourage the foundations attending this conference to pursue their self-imposed task of promoting the development of microenterprise. They have chosen an extremely useful and profitable area of work, one with high social returns. In fact, it is difficult to imagine anything more important. Through their efforts, they are supporting one of the most valuable tools for combating unemployment.

They are aiding microenterprise owners on a one-time basis, who generally expand or are at least able to put their businesses on a sound footing. Instead of ending in bankruptcy, as is normally the case of microenterprise owners receiving no such training and assistance, enterprises benefiting from training become a source of income and well-being for their respective proprietors.

This has been our experience with numerous microenterprises throughout Colombia. Such aid furthers the development of microenterprises, some of which, within a short period of time, employ as many as 25, 30 or even more workers and gradually become an integral part of the formal sector of the economy. They are the seeds of future big business, and it is highly satisfactory to know that our aid has contributed to their germination and growth.

PART V

Review of Assistance Programmes

Benefits, Costs and Sustainability of Microenterprise Assistance Programmes

MARIA OTERO

Introduction

The ubiquitous presence of microenterprises in all the major and secondary cities in developing countries is no longer a matter of dispute among academics, policy-makers and international assistance organizations. The analysis of the informal sector so appropriately crafted in the now famous ILO Study of over 15 years ago has led the way to our understanding and current concern with this important segment of the economy of developing countries.

The numbers grow before our eyes. Chronic unemployment, the apparently irreversible magnetic pull of the cities and the increasingly skewed income distribution patterns of many countries have placed on the development platter an enormous challenge: not only what to do about the growing mass of the self-employed but, more importantly, how to do it and do it quickly and efficiently.

The answers, of course, are quite complex and still elude our grasp. Nevertheless, the experience of the last decade signals a direction worth exploring, for there are rough and not-so-rough nuggets of wisdom that have emerged to guide our future decisions and our allocation of resources.

A cursory review of current experience provides useful background to this discussion. To date, most efforts to assist informal sector activities have consisted of programmes that distribute resources to those engaged in production and commerce at the smallest scale. Working capital loans, training and technical assistance, always in great demand, have emerged as the backbone of any microenterprise assistance programme. With few exceptions, the implementation of these programmes has been conducted through private development organizations with grants from donor institutions. The programmes have started small and in the successful cases have expanded to encompass ever-growing numbers of clients and also have acquired high levels of self-sufficiency.

The discussion in this paper focuses on several key issues related to microenterprise assistance programmes which can be summed up in the following questions:

MARIA OTERO is the representative in Washington, D.C., of ACCION International of Cambridge, Mass, an organization active in Latin America in supporting microenterprise development. Formerly she was Director of Operations of ACCION in Honduras.

1   what are the benefits derived from efforts to reach the informal sector?
2   what costs are incurred in the process?
3   how can these efforts become self-sustaining in the long term?

Benefits of microenterprise assistance programmes
A point of departure for this discussion considers the benefits that should be obtained through a well-implemented microenterprise assistance programme and relates these to the broader issues of economic development that underlie any such programme. Identifying and quantifying benefits may appear straightforward, but the question is often rife with complex philosophical and practical questions. How do we define benefits, what is an acceptable level of benefits obtained, and who should measure these benefits are three key areas to address before one even begins a programme intervention.

I suggest that we frame the discussion on benefits derived from microenterprise assistance programmes by considering benefits that the programme generates at three distinct levels: the direct beneficiaries; the implementing institutions; and the local context, better defined here as the policy climate[1,2].

The beneficiaries

These are the direct participants or clients of a programme, and constitute the first and most important group for whom benefits derived are most tangible and quantifiable. If it is possible to establish a causal relationship between a programme intervention and the benefits it generates, it is at this level that the relationship is most direct.

Two areas of benefit commonly are considered: the generation of additional income for the micro-producer and his family, and the creation or the maintenance of productive employment. The former, changes in income, involves a close study of the microenterprise itself, its performance as measured by changes in production, sales and net profit. Since most microenterprise programmes maintain that the infusion of working capital and technical assistance should enable a micro-producer to either improve the overall efficiency of his operation by lowering his costs, or to increase production, then changes in firm activity will probably lead to changes in family income.

The second key area, employment, constitutes one of the most important potential benefits of these programmes, since all developing countries face job creation needs of enormous proportions. Understanding the role of microenterprise assistance programmes in job creation entails a careful look at the two sub-components of employment in the informal sector: the creation of new jobs as a result of increased production, and the stabilization of existing but precarious jobs, often termed job maintenance.

The distinction between these two appears particularly relevant because almost all the persons employed in tiny shops are assured their post only as long as the enterprise can produce and sell at its current level or better. Once problems of liquidity or supply of raw materials plague the firm, then some of its workers are dismissed. If a programme's input stabilizes production, then it also strengthens the jobs already in place.

An example of benefits

The information on benefits that has been collected in many existing programmes allows us to assert that most micro-producers who receive loans and technical assistance, tend to increase their income as a result of increased net profit in their firms. These include impact evaluations of programmes in Colombia, Peru, Dominican Republic, Bolivia and others, and are available through Accion Internacional/AITEC. As illustration here, I will use the findings of a recent impact evaluation and survey of the micro-lending programme in Honduras to which I provide technical assistance through Accion Internacional/AITEC. The programme, Asepade (Asesores Para el Desarollo), extends credit, technical assistance and training to micro-producers and micro-vendors in eight cities, and can be considered a good example of an effective microenterprise assistance programme with the capacity to expand and become self-sufficient.

A survey of 85 existing firms which had received an average of US $820 in working capital loans over a period of a year yielded the following changes since they first entered the programmes.

Table I

Benefit	Percentage change
1 Percentage of firms that increased sales	62%
– Of these, firms that increased sales by more than 100%	22%
2 Average increase of sales among all firms	39%
3 Percentage of firms that increased fixed assets	25%
4 Percentage of firms that increased savings	95%
5 Average increase in income among all firms	27%

Source: Rebecca Reichmann, Impact Evaluation of Asepade, 1988.

The added working capital enabled 62 per cent of those surveyed to increase their sales, and nearly all of these — 50 per cent of the survey — experienced increases in income. The average increase in income among all borrowers was 27 per cent though there appeared to be no correlation between size of firm or type or activity and positive changes. While the largest changes were registered in women-owned firms the sample was to small to draw any gender-related conclusions. Since on the average each micro-producer made about $200 per month, the average annual increase in income per person was about $648, or $54 per month.

There is also information on the contribution these programmes make to employment creation and maintenance. The survey in Tegucigalpa, Honduras, demonstrated that for every enterprise assisted with an average of US$ 820 in working capital loans, .75 full-time jobs were created. Said a different way, for every four microenterprises assisted over a period of about a year, three new full-time jobs were created. Also, during this period, each firm generated one additional seasonal job, of an average of four months' duration.[3]

When one applies these data to a programme that reaches 500 new microentrepreneurs a year, as Asepade does, the findings show that about 375 new jobs are created in less than one year, as well as an equivalent of 166 full-time jobs in seasonal employment, or a total of 541 jobs.

Also relevant to this discussion is the finding that most of these employees earn wages higher than the minimum salary of US $90 per month. Among those surveyed (about 315 workers), 76.6 per cent earn between US $90 and US$ 400 per month, with the majority falling in the range US $100–$140. The firms surveyed employ an average of 3.4 full-time persons, and about 73 per cent of the microentrepreneurs pay an average of US $320 per month in wages. This relatively high level of wages may be explained in part because most employees earn by piece produced, and often work up to ten-hour days.

When we convert this information into increased income, we find that the aggregate annual increase in income among micro-producers is about $324,000. To this, one must add the annual income increase among the 541 new jobs created, which we average at $105 per job, yielding $681,660. However, there is little information on what their earnings were in previous jobs and hence one can only estimate the incremental annual wage payments or gross income. The assumption used is that 40 per cent of this income is newly generated, bringing the total annual increase in income of nearly $600,000.

The costs associated incurred for this level of activity include $410,000 in credit, $40,000 in operating costs (detailed below), $95,000 in technical assistance and $10,000 in bad debts, or $555,000. Hence just in terms of income generated this micro-assistance project yields a positive benefit cost ratio.

While the data on benefits based on income and employment changes are generally positive among well-implemented microenterprise assistance programmes, the information is still sweeping and broad in range, and does not allow us to conduct benefit analysis in the needed depth. Some of the issues that remain unclear but are beginning to make their way into data collection and analysis are the following:

1 As already suggested, most microenterprises are not one-person oper-

ations, and if they are, they don't remain so for long after receiving assistance. Many programmes — in the Dominican Republic, Colombia, Honduras, for example — for which there is information, show that the majority of microenterprises involved in production in Latin American countries employ two to three persons. Some are hired and paid a weekly wage, others are paid per piece completed, others receive part of their wages in lodging or meals, while still others are family members who are not paid. The variations are endless and the enterprise responds with surprising alacrity to changes in demand or in productive capacity.

Unlike the illustration used, systematic measure of the income benefits derived by these workers and their families is not often done, in part due to the cost and the complexity of the endeavour. Nevertheless, changes in income at this level are certainly data to be factored into the benefit equation of microenterprise assistance programmes.

2 The case is similar when attempting to measure what Kilby and D'Zmura have called 'indirect benefits,' that is, the benefits derived by the forward and backward linkages of microenterprise activity. As an example, Marcelina Santos Flores, a baker from Choluteca, a city in the drought ravaged southern region of Honduras, used to employ two full-time and one part-time persons in her bakery, and distributed the bread herself, directly to the *pulperias* or corner stores.

With working capital loans and technical assistance, she hired an additional worker, increased production and after a few months required a new distribution channel for her products. Today, the new channel consists of four or five independent microvendors, three of them previously unemployed, who purchase the product from the bakery, sell it directly to the consumer and also distribute it to many more corner stores than before. Marcelina now specializes in perfecting and expanding production and has added two new products: a Honduran version of cinnamon buns, and a sweet bread. In the process, she increased the number of employees in her bakery and as important, created or expanded jobs in the marketing of the product. Assessing the level of these benefits and quantifying them in terms of income generated and jobs created and maintained is difficult, and these linkages often are excluded from benefits stream calculations.

3 One also finds that the type of productive activity — carpentry, textiles, food, leather in manufacturing, or agricultural and consumer products in commerce and retailing, and repairs or other services — influences the benefit stream.

For example, the data collected in the Dominican Republic for the ADEMI programme (Asociacion Para el Desarrollo de la Micro-empresa) shows that over a period of one year micro-producers engaged in carpentry increased their sales an average of 49 per cent, while sales in food processing grew by about 28 per cent and seamstresses and tailors expanded sales by about 26 per cent. The information is based on 1,460 microentrepreneurs assisted by ADEMI for at least one year, of which 28 per cent were women.

This type of benefit analysis indicates, not surprisingly, that a programme obtains better returns to investment when it supports a certain type of activity, in this case carpentry. While this fact alone cannot constitute the basis for a programme's decision on whom to support, it is an important piece of the informal sector puzzle about which we still have little information.

4 Distinguishing between full-time, part-time and seasonal positions in the microenterprise is also essential since we find that many jobs in this sector are first created as part-time positions and later upgraded to full-time as production and demand allows. Also, during peak months of production, these firms generate thousands of person months of employment which often are ignored when one calculates jobs created.

In spite of advances in understanding how to measure employment creation and maintenance, we still lack precise tools for deciphering this crucial benefit area. Calculating the cost per job created or maintained, which is usually comparatively low in microenterprise assistance programmes ($1,025 in the Honduran example cited), is another area where the analysis is weak. It may be that standard methods for addressing these issues in the formal sector fall short when applied to a sector that escapes regulations, licensing, classification and clear parameters, and that new tools and assumptions are needed to better understand the benefits derived from microenterprise assistance programmes.

The institution

A second level of benefit analysis focuses on the implementing institution, sometimes called the intermediary, the private development organization or the financial institution. The successful implementation of programmes designed to assist microenterprises depends more than anything else on the existence of capable local institutions that view as their priority goal the promotion of self-sustained development. As a microenterprise assistance programme evolves and scales up from a pilot effort to a full-grown programme, the institution must also mature and expand its internal capacity to manage a growing programme.

The process of implementing a microenterprise assistance programme is in itself a learning experience that contributes to the creation of a cadre of competent local institutions with the capacity to manage and expand these programmes. One cannot emphasize enough the importance that building a human and institutional resource base holds for future assistance to the informal sector. Nevertheless, this key benefit derived from the implementation of programmes often is overlooked in benefit analysis.

Institutions benefit in at least three ways as a result of implementing microenterprise assistance programmes. First, if the microenterprise assistance programme is to move beyond the pilot phase, then the institution must review and upgrade its internal structure and management mechanisms.

Planning processes, communication flow, information systems, decision-making procedures, and established rules and regulations must all be adapted to fit the needs of the programme. In the process, these undergo improvements, leading to a stronger and more efficient institution.

Second, the institution must pay very close attention to its financial status and management. The proper implementation of a microenterprise assistance programme should strengthen both its financial analysis capacity and its monitoring and reporting techniques. More importantly, since the programme generates income through interest earned, the institution as an entity becomes more solvent, and less dependent on outside sources of funding. After three or more years of conducting a programme, an institution should begin to cover most or all of its operating costs from income earned through the programme. Data available on 19 programmes in seven countries that are currently receiving technical assistance from Accion Internacional/ AITEC, show that on the average these programmes cover close to 50 per cent of their operating costs, after two years of operation. Some of the more successful ones, notably Accion Comunitaria del Peru and ADEMI in the Dominican Republic, cover 100 per cent of their costs from income generated through the programme.

Finally, the institution over the course of programme implementation, develops staff capable of conducting microenterprise assistance programmes. The role these institutions play in building the needed local human resource base is essential as one witnesses increased donor and government involvement in this area. Current implementing institutions have become the training ground for professionals who will later participate in broader level decisions regarding policies and resources for this sector. As these persons move to mid- and high-level public or private sector posts, they will become instrumental in framing national level responses to these issues.

The benefits derived at the institutional and human resource development level from the implementation of a microenterprise assistance programme seldom are taken into account in benefit considerations. To date, we lack the means to quantify these benefits or to assess them in relation to benefits derived from alternative uses of money. Yet one can argue that the benefits derived at the institutional and human resource development level are the most essential at this stage of assistance to informal sector activities. The fragility of institutions in most countries constitutes a major roadblock. Without the creation of competent staff and stable organizations to conduct programmes, large scale future programming cannot succeed.

The local context
A third level of benefit analysis involves a study of how microenterprise assistance programmes are contributing to the evolution of a national political and policy climate favourable to addressing the needs of the informal sector. In the last five years, nearly every government in Latin America has

begun to study seriously this sector and to consider national level responses.

Regardless of how advanced this process is in each country, governments and interested entities have always turned first to existing programmes and utilized their experience to formulate solutions. The demonstration effects of effective microenterprise assistance programmes has been invaluable, and will continue to guide emerging public and private sector responses.

In Honduras, in the last two years, we have witnessed an evolution from very limited activity in the informal sector and no public sector interest in it, to the formation of a broad-based commission with representation from ministries, two private banks, universities, donor agencies and private development organizations. The commission's mandate is to formulate the first steps towards policy and legislation for the informal sector. It has detailed a workplan for itself and has met twice a month for the last three months. Not surprisingly, the leading force behind the commission are private development organizations who acknowledge that without government support and private sector financing their programmes will not grow.

While virtually impossible to calculate, benefit analysis of current microenterprise assistance programmes must take into account this level of impact. Unless current programmes have the vision to understand their roles in shaping national level agendas for this sector, their benefit, even in the well-implemented programmes, will be limited to the few hundred or thousand that they reach.

The costs of micro-assistance programmes

At one level, calculating the costs of a micro-enterprise assistance programme is considerably less complex than assessing its benefits. For the purpose of this discussion, one can summarize the cost stream as composed of the following:

Operating costs

These pertain to the costs of conducting a microenterprise assistance programme, and most often include the salaries, benefits and administrative expenses associated with the programme. Most efficient programmes operate out of low-rent offices with a staff composed mostly of young field workers or loan advisors each of whom handles a portfolio of borrowers — be these individual or group loans — and they spend most of their time outside the office in close contact with the borrowers.

The recurring costs of these programmes often are low, when compared to other development efforts. The cost per unit lent, which considers operating costs in relation to the amount of credit extended, often is used as an indicator of efficiency and of overall programme viability. In the more successful programmes which have achieved economies of scale, the cost per unit lent can be as low as US $.04 per dollar lent. Well-run, mature programmes should not need to spend more than 10–14 cents for every dollar they lend.

The Honduran example registers a cost of 9 cents per dollar lent.

There are start-up costs that can be considered in the cost stream of these programmes and, depending on the institution's situation, these are considered an investment or a sunk cost. Small office equipment, computers, vehicles and motorcycles are essential for any programme, and if not already available they must be included in the costs. In many countries, import taxes and other fees nearly double the cost of these items. Likewise, their maintenance and repair also figure as a high cost item in the operating budget.

Costs of money

Whether programmes operate on grants or not, the cost of money should be taken as a factor in the cost stream of a microenterprise assistance programme. Over the long term, a programme will become viable only if it can borrow and pay back capital in order to operate. Most of the time, soft or discounted lines of credit will be available, and the calculation of the cost of money should consider this factor rather than rely exclusively on commercial interest rates as a measure.

Microenterprise assistance programmes that are borrowing from banks and financial institutions are the exception. Most programmes currently operate on soft loans or grants from donor organizations.

Technical assistance costs

Invariably, a programme that is beginning or scaling up will require considerable infusions of technical assistance, often provided by an outside technical assistance organization. The level of the technical assistance effort will vary depending on both local institutional capacity and previous experience in microenterprise assistance programmes. Given my occupation, I am a strong advocate of technical assistance provision, which should be considered an essential component during the first years of a programme and factored into the cost stream.

Opportunity cost

A final key consideration in microenterprise assistance programmes is the opportunity cost of utilizing scarce resources to fund them as opposed to any benefit producing development efforts. This factor must be studied in relation to the benefits to the overall economy that one expects to derive from these or alternative programmes.

The debate about primary and secondary benefits and their relationship to costs in microenterprise programmes will persist in the literature. No one has a definitive answer on which of the above costs should appear in a benefit/cost analysis, or what benefit stream is the appropriate one. Kilby and D'Zmura's in-depth study of five projects in *Searching for Benefits* establishes some patterns by suggesting that from a benefit/cost perspective microenterprise assistance programmes are a smart use of scarce resources, if one factors into the equation the indirect benefits derived from the project. Other evaluations and my own experience support these findings. Indeed, when a microenterprise programme is well-implemented, its contribution to overall income and employment can be considerable, and its relative cost low.

While this discussion is instructive, remember that the assessment of benefits and costs is only one tool for decision making. There are many nonquantitative and noneconomic criteria for making decisions related to the informal sector, and we have not begun to touch those in this discussion. Social benefits, 'empowerment' issues and income redistribution, all important considerations in Latin American countries, are factors beyond this analysis. Tightening our understanding of the benefit cost-relationship in these programmes should be one ingredient in a decision-making process, but not a substitute for judgement that must also consider social and political factors.

A question that remains, then, is not whether to support microenterprise assistance programmes or not, but rather how to assure that those programmes that receive support are developing the capacity for long-term self-sustainment. In the paragraphs that follow I suggest a point of departure for this discussion, which must accompany any assessment of project benefits and costs.

Three ingredients for programme sustainability

The sustainability of a microenterprise assistance programme depends primarily on three factors: high volume of lending activity, appropriate institutional capacity to maintain and expand the programme and adequate repayment rate. These three factors are interrelated and must all be addressed at the same time in order to assure programme sustainability.

The question of volume

The impulse to grow should be the driving force behind any microenterprise assistance programme if it is to be self-sustaining over the long term. The only way a programme will have measurable impact and at the same time generate the income, through interest earned and other charges, which will enable it to cover its costs completely, is by a constant scaling up of its lending activity. In fact, the nature of the population reached requires that a programme gradually grow larger and larger, and eventually expand into a national scale.

If non-stop growth constitutes a goal from the outset, then all other factors in the programme will be designed and conducted with this in mind. The concept of growth behind a micro lending programme implies that a mentality of *gradual reduction of subsidies* underlines all its activities. Such an approach transforms the local institution from a grantseeker to a seeker of financial viability which invests time and energy into assuring its own capacity for self-sustainment. With this mentality, cost structures respond to a concern for greater efficiency, productivity is monitored and assessed and rates of growth are planned for the short and long term. In other words, the programme dedicates considerable time to planning its expansion and to determining the level of activity required in order to become self-sufficient.

The question of programme growth, viewed from the demand side, appears to be limitless. In every city in the developing world, there is enormous unmet demand for resources among those employed in the informal sector. Many programmes note that after initial promotion, word of mouth is the main reason for programme expansion. In Bolivia, for example, PRODEM (Fundacion Para la Promocion y Desarrollo de la Microempresa) increased its monthly lending from $1,000 its first month of operations to over $20,000 just months later.[5] Nine months into the programme, the monthly disbursement of credit has climbed to over US$55,000 and continued to grow, though at a lesser rate.

The supply side remains the biggest bottleneck to programme expansion, and various factors contribute to it
Programmes often are unable to grow because they cannot secure financial resources for credit lending in a timely manner, be it from donor organizations, financial institutions, or other sources, such as guarantee funds.

In fact, donor institutions — AID, the World Bank, the Inter-American Development Bank and others — often contribute to the bottleneck. In some cases, the amount of money made available to programmes is not adequate to the need. As successful programmes are launched (ADEMI, PRODEM and others), considerably more resources need to be allocated upfront and over time. The general practice of appropriating no more than $500,000 for lending is currently proving insufficient and cumbersome.

In other cases, donor and lending institutions attempt to support microenterprise assistance programmes but lack the internal procedures necessary to respond with agility and clarity to the resource needs of these programmes. The delays in decision-making and fund disbursement severely hamper the expansion of existing programmes. Some donor institutions, lacking firsthand experience with this sector, eye microenterprise assistance programmes through the prism of macro-economic analysis which does not render them any closer to clear policies and guidelines.

The mention of donor organizations in this context is not meant to undermine their current efforts or to imply that they are the major constraint to the scaling up of programmes. It is meant, however, to draw attention to this issue, and to urge that these institutions review their existing policies and aspire to develop effective and quick internal mechanisms for resource transfer to micro-lending programmes.

Institutional capacity
Indeed, the major bottleneck in the area of supply is not the funders but the capacity of local institutions to expand their programmes, a second key factor to programme sustainability. There are a variety of documents that provide guidance on how to determine if an institution has the capacity for engaging in these programmes, and most underline the following:

1   good financial management skills;
2   clear lending policies that include market interest rates;
3   monitoring systems that provide regular (weekly or monthly) information on portfolio movement and health, financial indicators, and key impact information;
4   first-hand knowledge of the characteristics of the population addressed;
5   a good track record implementing a programme on a small scale; and
6   a board of directors that understands the importance of agility in programme implementation and provides support and credibility.

Before an institution can scale up a microenterprise assistance programme, it must take at least the following steps:

1   develop a well-thought-out model for expansion based on decentraliza- and agility;
2   conduct intensive staff training;
3   computerize its portfolio management and financial functions.

Late repayment
As everyone who has worked directly in implementing a microenterprise assistance programme knows, there is nothing as fragile as an adequate repayment rate. Shortcomings in programme implementation or external factors or both can play havoc with a programme's repayment rate and jeopardize its sustainability. Factors beyond the programme's control can sometimes create serious setbacks. In my two years in Honduras, we have weathered two fires in the markets, affecting hundreds of borrowers, as well as police-led street sweeps of all vendors, many of them programme borrowers. These events required immediate emergency debt restructuring on the part of the programme.

Most often, however, the culprit is the programme itself. Poor follow-up with the borrower and an unbalanced emphasis on growth tend to be the main causes behind poor repayment. Unless repayments are monitored on a daily basis, and each field worker disaggregates late repayments and plans his or her work based on proper recovery rates, this factor will obstruct programme sustainability. One of the greatest advantages of a computerized system is the up-to-date information on this aspect of the programme.

Experience indicates that a 90 per cent timely repayment rate or above is very good, and that 80–89 per cent is good to adequate, with anything below registering as poor. This calculation is based on loans overdue as a percentage of the overall portfolio.

Conclusion

A programme that combines growth with the institutional capacity to propel it, and also maintains an adequate to very good repayment rate assures its own sustainability. Further, the benefits it generates at the suggested levels increase substantially in relationship to the costs, and constitute an important justification for supporting micro-assistance programmes that gather these characteristics.

Microenterprise assistance programmes are not every organization's bailiwick. Their recent proliferation would tend to suggest that many programmes do not gather the characteristics necessary for self-sustainability. The recent US legislation could exacerbate this situation. It becomes the funders' and the implementors' responsibility to determine with care which emerging or new programmes merit additional funds to expand, which require institutional strengthening as an intermediate step, and which should be abandoned. Only in this way will microenterprise assistance programmes achieve their full potential as contributors to the overall development of a country.

Comparative Experience with Microenterprise Projects

THOMAS A. TIMBERG

Micro- and small-industry projects have been pursued as a means to tap the potential micro-industries represent for efficient use of capital to secure production and employment and thus address the problems of the poor in society. This paper recounts the experience of various sorts of microenterprise promotion programmes and their impact. My own discussion of the issue of the merit of micro-industries is contained in an article of mine published elsewhere, for those who are interested.[1]

Though programmes of assistance to very small scale cottage enterprises and hawkers, especially credit schemes, have a hoary tradition and exist in some form in almost every country in the world — it is only in the last two decades that they have become critical elements in poverty elimination strategies and widely employed as such. Even now, the general experience with extensive programmes for very small non-agricultural enterprises is quite limited. Several of the countries of Asia — India, Indonesia, and Sri Lanka — have launched massive efforts and in Bangladesh efforts of similar magnitude have been launched by autonomous and voluntary organizations. These Asian efforts have involved hundreds of thousands of beneficiaries and permit some general conclusions on the potential society-wide impact of such programmes. Programmes of assistance to such very small enterprises in Africa are many fewer and newer and have typically emerged as a result of assistance to vocational school graduates or of cooperative credit activity, or the income generating programmes of voluntary organizations, sometimes two or three of these sources simultaneously. Among the most extensive efforts have been those funded by various NGOs in Kenya, the SEDOM Project in Malawi and the various programmes of the former Partnership for Productivity.

Latin American programmes in recent years have typically been launched by voluntary organizations, sometimes with expatriate funding and sometimes with support from the local elite, or in the case of Brazil, Colombia, Peru and now potentially Mexico, are partially publicly funded programmes

---

THOMAS A. TIMBERG is Director of ARIES (Assistance to Resource Institutions for Enterprise Support) Project, being carried out by Robert Nathan Associates Inc. for USAID, Washington, D.C., USA.

building on the experience of such voluntary groups. The volume of such Latin American programmes among non-agriculturalists is still small enough in the most extensive of programmes, so no systemic, society-wide effect can yet be recorded. The prototype programmes are those promoted by Accion, National Development Foundations (often affiliated with the Pan American Development Foundation or Solidarios), the Carvajal Foundation in Cali, and ADMIC in Monterey in Mexico.

Though some of the methods and aims of these microenterprise programmes are the same in all three continents there is some difference of motivation among the promoters. The Asian efforts are typically promoted primarily as equity measures and derive their support from those concerned about poverty in their societies. Much of the Latin American effort is informed by the work of Hernando de Soto and others about the informal sector and the political need to integrate it into the broader society. The African efforts are also concerned with the welfare of the poor, with less of an interest in systemic impact than in Asia.

I will now outline as best I can from available sources the experience of some of the most interesting and influential programmes: first, the Indian IRDP programme which is probably the most extensive and which is based on the longest experience, the Grameen Bank in Bangladesh and then the BKK in Indonesia. I will then give an overview of some recent programmes in Africa, though the experience there is generally too recent to be conclusive, and a shorter review of the Latin American experience which is being covered more extensively elsewhere in these sessions.

I will be using the following exchange rates: $1 = 13.3 Rs India; $1 = 33 taka Bangladesh; $1 = 2.05 Kwacha Malawi.

India-IRDP

India has a long history of attempts to assist craft and cottage producers including providing credit to them. This assistance was a concern of the Indian Nationalist Movement under the inspiration of Mahatma Gandhi and others, as well as of officially sponsored cooperative efforts before independence. Since independence, the government has extended the scope of services to small producers and the provision of credit to them through a wide variety of sources. For almost two decades, the Interest Rate Differential Programme has provided extensive commercial bank funds for such small producers; whole categories of production have been barred to larger units, and various protections extended to specific small-scale industries.[2] The latest material on the Differential Rate of Interest Scheme indicates that as of 31 December 1984 the number of accounts was 4.3 m and the outstanding credit 4.4 bn Rs (over $300 m or about 1 per cent of total bank advances). The banking system also extended 8.4 bn Rs (over $600 m) of credit to 3.8 m IRDP beneficiaries during 1984/85. Over 200,000 beneficiaries under the

Table 1 Indian Loan Programmes (approximate figures)

	Number (m)		Amount (bn)	Average (m)	
DRI	4.3	4.4	$300	1,000 Rs	($300)
IRDP	8.4	3.8	$600	2,000 Rs	($600)
TRYSEM	0.2	2.8	$200	14,000 Rs	($1,100)

Self-Employment Scheme for Educated Unemployed Youth received 2.8 bn Rs (over $200 m). These 15.5 bn Rs (over $1.1 bn) were out of a total credit extended of about 500 bn Rs ($37.5 bn).

In addition to the amounts advanced under these social programmes some of the 40 plus per cent of advances to priority sectors also served micro-units — particularly notable were schemes to assist handloom weavers, silk growers and scheduled tribes and castes (former untouchables). (*Reserve Banks of India Annual Report*, 1984–85, Supplemented to *Reserve Bank of India Bulletin* June 1985 and *Report on Trend and Progress of Banking in India*, Supplement to *Reserve Bank of India Bulletin*, September 1985). Though these efforts have not reached all small-scale producers, in some contrast to many other countries, the proportion benefited directly is often quite large.

In the 1960s, there emerged a consensus that poverty could be eliminated in India, through a combination of guaranteed public works employment and assistance to self-employment efforts, and public policy has moved in the direction of supporting these two thrusts. Dandekar and Rath, in their pathbreaking *Poverty in India* (1964), costed what applying these two thrusts would entail if they succeeded in ending absolute poverty. Mrs Gandhi's commitment to end poverty in her 1971 election campaign led to a number of state programmes and forerunners of the present national programme. These programmes were continued through the Antyodaya of the 1977–80 Janata years and with resumed enthusiasm by the Congress governments since then.

Under the IRDP, the poorest in each village are supposed to be selected each year, and assisted to rise out of poverty either by pension, loan or job depending on what seems feasible. According to the official Concurrent Evaluations the majority of beneficiaries meet the eligibility requirements and are benefited though this finding has been challenged by some observers.[3]

In the Sixth Plan (1980–85) the programme was intended to serve 15 m families. In fact, there were reported to be 16.56 m beneficiaries, on whom 16.6 bn Rs (about $1.3 bn) were spent. The total investment mobilized, including bank resources, was 47.6 bn or 2,975 Rs per beneficiary (about $3.6 bn or $220 per capita).[4] The Concurrent Evaluations show that 7 per cent of actual beneficiaries were over the income cutoff of 4,800 Rs (about $360) a year annual family income. Earlier studies reported an average misidentification of 15–20 per cent.[4] These misidentification figures seem far lower than those in the one or two detailed studies I have located, as you will see below, but perhaps these smaller studies are unrepresentative. The monthly surveys for the Concurrent Evaluations cover a rotating sample of 1,440 beneficiary households and is certainly well designed, but questions can always be raised about the accuracy of primary data gathering in this sort of survey and cross-check surveys are certainly desirable.[5] Unfortunately, the only general survey of such a sort with which I am familiar is the Consumer Expenditure Survey, collected every five years. The last one done in 1982-83 showed some apparent decline in absolute poverty, attributed by some observers to the various anti-poverty efforts of the government.

Leakages through mistargeting and poor administration are high enough to lead to some doubts of the value of the programme. In one study in Uttar Pradesh, only 46 per cent of the beneficiaries were actually eligible according to the income criteria. The costs of securing the benefits, including bribes, ranged as high as 400 Rs per loan. However, repayment of loans was 50-70 per cent, far higher than with normal bank credit. No impact data was collectible.[6] In Rajasthan, a survey indicated that 48.6 per cent of IRDP beneficiaries were above the income cut-off and there seemed a tendency for this percentage of ineligibles to rise over time. Despite provisions in the programmes, neither Uttar Pradesh nor Rajasthan seems to have utilized village level mass meetings to select beneficiaries as was prescribed. According to official sources only 60 per cent of beneficiaries were selected by village assembly,[4] but the individual studies at hand indicate that these assemblies are often pro forma and poor attended, and held away from the village itself even when they are conducted. Even those poor who were properly targeted had great difficulty maintaining the assets purchased, often livestock.[7]

Nonetheless, the scope of the IRDP programme is larger than anywhere else in the world; and the programme has largely included in its scope most of the kinds of voluntary agency activity recorded elsewhere. Two notable and well reported exceptions, the Working Women's Forum of Madras and the Self-Employed Woman's Association of Ahmedabad were founded before the IRDP.[8,9]

Bangladesh-Grameen Bank

Bangladesh has had various government programmes for small producers over the last several decades, but recent attention has focused on the Grameen Bank, a registered bank for very small borrowers which has had great success in reaching the poor. Though Grameen certainly has its roots in previous Bangladesh experiments such as the Comilla Project in the 1960s, and is paralleled by several other large volume small loan programmes, none of these can claim its success or the verified impact it has recorded. The Grameen Bank is not a voluntary organization, juridically it is a goverment-owned bank, but it operates largely autonomously of the rest of the government.

The Grameen Bank was started as a pilot project in 1976, and formally launched in 1979. Since 1982 it has been operating in five of the country's 24 old districts. Since April 1983, it has operated as a specialized credit institution for the rural poor. It has an authorized capital of 30 m taka (about $900,000), 40 per cent contributed by its members, 40 per cent by the government of Bangladesh, and 10 per cent each by two nationalized banks.

Only those owning less than a half acre of land or with total assets worth less than an acre of land are eligible to become members. Bank workers organize these members into groups of five with their own elected officers, which hold weekly meetings. Groups are organized separately for men and women and relatives may not belong to the same group.

After a month during which the group functions properly according to Grameen Bank's rules — undertaking credit and social education, collective physical exercises etc at their weekly meetings — two members are permitted to take a loan for any productive activity of their choice, to be repaid in equal weekly instalments. After the first two group members make payments regularly for several months other loans are extended to group members. If a member defaults on a payment loans are stopped to all group members.

Disbursements and collections are all handled by the salaried bank worker at the weekly meeting. A male bank worker should serve about 250 members, a female bank worker about 150. (These numbers may not be achieved in practice.)

The members must bring 1 taka in savings every week. They also deposit 5 per cent of the loan amount at the time of disbursement to form the Group Fund from which members can borrow on an interest free basis with group permission to meet emergency needs. Only one-sixth of the money available in Group Funds has in fact been borrowed. In addition to interest, now charged at 16 per cent, a sum of 25 per cent of the interest is due at the end of the cycle of equal weekly instalments — ie accounting for the last several payments. This sum is paid into an Emergency Fund, again available to meet emergencies threatening default. The Emergency Fund serves partially as a guarantee fund.

By 31 December 1986, the Grameen Bank had 295 branches and 234,000 borrower members and covered more than 6 per cent of the villages, and 3 per cent of the eligible borrowers in the country. The figure was 10 per cent of the eligible borrowers in the five districts Grameen Bank in fact served. Disbursement of loans in 1985 was 428 m takas (about $13 m) leaving an outstanding of 331 m takas (about $10 m) by the end of 1986. The Group and Emergency Funds amounted to 137 m taka (about $4 m) by the end of December 1986.

Sixty-nine per cent of the members are women, accounting for 55 per cent of the cumulative loan amount. Both proportions are rising rapidly. In 1985, livestock and fisheries accounted for about one-third and manufacturing and trading about a quarter each of the loan disbursements.

The Grameen Bank, despite what might be described as high administrative costs (14.2 per cent on loans and advances) makes a profit on a cash basis, with about half of its income coming from idle balances it keeps on deposit with other banks. It also benefits from two or three accounting practices which have been criticized. Grameen Bank's profit is also enabled by access to lower than average cost funds (an average annual cost of funds provided in 1985 of 5.8 per cent as against 8.5 per cent charged by the Bangladesh Bank for agricultural advances made by other banks). The Bank also benefits from a tax holiday, in contrast to other Bangladesh banks. Grameen Bank's returns should improve, however, as it no longer has to bear start-up costs for new branches. Those branches which are more than two years old just break even when charged with a 10 per cent cost of funds and not charged for central Bank overhead.

We should probably address one or two concerns raised by recent reports on the Grameen Bank which are not yet public. First, though overall arrears (overdue more than two years) are indeed rising, they are still well under 3 per cent, less than the 5 per cent originally planned for. However, one can agree that the Grameen Bank should make the proposed loss provision, and agree that taking training costs from rather than charging expenses to them is perhaps not called for. We should recognize that this costing of training is at least an open question in the case of a rapidly expanding programme like the Grameen Bank's — had these two provisions been made the Bank would have been sustainable in the long run (presuming the persistence of the slight interest and tax subsidies).

One could suggest, though I gather this is not the thinking of the current Grameen Bank leadership, that a 5 per cent arrearage rate is quite acceptable given the high risk nature of the ventures in which many borrowers are engaged and that the Bank has over-reacted in terms of curtailing its expansion, particularly among male borrowers. Ultimately Grameen Bank's viability may be as threatened by an inability to generate a sufficient volume of credit as by a slightly higher level of arrears. The leadership may be right, however, that an attitude which accepts 5 per cent easily leads to an attitude which accepts more. The rot has to be addressed at the start. The success of the bank leads all of us to be chary about challenging the managers' own decisions on these matters.

The fact that recent expansion has almost entirely been among women may also be a correct decision, given social and commercial priorities, but ultimately the bank will have to deal with men as well, if it wishes to deal with overall poverty problems.

Careful surveys indicate that 95 per cent of bank members meet the explicit target criteria and that performance in this respect seems to improve over time. Success in this matter is partly due, according to Mahabub Hossain, to the fact that the effective borrowing rate is higher and terms and conditions of borrowing more onerous than in other programmes to which the wealthier have access: 96.8 per cent of the loans were repaid within one year and 99.1 per cent within two years of due date at the time of the Hossain report. The average overdues rise to 8.3 per cent for older, more mature branches. Members increased assets and employment and had 50 per cent higher incomes than potential target group members in control villages where the bank did not operate and 17 per cent higher income than non-member target group people in their own villages.[10]

Though Grameen Bank's achievements are particularly impressive, it is only the most successful of numerous microenterprise schemes in Bangladesh, most of which are organized in roughly analogous fashion, though each one has some peculiarities. A survey of such schemes done for the Bangladesh Bank listed 22 such programmes ranging from those with under 100 to those with several hundreds of thousands of borrowers, and effective interest rates of up to 30 per cent, with many reporting repayment rates of 90–100 per cent.[11,12]

Indonesia-BKK

The BKK in Indonesia, by contrast, is closely integrated with the local government organization which oversees its detailed functioning. It, too, has succeeded in extending and collecting a larger number of loans to poor people, and improving their lot though no study of its general impact has yet been published. In addition, its target is less insistently the poorest of the poor in the society it serves.

The BKK (Badan Kredit Kecamatan) was created to provide small, short-term 'loans to rural families for off-farm productive' purposes. Between 1972 and 1982, it made 2.7 m loans amounting to over $55 m (an average of $20 each). The programme involves 486 BKK (subdistrict bodies) which are separately administered and autonomous though supervised by both central and provincial governments.

Small loans are made on the basis of character references from local officials and the amounts of such loans are raised with each repayment. Interest rates on loans are set to cover expenses including the cost of funds. (Rates ranged from 5.6 to 10.8 per cent per month.) On current loans, delinquency was only 6 per cent, but an overhang of old overdues represents 14 per cent of outstandings. The programme as a whole was making a profit (even after allowing for subsidies) of $333,000 in 1981, a 7 per cent return on its portfolio. One-third of BKKs, however, were either operating at low levels or closed.

Of the clients, 60 per cent were women, one-half owned some land with an average holding of 0.8 hectare (about average for the region), most were primarily engaged in trading, almost all used their loans for working capital and had increased the scope of their activities. Seventeen per cent of borrowers had hired someone since joining the programme. The average borrower created 0.3 full-time and 0.4 part-time jobs. The intended and effective target was somewhat better off than is the case of Grameen Bank and IRDP, though still way below those reached by most rural credit programmes.[13]

In many ways, the KUPEDES programme, founded in 1984, is more comparable to Grameen Bank in the size of credit extended. This programme is, however, explicitly limited to landowners or at least those who can provide collateral, which usually means land (47 per cent of the adults in Java are landless). Under the KUPEDES programme, by the end of 1986, 1.2 m borrowers had a total credit outstanding of $202 m or an average of $168. Cumulative payments missed as a percentage of due was 2.3 per cent in April 1987. The programme was turning in a profit with what appears to be 15–20 per cent interest charges and generating the bulk of its loanable fund as savings.

The loans are extended through Unit Desa, village banking units, of the Bank Rakyat Indonesia (BRI) for any productive purpose, though the bulk are taken nominally for trading and a fair number for livestock raising and 28 per cent for cultivation. However, since many households engaged in a number of these activities the actual use of funds may be hard to identify.[14]

Summary

If the Asian programmes did not reach the destitute, they did serve an absolutely poor clientele otherwise not reached by the credit system.

Table 2 Some basic comparative data

Country name	Population (m)	GNP per capita (1985) (US dollars)	% of household Income with highest 10%	Income with lowest 20%
Bangladesh	100.6	150	29.5	6.6
India	765.1	270	33.6	7.0
Indonesia	162.2	530	34	6.6
Philippines	54.7	580	37	5.2
Kenya	20.4	290	45.8	2.8
Senegal	6.6	370	—	—
Honduras	4.4	720	—	—
El Salvador	4.8	820	29.5	5.5
Ecuador	9.4	1,160	—	—
USA	239.3	16,690	23.3	5.3

Source *World Development Report 1987*, World Bank, Washington, D C 1987

Most of the beneficiaries in Bangladesh and Indonesia were women; they were able to make productive use of the money advanced and increase their incomes. The bulk of the activity in Indonesia was in trading, one-third of that in Bangladesh, little in India (because of explicit policy). A good proportion of the Indian loans and a quarter of those in Bangladesh were for animal husbandry. The remainder in all three countries was mostly for very small scale manufacturing.

The administrative and other costs were largely covered in Bangladesh and Indonesian cases, though elements of hidden subsidy remain. The Indian programme includes by design a considerable element of subsidy.

The Asian programmes as a whole have relatively small size clients and loans, which is logical enough given their relatively poor economies as compared to those in other continents (see Table 2).

Africa

In Africa, most of the successful programmes that have come to my attention are run by voluntary organizations, typically with an overhead cost that would be hard to justify on a continuing basis. Table 3 gives some indications of what kinds of cost are involved. The promoters are very much conscious of the cost factor and have experimented with various ways to reduce overhead, even while arguing that the dynamic advantages from the programme may justify them. Among these approaches are the minimalist approach now promoted by Malcolm Harper and several of his associates and embodied in the CEDP project in Senegal and an effort modelled on the Grameen Bank scheduled for implementation in Malawi. In the CEDP, costs were to be reduced by concentrating on the higher potential entrepreneurs and providing only the critical missing support for them, in this case credit.

This higher cost burden in African programmes is the case even where, as in the SEDOM programme in Malawi, expatriate salaries are not charged to the programme. SEDOM in Malawi (supported by the EEC) can extend loans up to 50,000 Kwacha (approximately $24,000) at an interest rate of 16 per cent a year. As of August 1986, it had extended over 1,610 loans with an average size of under 2,000 Kwacha ($975). Four-fifths of all loans were to manufacturers. Repayment and administrative costs have both been high. Arrears, though rising are still under 10 per cent of due. (*New Directions for Promoting Small and Medium Scale Enterprises in Malawi: Constraints and Prospects for Growth.* Malawi/USAID, Rural Enterprises and Agribusiness Development Institutions (READI). Report, June 1987).

SEDOM has lent roughly 3.8 m Kwacha ($1.85 m) during 1985. Arrearages of more than 30 days were 13.9 per cent of dues. Overall administrative costs were about 2.1 m Kwacha (about $1 m) but about one-third of that could be allocated to pure training and extension activity. The rest is hard to allocate between credit-connected and overhead activity with the data at

Table 3 Cost of African SME Loan Programmes

Organization	Average loan value ($)	Administrative cost per loan ($)	Administrative cost as a percentage of loan	Arrears Percentage of loan outstanding
PfP/Burkina Faso	$ 670	$1,238	185	23
Kaolack (Senegal)	(1.3 m CFA) 4,333[1]	$ 881[2] $1,215[3] (with expatriate)	20 28	No defaults 2.3% in late payment
VITA (Chad)	$6,025[4] $ 72[5]	$9,640[6]	66 (credit activities) 94 (business advisory services)	25
REP (Kenya)[7] Period 5/85 to 6/86	$1,277	$ 638	160 50 – just started – very rough figure	20

1 At $1 = 300 CFA.
2 Without cost of expatriate staff.
3 With cost of expatriate.
4 Loans made in Ndjamena only.
5 Loans made in Bongor (rural).
6 Includes both the credit cost and the cost of business advisory services. Includes expatriate cost (46.5 percent out of 66 percent is expatriate cost).
7 This is only for the credit activities of the NLOs in the sub-projects. The report on the project has stated that the figures are very rough. The cost on training/TA and institution building of the NGOs have been excluded. The performance indicators being used are mostly employment generation, cost of training and cost of credit has not been worked out.

hand, but perhaps we should say that the costs of credit administrator amounted to 30–60 per cent of annual loan disbursements (from computer printout of SEDOM) ($1 = 2.05 Kwacha).

There is some interesting experience in several African countries with small-scale support for technical school graduates and marketing assistance for craft producers, but I am not familiar with any impact studies on these programmes. Among the programmes of support to technical school graduates are the well-documented CNPAR in Burkina Faso (The Artisan Training and Credit Project of the Centre National de Perfectionnement des Artisans Ruraux), the Rural Vocational Training Centre programme of SIDO in Tanzania, and the Village Polytechnic scheme in Kenya. Among the artisan oriented marketing schemes are those surrounding the National Museum in Niger and the Artisan Centres in Tunisia. Similar programmes for technical school graduates and craft producers exist in Asia and Latin America as well.

Latin America

The Latin American experience with microenterprises is well enough represented at this meeting to require less attention in this paper. Many of the programmes are credit and training programmes for new and expanding entrepreneurs run by voluntary organizations often with considerable support from local businessmen. Often, as in the prototypical Carvajal Programme in Cali, these have a training focus and a bias toward manufacturing.

The business supported voluntary programmes have varying experience, but typically high enough costs so some level of subsidy is required, and often provided by outside donors. The model is used elsewhere and one might cite efforts especially in the Philippines, MIDAS in Bangladesh, the Birla Institute Programme in Ranchi etc.[15] The beneficiaries are typically much larger than in any of the microenterprise programmes cited earlier. ('The Informal Sector in Central America: A Preliminary Overview,' PADF Washington, D.C. January 1986; Donald Rhatigan, 'Evaluation of Solidarios and Selected National Development Foundations,' by Miranda Associates, Washington, D.C. for USAID, January 17, 1986; Ignacio Deschamps, 'Programas de Financiamento a Pequena Unidades Productivas Urbanas: Experiencia en la Reduccion de Costas de Administracion,' IDB, July 1986).

These business supported programmes contrast with efforts which stick closer to the UNO-ACCION-DDF Model, involving groups, smaller enterprises, many more non-manufacturers, working capital credit focus and lower administrative costs. These UNO programmes, too, are often run by voluntary groups, sometimes with an ideological or religious coloration, but include the Brazilian and Peruvian government programmes about which I have little data.

One scheme of classification
One way of looking at this diversity of programmes is presented in a series of ideal type models that were developed in some recent work at Harvard and are presented in Table 4.

General summary

Microenterprise promotion programmes differ in terms of the actual clientele they serve — of the size and type of enterprise they target — services needed etc. They range from those which support peripheral income generating activity especially for women, often in retailing and animal husbandry, to those which support units with several employees, some limiting themselves to manufacturing units. These differences in target groups are likely to have impact on the administrative costs of the programmes, and the extent to which they find themselves providing various social services. In Bangladesh, of the enterprises surveyed in the small and cottage sector, approximately one-third were not making a profit if labour costs were fully charged at the wage of an agricultural labourer, but the other two-thirds appeared to have a modal return of 50 per cent.[16,17]

Even the losing enterprises typically employed labour whose actual reserve price was quite low, much lower than that of agricultural labour. In fact, data from several sources including the Grameen Bank indicates that agricultural labourers may be less interested in small loans than others of the rural poor. In general, we know from our study of pre-modern economies (including neighbouring India's) that many activities were conducted at a loss when labour was charged at the normal market rate. Since most labour does not have alternative market use, when a labour market comes into play 'the market price of wage labour is incredibly high'.[17]

Since the goods sold by small microenterprise operators are typically sold in unsubsidized markets — sometimes in competition with subsidized goods from larger scale factories — we can presume that the enterprises are efficient and productive. In many countries, larger units have access to cheaper capital, subventions from the government budget, and cheaper than market inputs, though their labour costs may be inflated through legally mandated higher labour costs and manning levels beyond those justified by market returns. In the cases where larger scale units are subsidized and smaller scale ones survive in competition with them, the economic efficiency of SME is likely to be all the higher.

The situation might be different in a country like India where in some industries a significant share of the inputs used by small units are subsidized and the resulting products sold in protected markets, but India's is an almost unique situation.[2]

In any case, from a pure productivity point of view, the value of a subsidy where one is provided as compared to the other use of public funds needs to

Table 4 Small and microenterprise assistance models and examples of programmes that utilize them

1: Individual financial assistance
2: Integrated financial assistance and technical assistance/social promotion
3: Integrated and sequenced financial assistance, technical assistance, and training for individuals
4: Integrated and sequenced training, technical assistance, and financial assistance for individuals
5: Group-oriented social promotion, financial assistance, and technical assistance
6: Training

1	2	3	4	5	6
Banco del Pacifico[1]	CANAPI[6]	UNO[9]	DESCAP[3] (Carvajal)	PRODEME[7]	Calcutta Y Self-Employment Center[8]
PCIB Money Shops[2]	ADEPE[6]	NCCK[10]	CNPAR[10]	PRIDECO/ FEDEC-CREDITO[1]	Village Polytechnic Programme[10]
	CEOSS[7]	SEAP[12]	MSCI[2]	Working Women's Forum[8]	Lesotho Opportunities Industrialization Center[15]
Bank of Baroda[3]	NAESEY[8]	Carmona Social Development Center[2]	PROJUVE-NIUD[6]	CEOSS[7]	Rural Enterprise Extension Service[16]
					CEOSS[7]
ADEMI[4]		PfP/Upper Volta[11]	COLMENA[6]	SEDEMEX[11]	
BKK[5]		ASEPADE[1]	PRODEM[6]	Dominican Development Foundation[3]	
		SIDO[10]	Dominican Development Foundation[3]	FUCODES[6]	
		FUCODES[6]	PfP/ Botswana[12]	Banco Mundial de la Mujer[6]	
				Institute of Cultural Affairs Nairobi[10]	
				Women in Development, Kenya[13]	
				Grameen Bank[14]	

1 Fraser, Peter and William Tucker, 1981. *The Pisces Studies: Assisting the Smallest Economic Activities of the Urban Poor.* Washington, DC: US Agency for International Development (USAID)
2 Brown, Jason 1981a. 'Case Studies: The Philippines,' *The Pisces Studies: Assisting the*

Smallest Economic Activities of the Urban Poor. Washington, DC: US Agency for International Development (USAID), pp 253–336.
3. Smith, Cameron, and Bruce Tippett 1982. *Study of Problems Related to Scaling-up Microenterprise Assistance Programmes, Phase I.* Needham: Trade and Development International Corporation.
4. Wines, Sarah 1986. *Stages of Micro-Enterprise Growth in the Dominican Formal Sector.* Grassroots Development, Vol 9, No 2, 33–41.
5. Goldmark, Susan and Jay Rosengard 1983. *Credit to Indonesian Entrepreneurs: An Assessment of the Badan Kredit Kecamatan Programme.* Washington, DC: Development Alternatives, Inc.
6. Grindle, Merilee S 1986. Unpublished report of trip to Cali and Bogota, Colombia and San Jose, Costa Rica for ARIES project.
7. Ashe, Jeffrey, 1985. The PISCES II Experience: Local Efforts in Microenterprise Development, Vol I, Washington, DC: US Agency for International Development (USAID).
8. Brown, Jason 1981b. 'Case Studies: India,' *The PISCES Studies: Assisting the Smallest Economic Activities of the Urban Poor.* Washington, DC: US Agency for International Development, pp 337–378.
9. Tendler, Judith 1983. *Ventures in the Informal Sector and How They Worked Out in Brazil.* Washington, DC: US Agency for International Development.
10. O'Regan, Fred and Douglas Hellinger 1981. (in) *The Pisces Studies: Assisting the Smallest Economic Activities of the Urban Poor.* Washington DC: US Agency for International Development.
11. Lassen, Cheryl 1980. *Reaching the Assetless Poor: Projects and Strategies for their Self-Reliant Development.* Ithaca, NY: Cornell University Rural Development Committee.
12. Tuebner, Paul, Laurie Mailloux, Edward Butler, and Randolph Lintz 1984. 'Evaluation of Project No. 633–0228, Small Enterprise Development', USAID/Botswana.
13. Mbajah, E. 1984. 'Evaluation of the Partnership for Productivity Women in Development Project, Kenya.' Washington, DC: US Agency for International Development.
14. Houghton, Mary 1985. 'The Social Impact of a Micro-Enterprise Project on the Individual and the Community,' in Proceedings of a Conference Micro-enterprise Development in the Third World, Geneva Park, Ontario, Canada, April 22–24.
15. Hunt, Robert 1983. 'The Entrepreneurship Training Programme of the Lesotho Opportunities Industrialization Centre: An Evaluation of its Impact.' Washington, DC: Office of Private and Voluntary Cooperation, Bureau of Food for Peace and Voluntary Assistance, US Agency for International Development.
16. Lintz, Randolph 1981. 'Third Year Evaluation Project No. 633–0212, Partnership for Productivity: Rural Enterprise Service,' USAID/Botswana.

---

be examined. Where the amount of subsidy is small, and to some extent simply countervails subsidies for others present in organized financial markets, it is hard to argue with. (In economists' jargon it is a second best, optimal achievable solution.) Where subsidized inputs are more extensive, they need to be judged like other human capital investments, in terms of the increased productivity they bring in the long run. Investments of this human capital sort are powerful, contain a considerable element of public good in them, but suffer if too rapidly discounted. Societies which invest in education, training, research and development of the right sort — like Japan — may out-perform those with a shorter term perspective.

From a social point of view, and it seems that is what dominates the debate on micro-industry, investments in microenterprise programmes that work, may be justified because of their effects on income distribution and social integration, even at some cost in productive efficiency. The specific resolution

Characteristics of Enterprise Assistance Programme Models

Model	Cost	Beneficiary level	Staff skill	Labour intensity	New or established business	Beneficiary commitment
1	Low	I, II, III	Simple business	Low	Established	Low
2	Moderate	I, II, III	Simple business and community development	Moderate	New or established	Low
3	Moderate to high	II, III	Business	High	Established	Moderate
4	High	III and above	Business	High	Established	High
5	Moderate to high	I, II	Community development	Moderate	New or established	High
6	High	I	Specialized	Moderate	New high	High

of how much to spend for microenterprise will obviously differ according to the circumstances of each programme, country, and set of policies adopted.

The character of the micro-units, obviously, also effects the level and type of services which are required — minimalist approaches such as that of the Grameen Bank are based on the existence of a clientele which has usable technologies and has access to markets. Minimalist approaches also imply a pessimism about the potential for outside engineered improvement in the technologies used by small units. On the other hand, more ambitious programmes, generally envisage some of their clients growing and graduating into larger categories. The question is clearly how realistic either of the set of assumptions are and how functional to the general social and economic goals society wishes to pursue.

Support for Women in Microenterprises in Africa

MARY E. OKELO

Introduction

The economic crisis in Africa, rather than diminishing, has increased considerably in intensity over the past few years. Production in both industry and agriculture is declining, inflation is rising with concomitant effect on household incomes. Exporters are having serious problems finding markets at equitable prices. Servicing of external loans contracted previously is getting to be impossible. Capital flows are negative for many countries. The servicing of external debt as a percentage of export earning or GNP has attained alarming proportions.

Given these circumstances, many African countries are seriously rethinking their development strategies and the structure of their economies. Individuals too, some of whom have been adversely affected by the crisis, are looking for avenues to support themselves and their families and in some way contribute to the development of their economies.

Since independence in the 1960s, African countries have lived in one way or another through various sizes of enterprises. These were large scale public enterprises, large scale private enterprise, after which emphasis was and is still put on medium- and small-scale enterprises. The large enterprises, especially the public ones on which concentration was put, have failed to give satisfaction, riddled as they were with deficits, debts, heavy staff expenditure and general mismanagement. These have in fact contributed in some way to the present economic crisis of these countries.

The response of individuals as it were to the every-day hardship imposed by the present situation has manifested itself in the emergence of individual initiatives, some of which we classify as microenterprises. For the purpose of this paper, the term refers to very small non-farm income generating units in the informal sector and/or engaged in artisan operations, family business or cottage industries employing five or less persons and with minimum capital assets.

Many of these microenterprises have developed mainly in a crisis situation. Some are doing well, others are having problems, but all are generally in a large way fulfilling some of the demands of their promoters. They are also

---

MARY E. OKELO of Kenya is Senior Advisor on Women in Development at the African Development Bank, Abidjan, Ivory Coast.

contributing to the development of the various economies by providing employment, producing goods and services and generally filling the gap left by the large-scale public enterprises.

Since the mid-1970s, the role of small or microenterprises in the development of African economies has become a major concern among policy makers and the international donor community. In 1980, for example, the African Heads of State met in Lagos to seriously review the development of the continent, its problems, constraints and possible solutions, and they drew up a strategy and agenda for future action, the Lagos Plan Action.

This paper will attempt to analyse the problems of microenterprise development, particularly those encountered in helping women, and propose ways in which governments, business community and donors could assist in microenterprise development.

Major characteristics of microenterprises in Africa

The major characteristics of microenterprises could be summarized as follows: small size, loose informal structure, ease of entry, requiring very little capital to start up, high flexibility, little or no formal education required, tends to be labour intensive, generally a one person or family business, depends on the business acumen of proprietor/promoter. A large percentage of these are operated by women, they often use local raw material/input and cater for local/surrounding markets.

The bulk of microenterprises in Africa are concentrated in production of simple consumer goods and services catering primarily for the needs of relatively low income urban and rural households. Microenterprises cover a whole range of activities in manufacturing, trade and services. The most important types are: clothmaking and tailoring, food processing and vending, dry cleaning, restaurants and food kiosks, handicrafts, vehicle, shoe, electrical and bicycle repairs, grainmilling, hairdressing and butchers.

In unfavourable economic conditions where the majority of the population is still rural, raw materials and markets are dispersed, transport is costly and difficult and markets are small, microenterprises are becoming more important and also efficient providers of incomes, good and services. They also provide a tool for more equitable income distribution as the rural and urban poor, the landless and women who fail to share in the returns of agriculture and formal industrial development, depend on non-farm microenterprises.

While some businesses are one-man units, others work on a family basis and some hire labour or train apprentices. Though hired labour is a minor component of these activities, apprentices play a major role in these operations, especially in West Africa. The proprietors and family workers involved in microenterprises usually have little formal education, generally acquired technical skills as apprentices in other small enterprises of family business and lack training in marketing, finance and management.

Women and microenterprises

As we saw earlier a large percentage of the microenterprises in Africa is operated by women. One therefore wonders why this is so. A look at the major characteristics of microenterprise might help us find some answers. Some of the features which account for women's predominance are: ease of entry, loose and informal structure, requiring very little capital to start, little or no education required, high flexibility in terms of time. This enables women to reconcile more easily their different roles. Apart from those women who are managers, many of the microenterprises employ women.

Women in microenterprises are involved in both production and services. The most common activities are the garment industry, handicrafts, spinning and weaving, food processing, oil extraction, fish smoking, beer brewing, leather works and soap manufacturing. Service industrial activities operated by women in households, road sides and market places include: food kiosks, hairdressing, baking, retail and grocery shops, butchery and transportation.

It may be appropriate here to discuss those characteristics or factors which tend to give strength to microenterprise and so make them a dynamic developmental force. The first factor is the high motivation of the promoter. The fact that one is working for oneself gives impetus to the business. There is no rigid timetable and one can work until a late hour. The drive to obtain one's objective is high. The fact that personal profit or income could be a function of one's own action helps maintain the momentum. In fact, the time spent by the promoter in various activities related to the smooth running of the business is hardly ever quantified and costed.

Microenterprise generally requires little capital to start. This could be obtained from one's own savings, friends or relatives. Few microenterprise promoters have recourse to formal credit institutions with their interminable questions and paperwork. This helps to make decisions to start up microenterprises easier and accounts for their proliferation. The small size of capital required limits expansion but makes it such that only a limited surrounding market is catered for.

The flexibility, another factor, further ensures that the product or its packaging is adapted to client's tastes, no boards of directors or committee has to meet first. Let us take the case of women in Cocody, Abidjan, Ivory Coast making and selling *atieke* (prepared food made from cassava). These women employ about three to four girls or young women in the preparation. The atieke is prepared starting from late evening around 16.00–17.00 hours, by 19.00 hours the processing is finished and the girls then take the finished product to the nearby local market. In the late 1970s the atieke was sold wrapped in broad leaves. These do not retain heat well (atieke is best eaten when hot just after preparation) and are not the best from the hygiene point of view.

This packaging is suitable for those like industrial workers, who, after work, want to eat it with their fish on the spot or in nearby eating kiosks, but as the clientele broadened to the middle level white collar and professional groups and under pressure from the authorities the packaging changed; small plastic packets are now used.

Another element of dynamism of these microenterprises could be in their possibility of adaptation and should we say diversification. In the Seychelles, where tourism is a major industry, formal reception structures such as hotels are not always sufficient, depending on the period of the year. Individuals have taken up the challenge and are providing these services in guest houses. These are mainly owned and run by women who make extra income through letting out two or more spare rooms. In this way they supplement the income earned by their husbands.

In one particular case with which we are familiar, the proprietress has always been approached by guests/tourists who would like souvenirs. Because of these frequent and persistent requests, the lady has diversified into making small, inexpensive objets d'art at home and printing 'made in Seychelles' type T-shirts. This has now grown to the extent that as her few guests cannot absorb the output of herself and her three helpers, she has now been able to rent a shop in the town centre to sell her goods. Because the shop is there, other small guest house owners who produce similar souvenirs have asked her, for a consideration, to display their goods as well.

Microenterprises thus have features which, if exploited, and if the energies of their promoters are carefully harnessed, can make them more dynamic forces at the level of the 'quartier'. Of course, there are certain areas which given their size and other characteristics, they can not enter or cannot do with the same efficiency. In fact we do not want to convey the impression that all microenterprises, or even all microenterprises run by women, are successful. There are things which need small and/or medium enterprises to function effectively or efficiently. Many microenterprises would function more efficiently and contribute much more to the provision of income and employment if certain constraints were removed and problems they encounter could be solved.

In the following paragraphs these constraints and problems are discussed and possible ways of support enumerated.

Constraints to microenterprise development

The major constraints to and problems of the development of microenterprises in Africa revolve around: financing, markets, appropriate low cost technologies, government policies, data on microenterprises and social norms, as well as institutional and legal structures, poor management, weak accounting methods and, in certain areas, poor product finishing.

Shortage of financing

The available evidence indicates that the main sources of microenterprise financing are personal savings, friends, occasionally retained earnings and very limited funding from formal financial institutions. Access to formal institutional credit is difficult for most small scale entrepreneurs, especially women, because of the small nature of their operations which makes their needs small and loan administration becomes costly and unattractive to established credit institutions. Lack of adequate collateral and unfamiliarity with complicated loan application procedures and paper work futher limits microenterprises' access to formal credit. The problem of collateral affects women more seriously, since in some African societies they have no legal right to ownership of tangible property like land. They usually have to rely on their husbands or male relatives to obtain formal credit, no matter how viable their ventures are.

Though the minimum start-up capital required for establishing microenterprises makes entry easy, in absence of funding for expansion, it leaves the microentrepreneurs caught up into a vicious cycle of low investment, low incomes, low profits and savings for reinvestment. There is also the problem of insufficient network of financial institutions with enough branches to permeate the rural areas where the majority of microenterprises are located. All these problems, coupled with small scale entrepreneurs' lack of basic management skills necessary for keeping proper records and financial accounts normally required by the credit system, terribly limit their access to financing.

Marketing problems

The products and services of microenterprises primarily target the needs of relatively low-income urban and rural households. These primary markets are nearby and small. They are defined not only by local effective demand but also the entrepreneur's ability to reach the market, know the preferences of the market channels and competition and to deliver the goods and services to the market.

While nearby markets are easily accessible, they tend to have the disadvantages of low effective demand because of relative poverty, especially in the rural areas, and saturation of products due to commonality of raw materials and skills in most areas. Though often the microentrepreneurs are capable of production activities, they hardly have any product design and not much marketing skills. Hence they produce standard products for sale in slowly growing markets. Women entrepreneurs are the most lacking in marketing skills and usually plunge into production without any marketing advice. We find at times one promoter having set up a dress making workshop or hairdressing saloon being followed by several others in the same street. This tends to increase competition considerably and may have a negative effect on income earning and employment generation. The weak linkage between large and small scale enterprises aggravates the market situation as it limits subcontracting arrangements.

Inadequate access to technological information

Microenterprises are often unaware of technological options which could assist them in increasing their productivity and business income. Though not in abundance, there are some simple low-cost appropriate technologies and tools which microenterprises could benefit from. Usually microenterprises have no access to such information partly because of deficiencies in the institutional network (eg industrial extension services), especially its inability to supply such information at a cost affordable to microenterprises and in simple packages they can readily utilize. The little information on simple technologies is often not tailor-made to match the absorption capacity of small entrepreneurs, leaving personal contact and simple imitation through observation as the main limited forms of disseminating technological information.

Weak accounting

Many microenterprises have weak accounting methods and often no accounts are even kept. A man I know who runs a small automobile repair workshop hardly keeps any records at all. It is not uncommon to see him draw open his till, take some money out to give to his spouse to go to the market or to his children to buy their lunch. No record is kept of such non-business expenditure.

Government policies

Since the mid-1970s many African government policies have shown support for the growth of small-scale enterprises. Most policies on industrial development, interest rates, foreign exchange, trade and tariffs are rather biased in favour of large and medium scale producers, often to the disadvantage of small entrepreneurs.

Interest rate ceilings make it unprofitable for financial institutions to lend to small entrepreneurs because of the high administrative cost involved and the higher possibility of default than is expected of more established firms. In the absence of personal savings, microentrepreneurs are forced to resort to more expensive forms of credit for their needs. Thus the government policy aimed at protecting small borrowers from bearing the full cost of their credit needs forces them to more costly alternatives like money lenders who in some cases charge over 100 per cent interest rate.

Due to inadequate lobbying on the part of small entrepreneurs and inadequate sensitization on the part of policy makers, the formulation of trade and foreign exchange policies often takes little account of the needs of this group of entrepreneurs. An example of this is that in Rwanda microenterprises do not benefit from import subsidies granted for industrial stimulation because, unlike medium and large scale enterprises, they do not import their materials directly but buy from local importers who are subject to higher tariff rates. This bias is also evident in countries like Nigeria, Ghana, Sierra Leone where well-established textile industries co-exist with small textile producers. The large textile producers, under the cover of the country's industrial incentives, can import industrial machines duty-free while the basic equipment of the micro-scale tailor, the sewing-machine, is classified as luxury goods and taxed accordingly. This differential treatment with regard to foreign exchange and tariffs affects most imported goods.

Small enterprises are often at a disadvantage with regard to access to raw materials. In situations where the government controls distribution of industrial inputs to avoid excessive mark-ups or to regulate supplies of imported inputs, there tends to be a bias in favour of larger producers at the expense of small entrepreneurs.

Social values, institutional and legal structures

Women microentrepreneurs are the ones most affected by these constraints. Social attitudes concerning women's values, abilities and proper roles, often encouraged by women themselves, tend to be limiting factors to women's entry and success in microenterprises. This, combined with their family commitments and responsibilities, tends to limit their performance as entrepreneurs.

In many African societies, a task is devalued when it becomes 'women's work'. Planners and policy makers often reflect societal attitudes regarding women and their productive activities as non-existent, unproductive or limited by child-bearing and rearing roles, thus undermining government support to women in microenterprises and other sectors of the economy. Due to certain societal constraints, however, the wealth and value contributed by women to their economies do not accrue to the producers in full.

Institutions normally reflect societal norms that often create administrative and organizational barriers to the development of microenterprises, particularly for women. Various aspects of the legal framework in most African countries, especially concerning succession/inheritance and property ownership, are biased against women and impede their access to and control of key productive resources like land and capital. In the Akan group of tribes in West Africa, for example, at the death of her husband, a woman has to surrender all valuable assets including furniture and household goods, acquired over years by the family, to the relatives of her deceased husband. It is not uncommon for instance to find successful business women being denied credit until a guarantee is obtained from a man.

Unavailability of data

There is very limited data on microenterprises for planners and policy makers to go on. Despite the greater recognition lately given to the importance of small scale enterprises in development, most of them are very difficult to quantify especially in rural areas. This problem of invisibility is even more severe with women's microenterprises because often neither they nor the rest of the society think of them as business people. Women entrepreneurs are often on the borderline with their subsistence occupations. Working without remuneration makes women's participation in microenterprises even less visible. Due to lack of data the contribution of microenterprise goes largely unrecorded, making it difficult for planners to take their participation and contribution into consideration during policy formulation.

Suggestions on possible solutions

In the past, African governments' and donors' attention to small scale enterprise development has focused on targeted projects and programmes as opposed to policies, practices and attitudes which seem to be major impediments to microenterprise development. In the absence of supportive policies and incentives, past efforts in microenterprise development were not as effective as originally expected. There is therefore urgent need for both governments and donors to review and revise the existing policies and practices with a view to promoting the development of small scale enterprises to enable them to make their full potential contribution to economic and social development. With regard to this the following actions are proposed.

The following actions could increase microenterprises' access to financing. Both governments and donors should explore ways of developing innovative credit programmes using intermediary channels or institutions closer to the target groups, such as entrepreneurs' associations, cooperatives, women's associations/clubs and other grassroots associations. It may be worthwhile to try out the sort of group lending methods which have proved quite successful in some parts of Africa like Ghana and Zimbabwe. Given the status of target borrowers, credit under such programmes should be screened on the basis of character, project viability and not purely on the availability of collateral. To ensure effective use of business credit, mechanisms should be developed which could allow for awarding credit for personal consumption in times of need. It would be impossible for a microentrepreneur not to use money, even if it is business credit, to pay hospital bills or buy medicines for a sick child. Whenever feasible, credit in kind should be seriously considered.

Interest rates and loan terms should be flexible enough to allow for the repayment capacity of the different microentrepreneurs. No-one is saying that they have to be very low, otherwise local banks may be unlikely to step in and continue the credit flow on termination of the subsidized government or donor funding.

Recent microenterprise studies have revealed that working capital rather than fixed capital is the primary financial constraint to microenterprise development. Credit programmes should therefore focus on working capital in order effectively to address financial problems of microenterprises. In the consideration of credit to microenterprises, caution should be exercised with regard to the assessment of the real needs of the target group for these kinds of credit programmes.

Governments and donors could also take the following steps to encourage formal credit institutions to finance microenterprise developments:

1   help to pay a share of the administrative cost for financial institutions or other financial intermediaries;
2   some countries like Ghana and Sierra Leone have credit guarantee schemes for small borrowers. This could be extended to other countries to enable credit institutions to learn about lending to small producers and so develop confidence in that type of credit portfolio;
3   provide technical assistance to financial institutions to enable them to develop low-cost screening mechanisms for lending to small producers and assist them in modifying the loan procedures to meet the need for small scale entrepreneurs.

To have access to formal credit, microenterprises are required to keep clear records of their operations. Most small entrepreneurs, particularly women, do not possess the basic managerial skill it takes to keep such records. Governments and donor agencies could contribute considerably to the development of microenterprises through technical assistance programmes for small scale entrepreneurs in basic managerial skills like bookkeeping, inventory management, record keeping etc. Such programmes would be more cost-effective if they are based on existing formal institutions like vocational training centres or informal ones like apprenticeship, which is particularly dominant in West Africa. A simple package of technical assistance covering basic managerial skills with emphasis on financial management, simple marketing and product design, aimed at increasing the small entrepreneurs' ability to manage their operations, could go a long way in easing their two most critical problems of finance and marketing.

The marketing problems faced by small producers can best be addressed through supportive government policies geared at increasing rural incomes which form the bulk of the market for microenterprises. Such government policies, particularly agricultural pricing and other supportive policies, would have significant multiplier effects on the development of microenterprises.

Assistance for microenterprise development should ideally focus on basic training in marketing and product design to increase the small producer's knowledge of the market as well as their ability to reach these markets. As far as possible government policies should encourage strong linkages between small-, medium- and large-scale enterprises as this would provide more opportunities for increasing the market for small producers through subcontracting arrangements. For instance, in the 1970s, the subcontracting arrangement between handicraft microenterprises and the large Botswana craft company provided the missing marketing link that was needed to support commercial production of handicrafts in rural Botswana. A similar subcontracting arrangement with a view to providing a more effective link with external markets would provide a breakthrough for microindustries like those making cloth in several African countries, whose products seem to be in fairly high demand in Western markets.

The demand for microenterprise products and services could also be increased through elimination of unfair competition in the form of subsidies given to large-scale producers. Often, barriers to the trading companies which market the products of small firms exist and these should be eliminated. Governments can also directly enlarge the markets for microenterprises, through, among other things, improvement of the infrastructure in rural and poor urban areas.

With regard to availability of appropriate technology for microenterprise development, changes in government policies leading to a reduction in subsidies for imported machinery would stimulate domestic engineering industry and machine shops potentially important for addressing technological needs of small producers. Technological information can be disseminated to small scale producers through demonstration of technological alternatives using exhibitions, trade fairs, films etc. In the absence of such facilities, informal arrangements like apprenticeships and trade associations can be channels for dissemination of technological information. Research in appropriate technologies for microenterprises would greatly enhance microenterprise development efforts.

African governments and the donor community need to adopt supportive policies for promotion of microenterprise development. Differential treatment of large and medium scale operations with respect to foreign exchange, access to inputs, credit and tariffs, which tends to be biased against microenterprise development should be reviewed and, whenever possible, eliminated. With regard to access to industrial inputs, the governments should work towards a system based on reduced control and intervention in distribution of inputs. On the whole, governments should strive regularly to review and revise their existing policies with a view to providing incentives and opportunities for more effective microenterprise development.

Social, institutional and legal constraints are the most difficult to address as they require change of attitudes which take a long time to achieve. Increased sensitization of policy makers, decision makers and microentrepreneurs themselves, particularly women, with a view to bringing about a change of attitudes and review of institutional and legal framework impeding development of women entrepreneurs need to be vigorously conducted by all concerned. This could be done through training programmes aimed at increasing the awareness of all parties concerned and through policy dialogues.

Microenterprise data bases should be developed at country levels to quantify the contribution of microenterprises to the development process and to facilitate planners and decision makers in planning for more effective and integrated development of microenterprises. Governments and the donor community should cooperate in providing technical and financial assistance for development of these national microenterprise data bases.

Conclusions

Because of certain dynamic elements in their characteristics, microenterprises contribute significantly to the development of African countries, particularly in employment creation and resource utilization, as well as income generation and distribution.

In the past, effective development of microenterprises encountered limitations some of which could be traced to government policies. The other major constraints hindering development of microenterprises related to deficient demand, shortage of financing, especially working capital, inadequate technological information and social, institutional and legal structures which do not take into account the needs of the small producers.

In order effectively to address these problems and foster development of microenterprises, African governments and the donor community must adopt a more comprehensive view of looking beyond the traditional sphere of industrial policy and should also include agricultural pricing and income policies as well as general trade and foreign exchange policy. They must also strive to develop innovative credit programmes and appropriate packages of technical assistance suitable for the needs of the small entrepreneurs.

Appendix

Papers Submitted for the International Microenterprise Conference Washington D.C., USA 6–9 June 1988

Paper number	Paper title	Author
1	The Role of Informal Credit Markets in Support of Microbusinesses in Developing Countries	ANAND G. CHANDAVARKAR
2	Comparative Experience with Microenterprise Projects	THOMAS A TIMBERG
3	Microenterprise Assistance Programmes: Their Benefits, Costs, and Sustainability	MARIA OTERO
4	Whatever Happened to Poverty Alleviation?	JUDITH TENDLER
5	Financial Innovations for Microenterprises: Linking Informal and Formal Financial Institutions	HANS DIETER SEIBEL
6	Entrenamiento y Asistencia Técnica para Microempresas	PETER LUTZ (Spanish)
7	Formation et Assistance Technique aux Petites Entreprises	PETER LUTZ (French)
8	Training and Technical Assistance for Microenterprise	MALCOLM HARPER
9	Training and Technical Assistance for Microenterprises	PETER LUTZ
10	The Role of Technology in Microenterprise Development	MATTHEW GAMSER and FRANK ALMOND
11	Financial Services for Microenterprise: Programmes or Markets?	RICHARD L. MEYER
12	Systems of Institutional Decentralization and Technology Transfer for Rural Small-Scale Enterprises	ENYINNA CHUTA

13	Institutional Aspects of Microenterprise Promotion	MARILYN CARR
14	Grameen Bank: Organization and Operation	MUHAMMAD YUNUS
15	Venture Capital for Microenterprise Development: The VCAT Model	JACK CROUCHER and S. K. GUPTA
16	Microlevel Strategies for Supporting Livelihoods, Employment, and Income Generation of Poor Woman in the Third World: The Challenge of Significance	KATHARINE MCKEE
17	Support for Microenterprises: Some Issues	MEINE PIETER VAN DIJK
18	Banking on the Informal Sector: Suggestions to Reach Microenterprises in Developing Countries	HENRY R. JACKELEN
19	La Microentreprise: L'Investissement Social le Plus Utile	JAIME CARVAJAL (French)
20	Programme d'Assistance aux Microentreprises: Avantages, Coûts et Durabilité	MARIA OTERO (French)
21	Soutien des Microentreprises: Quelques Problèmes s'y Rattachant	MEINE PIETER VAN DIJK (French)
22	¿Que Ocurrió Con el Alivio de la Pobreza?	JUDITH TENDLER (Spanish)
23	Systèmes de Décentralization Institutionnelle et de Transfert de Technologie pour les Petites Entreprises Rurales	ENYIANNA CHUTA (French)
24	El Papel de la Technología en el Desarrollo de la Microempresa	MATTHEW GAMSER and FRANK ALMOND (Spanish)
25	Innovations Financières pour le Microentreprises: Liaisons de Institutions Financières Formelles et Informelles en Afrique et en Asie	HANS DIETER SEIBEL (French)
26	Capacitación y Asistencia Técnica para Microempresas	MALCOLM HARPER (Spanish)

27	Los Programas de Asistencia a las Microempresas: Beneficios, Costos y Posibilidad de Mantenerlos	MARIA OTERO (Spanish)
28	El Crédito al Sector Informal Sugerencias sobre el uso de las instituciones financieras para llegar a las microempresas en los paises en desarrollo	HENRY R. JACKELEN (Spanish)
29	Le Role de la Technologie dans le Developpement des Microentreprises	MATTHEW GAMSER and FRANK ALMOND (French)
30	Banque Grameen: Organization et Opérations	MUHAMMAD YUNUS (French)
31	Sistemas de Descentralizacion Institucional y Transferencia de Tecnología para Empresas Rurales de Pequena Escala	ENYINNA CHUTA (Spanish)
32	Algunos Puntos Sobre el Apoyo a las Microempresas	MEINE PIETER VAN DIJK (Spanish)
33	El Banco Grameen: Organizacion y Operaciones	MUHAMMAD YUNUS (Spanish)
34	Papel de los Mercados de Crédito no Estructurados en Apoyo de la Microempresa en los Paises en Desarollo	ANAND G. CHANDAVARKAR (Spanish)
35	Services Financiers pour les Microentreprises: Programmes ou Marches?	RICHARD L. MEYER (French)
36	De la Pluriactivité à l'Industrialization Rurale: Le Role des Microentreprises dans le Developpement	MARIA NOWAK (French)
37	La Microempresa: La Mas Util Inversión Social	JAIME CARVAJAL (Spanish)
38	Le Role des Marchés de Credit non Institutionnalisés dans le Financement des Microentreprises dans les Pays en Developpement	ANAND G. CHANDAVARKAR (French)
39	L'Impact des Politiques d'Ajustement sur les Microentreprises	PHILIPPE HUGON (French)

40	Innovaciones Financieras para la Microempresa: Vinculacion de las Instituciones Oficiales y no Oficiales en Africa y Asia	HANS DIETER SEIBEL (Spanish)
41	Qu'est-il Advenu de la Lutte Contre la Pauvreté?	JUDITH TENDLER (French)
42	The International Development Research Centre's Intervention in the Field of Microentreprises	MOUSSEAU TREMBLAY
43	The Netherlands'-Pakistan Programme on Small-Scale Industrial Development: a Report	HENK THOMAS
44	Breaking the Entrepreneurial Bottleneck in the late-developing Countries	PETER KILBY
45	Small-scale Industrialization: A New Perspective on Urban Employment Policies	HENK THOMAS
46	Trickle-Up Programme: Global Report for the Year Ending December 1987 with Summary Information for the Period from the Start of the Programme in 1979 through 1987	GLEN LEET and MILDRED ROBBINS LEET
47	Les Banques et le Secteur Non Structure: Propositions Concernant l'Utilization des Institutions Financières pour Atteindre les Microentreprises des Pays en Developpement	HENRY L JACKELEN (French)
48	Credit Programmes for Microenterprises: The Need for Exchange of Relevant Information	M. F. DE JONG
49	Can NGOs, Private Voluntary Organizations and Local Initiatives for Development of the Poorest Southern Countries Help Eradicate Famine and Malnutrition?	BERTRAND SCHNEIDER
50	Les Ong, les Agences Privées de Volontaires et les Initiatives Locales dans le Developpement des Pays du Sud les Plus Pauvres	BERTRAND SCHNEIDER (French)

	Peuvent-Elles Contribuer à Eliminer la Famine et la Malnutrition?	
51	Aspectos Institucionales del Fomento de la Microempresa	MARILYN CARR (Spanish)
52	Los Programas para las Microempresas: Comparacion de Experiencias	THOMAS A. TIMBERG (Spanish)
53	Programmes de Microentreprise: Comparaison des Experiences	THOMAS A. TIMBERG (French)
54	The Impact of Adjustment Policies on Microenterprises	PHILIPPE HUGON
55	From Multiple Rural Activity to Rural Industrialization: The Role of Microenterprise in the Development Process	MARIA NOWAK
56	Microenterprise: The Most Profitable Social Investment	JAIME CARVAJAL
57	The Informal Sector in Central America: A View on Conceptual and Operational Environments	GASTON R. LEAL
58	Serving Micro-Businesses in Two African Countries	MICHAEL SCHULZ
59	An Example of Collaboration Between a Federation of Rural Grassroots Organization to Mobilize Rural Savings and to Facilitate Access to Credit to a Large Number of Rural Poor	MOUSSA BA
60	Institutional Shortcomings of NGOs and Donor Agencies Affecting Microenterprise Support Activities	PIETER BUIJS
61	Support for Woman in Microenterprises in Africa	MARY E. OKELO
62	Difficulties of Lending to Poor Target Groups	TH. WOLLENZIEN
63	Supporting the Informal Sector: Micro Level Interventions with a Macro Perspective	VICTOR E. TOKMAN
64	Structural Adjustment and the Informal Sector	HERNANDO DE SOTO

Appendix II
AGENDA

Monday, 6 June 1988

8:00 a.m.   REGISTRATION

9:00 a.m.   OPENING SESSION

Chairman: JACOB LEVITSKY (Secretary, Donor Agencies Committee)

Speakers

ENRIQUE V IGLESIAS (President, Inter-American Development Bank)

ALAN WOODS (Administrator, U.S. Agency for International Development)

DAVID W HOPPER (Senior Vice President, The World Bank)

BENJAMIN GILMAN (Representative, U.S. Congress)

11:00 a.m.   PLENARY SESSION

Chairman: MICHAEL FARBMAN (USAID)

Speakers

HERNANDO DE SOTO (President, Instituto Libertad y Democracia, Peru)
Policies for Microenterprise Development

BERTRAND SCHNEIDER (Secretary-General, Club of Rome, Paris)
Role of NGOs in Aid Programmes

2:00 p.m.   PLENARY SESSION

Chairman: KENNETH COLE (Inter-American Development Bank)

Speakers

GERARD LATORTUE (Minister of Foreign Affairs, Republic of Haiti – formerly Division Chief, UNIDO)
Informal Sector in Developing Countries

VICTOR TOKMAN (Chief, Employment Development Department, ILO Geneva – formerly PREALC, Santiago)
Role of Microenterprise in Economic Development

MUHAMMAD YUNUS (Managing Director, Grameen Bank, Bangladesh)
Review of Experience of Grameen Bank: A Special Bank for the Poor

DISCUSSION GROUPS

4:00 p.m. *Group I – Credit Programmes*

Chairman: JON WILMSHURST (Overseas Development Administration, United Kingdom)

Presentations

Professor RICHARD MEYER (Ohio State University)
Financial Services for Microenterprises

ANAND CHANDAVARKAR (India – formerly with International Monetary Fund)
Role of Informal Credit Markets in Support of Microenterprises

HENRY R. JACKELEN (U.S./Brazil Financial Consultant
Banking on the Informal Sector

Group II – Training and Technical Assistance

Chairman: STIJN ALBREGTS (ILO)

Presentations

Professor MALCOLM HARPER (Cranfield School of Management, United Kingdom)
Training and Technical Assistance for Microenterprises

PETER LUTZ (Swiss Contact)
Case Study of Training

MATTHEW GAMSER (Intermediate Technology Development Group, London)
Role of Technology in Microenterprise Development

Group III – Collective Groups and Institutional Aspects

Chairman: PETER KUNZI (Switzerland)

Presentations

Professor HANS SEIBEL (University of Cologne, Germany)
Linking Informal and Formal Financial Institutions: Asia and Africa

MS V.A NYAMODI (General Manager, Kenya Industrial Estates, Nairobi)
Women in Microbusinesses in Africa

MEINE P. VAN DIJK (Royal Tropical Institute, Amsterdam)
Support of Microenterprises: Some Institutional Issues

6:00 p.m. RECEPTION
Hosted by USAID, U.S. Department of State

Tuesday, 7 June 1988

9:00 a.m.   PLENARY SESSION

Chairman: ALEX FRENZ (GTZ, Germany)

Speakers

MARILYN CARR (Advisor on Technology and Small Enterprise Development, United Nations Development for Women – UNIFEM)
Institutional Aspects of Microenterprise Promotion

ENYINNA CHUTA (Federal University of Technology, Yola, Nigeria)
Systems of Institutional Decentralization and Technology Transfer for Rural Small-Scale Enterprises

S.K. GUPTA (Deputy General Manager, Industrial Development Bank of India)
Venture Capital for Microenterprise Development

11:00 a.m.   Chairman: MILLARD LONG (The World Bank)

Speakers

Professors JUDITH TENDLER and MICHAEL PIORE (Massachusetts Institute of Technology)
Implications of Policies on Microenterprise Development

Professor PHILIPPE HUGON (University of Paris, France)
Impact of Structural Adjustment on the Informal Sector in Africa

2:00 p.m.   PLENARY SESSION

Chairman: GASTON LEAL (Canadian International Development Agency)

Speakers

MARIA NOWAK (Chief, Division of General Studies, Caisse Centrale de Cooperation Economique, France)
Role of Microenterprise in Rural Development

THOMAS TIMBERG (Director, ARIES Project, Robert Nathan Associates, Washington, DC)
Comparative Experience with Microenterprises

MARIA OTERO (Director, ACCION/AITEC, Tegucigalpa, Honduras)
Microenterprise Assistance Programmes: Their Benefits, Costs and Sustainability

4:00 p.m.	CONCLUDING SESSION
	Reports of Discussion Groups
	Discussion
	Concluding Remarks
6:30 p.m.	RECEPTION
	Hosted by The World Bank
	World Bank, E Gallery, 701 19th Street, N. W.

Wednesday 8 June 1988

9:30 a.m. Opening remarks on objectives of second part of conference and review of first two days
— JACOB LEVITSKY

10:30 a.m. *Working Groups (3) – I*

Review and Analysis of Different Programmes for Providing Financial Assistance to Microenterprises
Moderator/Rapporteur: REINHARD SCHMIDT (Professor, University of Trier, Germany)

Discussions of respective roles of different institutions, including development banks, commercial banks, NGOs, saving and credit cooperatives, informal credit groups, and of:
- degree of replicability of successful programmes
- problems of 'scaling up' successful programmes
- achieving self-sustainability of programmes
- methods of achieving a high repayment rate
- forms of mutual guarantee arrangements and guarantee schemes
- the case for, and against, combining credit programmes with training and technical or management assistance

1:00 p.m. Lunch – hosted by sponsoring committee – State Plaza Hotel

2:30 p.m. *Working Groups (3) – II*

Government Role: Policies and Regulations
Moderator/Rapporteur: WILLIAM STEEL (World Bank)

Discussion of government role and of approaches, and experience presented during the first part of the conference and of:
- policies and regulatory framework
- problems of growth and graduation of microenterprises to the formal sector
- potential and limitations of government support for microenterprises

- role of private sector, the business community and of NGOs
- links with other programmes, e.g., promoting women in business, stimulating savings, developing entrepreneurship, etc.

4:30 p.m. *Working Groups (3) – III*

International Support for Microenterprises
Moderator/Rapporteur: KATHERINE MCKEE (Ford Foundation)

Discussion of
- respective roles of donor agencies and NGOs
- comparative advantages and disadvantages of bilateral agencies and multilateral organizations and banks in providing assistance to microenterprises
- mobilizing domestic resources of national and international voluntary foundations
- proposals to donor agencies for increasing support to microenterprises and/or of rendering aid more effective

Thursday, 9 June 1988

9:00 a.m. *Report of Working Groups I, II, and III of Previous Day*

11:30 a.m. *Concluding Session* – Chairman: JACOB LEVITSKY

Panel of representatives from developing countries and donor agencies

Discussion

Closing statements.

Abbreviations

ACORD	Agency for Cooperation and Research in Development
ADBN	Agricultural Development Bank of Nepal
ADEMI	Asociacion Para el Desarrollo de la Micro-empresa
APDDCFL	Dairy Development Federation of the Indian state of Andhra Pradesh
APRACA	Asian and Pacific Regional Agricultural Credit Association
ARIES	Assistance to Resource Institutions for Enterprise Support
ATI	Appropriate Technology International
BKK	Badan Kredit Kecamatan, Indonesia
BNDA	Agricultural Development Bank, Ivory Coast
BRAC	Bangladesh Rural Advancement Committee
CEDP	Community and Enterprise Development (Senegal)
CMDT	Compagnie Malienne de Développement Textile (southern Mali)
CNPAR	Centre National de Perfectionnement des Artisans Ruraux, Burkina Faso
EQI	Environmental Quality International
ESCAP	Economic and Social Commission for Asia and the Pacific (UN)
GTZ	Gesellschaft fur Technische Zusammenarbeit (Agency for Technical Cooperation), Federal Republic of Germany
IDB	Inter-American Development Bank
IFAD	International Fund for Agricultural Development
ILO	International Labour Office
IRDP	Interest Rate Differential Programme, India
ITDG	Intermediate Technology Development Group, UK
ITTU	Intermediate Technology Transfer Unit, Ghana
KENGO	Kenya Energy Non-Government Organisations Association
KUPEDES	Kredit Unit Pedasaan (Rural Credit Scheme of Bank Rakyat), Indonesia
KVIC	Khadi Village Industries Commission, India
LEIG	Livelihood, Employment and Income Generation (Ford Foundation), US
MYRADA	Mysore Resettlement and Development Agency
NGO	Non-Governmental Organization
PfP	Partnership for Productivity

PISCES	Program for Investment in the Small Capital Enterprise Sector –USAID
PRADAN	Professional Assistance for Development Action
PRODEM	Fundacion Para la Promocion y Desarrollo de le Microempresa, Bolivia
PVO	Private Voluntary Organization
ROSCA	Rotating Savings and Credit Association
RSA	Rotating Savings Association
SEWA	Self-Employed Women's Association, Ahmedabad, India
SHPI	Self-Help Promotion Institution
SIFFS	South India Federation of Fishermen's Societies
SIRTDO	Small Industries Research and Training Association, Ranchi, India
TCC	Technology Consultancy Centre, Ghana
UMN	United Missions to Nepal
UNIDO	United Nations Industrial Development Organization
UNIFEM	United Nations Development Fund for Women
USAID	United States Agency for International Development
VITA	Volunteers in Technical Assistance
WWF	Working Women's Forum, Madras, India

References

Tokman

1. de Soto (1986)
2. Bhatt (1988)
3. Tokman (1978)
4. Tokman (1987)
5. McKee (1988)

Tendler

1. Hirschman (1967)
2. Rial & Howell (1986)
3. Kilby (1979)
4. DAI (1979)
5. Farbman (1981)
6. Ashe (1985)
7. Kilby (1985)
8. Tendler (1982)
9. Paul (1982)
10. Chen (1984), (1986)
11. Kilby (1985)
12. James & Rose-Ackerman (1986)

Nowak

1. Kilby & Liedholm (1986)
2. Baumann (1984)
3. Garin (1988)
4. Capecchi (1988)
5. Chaponniere (1985)
6. Judet (1985)
7. Coussy, Hugon & Sudrie (1984)
8. Humbert-Gret (1986)
9. Courlet (1985)
10. Tu Nan (1986)
11. Streeten (1983)
12. Haggblade (1986)
13. Bekolo-Ebe (1985)
14. Swaminathan (1986)

Chandavarkar

1. Bouman (1977)
2. Miracle, Miracle & Cohen (1980)
3. Timberg & Aiyar (1983), (1984)
4. Holst (1984)
5. Chandavarkar (1984), (1987)
6. Holst (1984)
7. Vogel & Burkett (1986)
8. Anderson & Khambatta (1966)
9. Begashaw (1978)
10. Katzin (1959)
11. Manhertz & Marston (1979)
12. Christen & Vogel (1984)
13. Ghai (1984)
14. Thingalaya (1978)
15. Choucri (1986)
16. Bakht & Mahmud (1987)
17. Chandavarkar (1980)
18. Timberg & Aiyar (1980)
19. Page (1979)
20. Liedholm & Chuta (1977)
21. Child (n.d.)
22. Little, Mazumdar & Page (1987)
23. Cortes, Berry & Ishaq (1987)
24. Park (1976)
25. Ho (1980)
26. SEACEN Centre Report (1986)
27. Anderson & Khambatta (1981)
28. Patel (1978)
29. Cole and Park (1975)
30. Achanja & Madhur (1984)
31. Pereira, Leite & Vaez-Zadeh (1986)

Seibel

1 Shrestha & Seibel (1988)
2 Portes & Sassen-Koob (1987)
3 Bouman (1979)
4 Ardener (1964)
5 Seibel & Damachi (1982)
6 Seibel & Marx (1987)
7 Seibel (1987b)
9 Seibel (1987a)

Meyer

1 Hunt (1985)
2 Ashe (1985)
3 Timberg (1988)
4 Bhatt (1988)
5 Heimenz & Bruch (1983)
6 Levitsky & Prasad (1987)
7 Cuevas & Graham (1984)
8 Ahmed & Adams (1987)
9 Sen (1987)
10 McLeod (1984)
11 Hossain (1988)
12 Sacay (1985)
13 Marion (1987)
14 Farbman (1981)
15 Tendler (1982)

Gamser and Almond

1 Liedholm & Mead (1987)
2 Tendler (1987)
3 Marshall (1983)
4 Spiropoulos (1985)
5 Wingate (1985)
6 Carr (1989)
7 Standards . . . (1987)
8 Spence (1974)

9 Fibre Concrete . . . (1986)
10 Whitcombe & Carr (1982)
11 Hislop (1988)

Otero

1 Goldmark & Rosengard (1985)
2 Otero (1987)
3 Cruz (1988)
4 Gomez & Saladin (1987)
5 Jackelin (1987)

Timberg

1 Timberg (1986)
2 Little, Mazumdar & Page (1987)
3 Sinha (1986)
4 Saxena (1987)
5 Stone, Shreshta & Campbell (n.d.)
6 Sinha (n.d.)
7 Gianchandani, Sharma & Narula (1987)
8 Selbstad (1982)
9 Arunchalam (n.d.)
10 Hossain (1986)
11 Maloney (1986)
12 Al Hussainy (1986)
13 Goldmark & Rosengard (1983)
14 Patten & Snodgrass (1987)
15 Carr (1981)
16 Ahmad (1984)
17 Jehan (1985)
18 Kula (1976)

Summary report

1 Kilby & D'Zmura (1985)
2 Hirschman (1967)

Bibliography

Acharya, S. and Madhur, S., 'Informal credit markets and monetary policy', *Economic and Political Weekly* XIX, No 36, 8 September 1984.
Ahmad, Q. K. (ed), *The Bangladesh Development Studies XII*, Special issue on rural industrialisation in Bangladesh, 1984.
Ahmed, H. Ahmed and Adams, Dale W., 'Transaction Costs in Sudan's Rural Financial Markets', *Savings and Development, Supplementary Issue*, Finafrica, Milan, 1987.
Al-Hussainy, S. M., 'Bridging the gap: Experience of Swanirbar Bangladesh in self-actuation and employment generation', November 1986.
Anderson, D. and Khambata, F., *Small enterprises and development policy in the Philipppines: a case study*, World Bank staff training paper 468, Washington DC, 1981.
Anheier, H. and Seibel, H. D., *Small-scale industries and economic development in Ghana: business behaviour and strategies in informal sector economies*, Breitenbach Publishers, Saarbrucken and Fort Lauderdale, 1987.
Annis, S., 'Can small-scale development be a large-scale policy?', Development alternatives: the challenge for NGOs, *Supplement to World Development* 15, Pergamon, Oxford, 1987.
Ardener, S., 'The comparative study of rotating credit associations', *Journal of the Royal Anthropological Institute* 94, pp. 201–29, London, 1964.
Arunachalam, Jaya, 'Credit Needs of Women Workers in the Informal Sector: Case Study of the Working Women's Forum, India', n.d.
Ashe, J., *The Pisces II experience: local efforts in microenterprise development*, USAID, Washington DC, April 1985.
Ashe, J., *The Pisces II experience: case studies*, USAID, Washington DC, 1985.
Bahkt, F. and Mahmud, R., 'Overseas remittances and informal financing in Bangladesh', unpublished, May 1987.
Bangladesh: selected issues in rural development, World Bank, Washington DC, March 1983.
Bank of Thailand staff papers on unorganized money markets. 'Report on the seminar on unorganized money markets in the SEACEN countries, 20–22 November 1985, Yogyakarta, Indonesia', SEACEN Research and Training Centre, Kuala Lumpur, April 1986.
Barclay, A. H. (jr), Hoskins, M. W., Njenga, W. K. and Tripp, R.B., 'The development impact of private voluntary organizations: Kenya and Niger', DAI, Washington DC, February 1979.

Baumann, E., *Activites informelles en milieu rural – le cas du centre rural de Saa centre-sud du Cameroun*, University of Bordeaux, France, 1984.

Begeshaw, G., 'The Economic Role of Traditional Savings and Credit Institutions in Ethiopia', *Savings and Development*, 4, Finafrica, Milan, 1978.

Bekolo-Ebe, Bruno et al., *Etude sur la stratégie d'intervention du fonds de garantie aux PME*, Centre Universitaire de Douala, Douala, Cameroon, 1986.

Bhatt, E., 'Women and small-scale enterprise development in a new era', paper submitted to the Ford Foundation symposium on expanding income earning opportunities for women in poverty: a cross-regional dialogue, Nairobi, Kenya, 1–5 May 1988.

Biggs, S. and Grosvenor-Alsop, R., *Developing technologies for the rural poor*, ITDG Occasional Paper 2, Intermediate Technology Publications, London, 1984.

Bouman, F. J. A., 'Indigenous savings and credit societies in the Third World: a message', *Savings and Development* 4, pp. 181–209, Finafrica, Milan, 1977.

Bouman, F. J. A., 'The ROSCA: financial technology of an informal savings and credit institution in developing countries', *Savings and Development* 4, pp. 1–24, Finafrica, Milan, 1979.

Buatsi, S., *Technology Transfer: Nine case studies*, Intermediate Technology Publications/UNESCO, London, 1988.

Buatsi, S., *Small-scale Industries Promotion in India*, Intermediate Technology Publications, London, 1987.

Capecchi, Vittorio, 'I fattori di sviluppo di una economia regionale', Caisse Centrale de Coopération Économique, Paris, 1988.

Carr, M., *Developing Small-scale Industries in India: An integrated approach*, Intermediate Technology Publications, London, 1982.

Carr, M., *Appropriate Technology and Rural Industrialization*, ITDG Occasional Paper 1, Intermediate Technology Publications, London, 1982.

Carr, M., *Blacksmith, Baker, Roofing-sheet Maker – Employment for rural women in developing countries*, Intermediate Technology Publications, London, 1984.

Carr, M., *Sustainable Industrial Development*, Intermediate Technology Publications, London, 1988.

Carr, Marilyn, (ed), *Women and the Food Cycle*, Intermediate Technology Publications, London, 1989.

Chandavarkar, A. G., 'Use of migrant's remittances in labour-exporting countries', *Finance and Development*, June 1980.

Chandavarkar, A. G., *The informal financial sector in developing countries: analysis, evidence and policy implications*. Occasional Papers No 2, SEACEN Research and Training Centre, Kuala Lumpur, 1987.

Chandavarkar, A. G., 'The non-institutional sector in developing countries: macroeconomic implications for savings policies', *Savings and Development* 2, Finafrica, Milan, 1984.

Chaponniere, J. P., *La puce et la riz – la croissance dans le sud-est asiatique*, Armand Collin, 1985.

Chen, M., 'Development projects for women: Oxfam America's programme in India and Bangladesh', presented at the conference 'The International Womens' Decade and Beyond', American Association of University Women, New York, 12–13 October 1986.

Child, F. C., *An empirical study of small-scale rural industry in Kenya*, Institute of Development Studies Working Paper 127, University of Nairobi, Kenya, (no date).

Child, F.C., *Small-scale rural industry in Kenya*, Occasional Paper 117, African Studies Centre, University of California, 1977.

Choucri, N., 'The hidden economy: a new view of remittances in the Arab world', *World Development* 14, No. 6, Pergamon, Oxford, 1986.

Christen, R. P. and Vogel, R. C., 'The importance of domestic resource mobilization in averting financial crises: the case of credit unions in Honduras'. Conference on Financial Crises, Foreign Assistance and Domestic Resource Mobilization in the Caribbean Basin, Ohio State University, Columbus, 1984.

Coelho, Antonio de Almeida and Fuenvalidd, L. A., *An appraisal of UNDP programmes in Bahia and Recife: preliminary results*, Masters Programme in Economics, Universidade Federal de Bahia, Salvador, May 1980.

Cole, D. C. and Park, Y. C., *Financial Development in Korea 1948–78*, Harvard University Press, Cambridge, Mass., 1983.

Cortez, M., Berry, A. and Ishaq, A., *Success in Small- and Medium-scale Enterprises: The evidence from Colombia*, Oxford University Press, New York, 1987.

Courlet, C., 'Accumulation du capital, dynamiques sociales et restructuration industrielle dans les pays industrialises, IREP–Developpment, Grenoble, 1985.

Coussy, J., Hugon, P. and Sudrie, O., *Dependance alimentaire et urbanisation en Afrique sub-saharienne*, CEREP, 1984.

Credit to the poorest: the Grameen Bank, Bangladesh and the Small Farmers' Development Programme, Nepal, IFAD, Rome, March 1987.

Cruz, Julian, Un estudio de la Microempressa en Honduras, unpublished paper, Honduras, 1988.

Ceuvas, Carlos E. and Graham, Douglas H., 'Agricultural Lending Costs in Honduras', *Undermining Rural Development with Cheap Credit*, Dale W. Adams et al., Westview Press, Boulder, 1984.

de Soto, H., *El otro sendero: la revolucion informal*, Editorial El Barranco, Lima, Peru, 1986.

DGAP, *Identification and assessment of local institutions and mechanisms appropriate for the implementation of World Bank supported employment-generating purposes: Brazil and Cameroon* (Pt II Brazil), World Bank, Washington DC, July 1978.

Elkan, W., 'Policy for small-scale industry: a critique', Discussion Papers in Economics No 8701, Brunel University, 1987.

Farbman, M. (ed), *The Pisces studies: assisting the smallest economic activities of the urban poor*, USAID, Bureau for Science and Technology, 4, Washington DC, September 1981.

Fibre Concrete Roofing: A State of the Art Report, Intermediate Technology

Publications/SKAT, London, 1986.
Financing small enterprises, GTZ, Eschborn, 1986.
Fricke, T., *High impact appropriate technology case studies*, ATI, Washington DC, 1984.
Fuglesang, A. and Chandler, D., *Participation as a process: what we can learn from Grameen Bank, Bangladesh*, Norwegian Ministry of Development Cooperation, Norway, 1986.
Garin, M., *Pluralactivite rurale en Thailande*, IREP, Grenoble, 1988.
Ghai, D., 'An evaluation of the Grameen Bank project', IFAD, Rome, 1984.
Ghosh, A., 'Monetary targeting and the banking sector', *Economic and Political Weekly*, January 3–10 1987.
Gianchandani, D., Sharma, R. and Narula, R. R., *A target missed: an evaluation of IRDP in northern and eastern Rajasthan*, Institute of Development Studies, Jaipur, 1987.
Goldmark, S. and Rosengard, J., *Credit to Indonesian entrepreneurs: an assessment of the Badan Kredit Kecamatan programme*, USAID, Washington DC, May 1983.
Goldmark, S. and Rosengard, J., *A manual to evaluate small-scale enterprise programmes*, USAID, Washington DC, 1985.
Gomez, Arelis and Saladin, Vanessa, Programa de Financiamient a Microempressas y Grupas Solidarios: Informe de Evaluacion de Impacto, Sando Domingo, ADEMI, 1987.
Grameen Bank Annual Report, Bangladesh 1984 and 1986.
Grindle, M. et al., *Capacity building for resource institutions for small and microenterprises: a strategic overview paper*, USAID, Washington DC, October 1987.
Haggblade, S., Examination of the clothing and textile sector in Rwanda, September 1986.
Haggblade, S., 'Africanization from below: the evolution of Cameroonian savings societies into western-style banks', *Rural Africana* (New Series 2), pp. 35–55, Autumn 1978.
Haggblade, S., Defay, J. and Pitman, R., *Small manufacturing and repair enterprises in Haiti: survey results*, Michigan State University Working Paper 4, East Lansing, 1979.
Harper, M. and Ramachandran, K., *Small Business Promotion: Case studies from developing countries*, Intermediate Technology Publications, London, 1984.
Harper, M., *Small Business in the Third World: Guidelines for practical assistance*, Intermediate Technology Publications/J. Wiley and Sons, London, 1984.
Harrington, John J. (jr), *People's banking: the Grameen Bank*, Seton Hall University, South Orange, 1987.
Hiemenz, Ulrich and Bruch, Mathias, *Small- and Medium-scale Manufacturing Establishments in Asian Countries: Perspectives and Policy Issues*, Asian Development Bank Economics Staff Paper No. 14, Manila, Philippines, 1983.
Hirschman, A. O., *Development projects observed*, The Brookings Institu-

tion, Washington DC, 1967.
Hislop, D. (Carr, M. (ed)), 'The micro-hydro programme in Nepal', *Sustainable Industrial Development*, Intermediate Technology Publications, London, 1988.
Ho, S., *Small-scale Enterprises in Korea and Taiwan*, World Bank Staff Working Paper 384, Washington DC, 1980.
Holst, J. U. (ed Kesler, D. and Ulmo, P. A.), 'The role of informal financial institutions in the mobilization of savings', *Savings and Development*, Paris, 1984.
Hossain, M., *Credit for the rural poor: the experience of Grameen Bank in Bangladesh*, Research Monograph 4, Bangladesh Institute of Development Studies, Dhaka, 1984.
Hossain, M., *Credit for alleviation of rural poverty: the experience of Grameen Bank in Bangladesh*, Working Paper 4, Grameen Bank Evaluation Project, Bangladesh Institute of Developmental Studies, Dhaka, September 1986.
Hossain, Mahubub, 'Credit for Alieviation of Rural Poverty: The Grameen Bank in Bangladesh', Research Report No. 65, International Food Policy Research Institute, Washington DC, 1988.
Humbert-Gret, E., Artisanat utilitaire a Madaagascar, 1986.
Hunt, R., *Private voluntary organizations and the promotion of small-scale enterprises*, USAID, Washington DC, July 1985.
Hunter, J., *Things fall apart: an analysis of the problems of thirteen Botswana firms*, Institute of Development Management, Gaberone, 1978.
Jackelen, H., Blayney, R.G. and MaGill, J., 'Evaluation of PRODEM program on Bolivia', USAID Report, Washington DC, 1987.
Jain, D., 'Pappad sellers of Lijjat', *Womens' quest for power*, Vikas, Delhi, 1980.
James, E. and Rose-Ackerman, S., *The non-profit enterprise in market economies*, Harwood Academic Publishers, New York, 1986.
Jehan, S., *Income-generating organizations in Bangladesh*, CIDA, DANIDA and MIDAS, July, 1985.
Judet, P., *Pour un vrai partenariat industriel avec l'Afrique – Bilan et perspectives*, Institut de l'Entreprise (Centre Nord-Sud), Paris, May 1985.
Katzin, M. F., 'Partners: an informal savings institution in Jamaica', *Social and Economic Studies* 8, 4 December 1959.
Kilby, P., 'Evaluating technical assistance', *World Development* 7, pp. 309–323, Pergamon, Oxford, 1979.
Kilby, P. and D'Zmura, D., *Searching for benefits*, AID Special Study 28, USAID, Washington DC, June 1985.
Kilby, P. and Liedholm, C., *The role of nonfarm activities in the rural economy*, World Congress of International Economics Association, New Delhi, December 1986.
Korten, V. C., 'Third generation NGO strategies: a key to people-centred development', Development Alternatives: the Challenge for NGOs, supplement to *World Development* 15, Pergamon, Oxford, Autumn 1987.
Kruft, A., *Intermediate Technology in Indonesia: A review of the Develop-*

ment *Technology Centre*, ITDG Occasional Paper 13, Intermediate Technology Publications, London, 1985.
Kula, W. (Garner, L. translator), *The economic theory of the feudal system: towards a model of the Polish economy 1500–1800*, Verso, London 1976.
Kurien, J. (Carr, M. (ed)), 'The introduction of plywood boats in South India', *Sustainable Industrial Development*, Intermediate Technology Publications, London 1988.
Lecompte, B., Maldonado, C. and Ransoni, P., 'La promotion du "secteur structure": le cas de Kigali', *Revue Tiers Monde* 27, No 106, pp. 439–55, 1986.
Levitsky, J., *Review of World Bank lending to small enterprises*, World Bank, Washington DC, 1985.
Levitsky, Jacob and Prasad, Ranga, N., *Credit Guarantee Schemes for Small and Medium Enterprises*, World Bank Technical Paper 58, Industry and Finance Series, World Bank, Washington DC, 1987.
Liedholm, C. and Chuta, E., 'The economies of rural and urban small-scale industries in Sierra Leone', *African Rural Economy* Paper No 14, Michigan State University, East Lansing, 1977.
Liedholm, C. and Mead, D., 'Small-scale industries in developing countries: empirical evidence and policy implications', International Development Paper No 9, Michigan State University, East Lansing, 1987.
Little, I. M. D., Mazumdar, D. and Page, J. M., *Small Manufacturing Enterprises: A Comparative Study of India and Other Economies*, World Bank, Washington DC, and Oxford University Press, Oxford, 1987.
Maloney, C., Report on NGO programmes in rural savings and credit in Bangladesh, May 1985.
Manhertz, H. G. and Marston, D., 'Savings behaviour in the rural sector: the Jamaican experience', *Savings and Development* 3 No 2, pp. 136–47, Finafrica, Milan, 1979.
Marion, Peter J., *Building Successful Financial Systems: The Role of Credit Unions in Financial Sector Development*, World Council of Credit Unions, Madison, Wisconsin, 1987.
Marshall, K., *Package Deals: A study of technology development and transfer*, Intermediate Technology Publications, London 1983.
McKee, K., Micro level strategies for supporting livelihood, employment and income-generating for poor women in the Third World: the challenge of significance, paper submitted to the Ford Foundation symposium on expanding income earnings opportunities for women in poverty: a cross-regional dialogue, Nairobi, Kenya, 1–5 May 1988.
McLeod, Ross, *Case Studies of Small Businesses Financing in Indonesia*, Working Paper No. 101, Working Papers in Economics and Econometrics, Australian National University, 1984.
Milimo, J. T. and Fissena, T., *Rural small-scale enterprises in Zambia, results of a 1985 country-wide survey*, Working Paper 28, Michigan State University, East Lansing, 1986.
Miracle, M. P., Miracle, D. S. and Cohen, L., 'Informal savings mobilization in Africa', *Economic Development and Cultural Change*, July 1980.
Molenaar, N. et al., Small-scale industry promotion in developing coun-

tries, RIMS, Delft, 1983.
Nordic Consulting Group, *Substantive issues within assistance to small-scale enterprises*, NORAD/NCG, Draft, Norway, October 1986.
Opole, M. (Carr, M. (ed)), 'The introduction of the Kenya Stove: a Kengo experience', *Sustainable Industrial Development*, Intermediate Technology Publications, London 1988.
Osborne, D., 'Bootstrap Banking', inc, August 1987.
Osorio, A. M. T., 'An evaluation of a project for generating employment in the informal sector of the metropolitan area of Recife, Brazil', Development Planning Unit, Bartlett School of Architecture and Planning, University College, London, July 1981.
Otero, M., *A question of impact*, PACT, Tegucigalpa, Honduras, October 1987.
Page, J. M. (jr), *Small enterprise in African development: a survey*, World Bank staff working paper 363, Washington DC, 1979.
Page, J., *Some economic considerations in small enterprise development*, World Bank, Washington DC, 1983.
Park, Y. C., *The unorganized financial sector in Korea 1945–78*, World Bank Finance Studies 28, Washington DC, 1976.
Patel, V. G., *Innovations in banking: the Gujarat experiments*, World Bank Domestic Finance Studies 51, Washington DC, 1978.
Patten, R. H. and Snodgrass, R., 'Monitoring and evaluating KUPEDES', Development Discussion Paper No 249, HIID, Harvard, USA, November 1987.
Paul, S., *Managing development programmes: the lessons of success*, Westview Press, Boulder, 1982.
People's Republic of Bangladesh Small Farmer Agricultural Credit Project: mid-term evaluation report, IFAD, Rome, April 1984.
Pereira Leite, S. and Vaez-Zahed, R., 'Credit allocation and investment decisions: the manufacturing sector in Korea', *World Development* 14 No 1, Pergamon, Oxford, 1986.
Policy considerations for improving the design of UNDP projects dealing with credit, UNDP, New York, March 1988.
Portes, A. and Sassen-Koob, S., 'Making it underground: comparative material on the informal sector in western market economies', *American Journal of Sociology* 93, pp. 30–61, 1987.
'The promotion of small- and medium-scale enterprises', International Labour Conference 72nd session 1986, report VI, ILO, Geneva, 1986.
Quinones, B. R. (jr), *Linkages between formal and informal sectors in rural financial markets: the role of self-help groups*, APRACA, Bangkok, 1986.
Rahman, A., *Demand and marketing aspects of Grameen Bank: a closer look*, University Press, Dhaka, 1986.
Rahman, A., *Consciousness raising efforts of Grameen Bank*, Working Paper 3, Grameen Bank Evaluation Project, Bangladesh Institute of Development Studies, Dhaka, July 1986.
Rahman, A., *Impact of Grameen intervention on the food availability and the nutritional status of its members*, Working Paper 5, Grameen Bank Evaluation Project, Bangladesh Institute of Development Studies,

Dhaka, June 1987.

Rhaman, A., *Impact of Grameen Bank intervention on the rural power structure*, Working Paper 2, Grameen Bank Evaluation Project, Bangladesh Institute of Development Studies, Dhaka, July 1986.

Rahman, R. I., *Impact of Grameen Bank on the situation of poor rural women*, Working Paper 1, Grameen Bank Evaluation Project, Bangladesh Institute of Development Studies, Dhaka, July 1986.

Ray, J. K., *To chase a miracle: a study of the Grameen Bank, Bangladesh*, University Press, Dhaka, September 1987.

Report of the Banking Commission, Government of India, New Delhi, 1972.

Rial, C. and Howell, C., *Final report on PRI financial intermediaries. Report to the Ford Foundation programme related investments*, Ford Foundation internal report, New York, 10 January 1986.

Sacay, Orlando J., Agabin, Meliza H., and Tanchoco, Chita Irene E., *Small Farmer Credit Dilemma*, Technical Board for Agricultural Credit, Manila, Philippines, 1985.

Savings for development: report on the third international symposium on the mobilization of personal savings in developing countries, UN, New York, 1986.

Saxena, A. P., 'Concurrent evaluations of IRDP: selected aspects for administrative follow-up', *Economic and Political Weekly*, 26 September 1987.

Schmidt, R. and Dedorath, G. W., *Small-scale financing and credit intermediaries*, GTZ, Eschbron, 1985.

Schmidt, R. H. and Kropp, E. (ed), *Rural finance: guiding principles*, GTZ, Eschborn, 1987.

Schneider, B., *The Barefoot Revolution: A Report to the Club of Rome*, Intermediate Technology Publications, London, 1988.

Schreiber, J. G., *Analise de CUATE Beneficio de Programo UND*, Recife, 1985.

Seibel, H. D. and Damachi, U. G., *Self-help organizations: guidelines and case studies for development planners and field workers*, Freidrich-Ebert Foundation, Bonn, 1982.

Seibel, H. D. and Marx, M. T., *Dual financial markets in Africa: case studies of linkages between informal and formal financial institutions*, Breitenbach Publishers, Saarbrucken and Fort Lauderdale, 1987.

Seibel, H. D. and Marx, M. T., *Mobilization of personal savings through cooperative societies or indigenous savings and credit associations?*, UN 1986, pp. 107–12, 1986.

Seibel, H. D., 'Saving for development: a linkage model for informal and formal financial markets', *Quarterly Journal of International Agriculture* 24, pp. 390–98, Berlin 1985.

Seibel, H. D., *Rural development as an exchange process: indigenous social systems, governmental development organizations and informal financial institutions in Ivory Coast*, Breitenbach Publishers, Saarbrucken and Fort Lauderdale, 1987a.

Seibel, H. D., *Landliche Selbsthilfeorganisationen in der VR Kongo: An-*

satzmoglichkeiten fur eine Verknupfung informeller und formeller Finanzinstitutionen, Breitenbach Publishers, Saarbrucken and Fort Lauderdale, 1987b.

Selbstad, Jennifer, 'Struggle and Development among Self-Employed Women: A Report on the Self-Employed Women's Association, Ahmedabad, India', USAID, Washington DC, 1982.

Sen, Biswajit, 'NGO Self-Evaluation: Issues of Concern', *World Development* 15, Pergamon, Oxford, 1987.

Sethuraman, S. V. (ed), *The urban informal sector in developing countries: Employment, Poverty and Environment*, ILO, Geneva, 1984.

Shrestha, B. P. and Seibel, H. D., 'Dhikuti: the small businessman's informal self-help bank in Nepal', *Savings and Development*, Finafrica, Milan, 1988.

Sinha, S., 'Monitoring Poverty Alleviation: Information Systems for the IRDP in Uttar Pradesh', Economic Development Associates for the Rural Development Department, Government of Uttar Pradesh.

Sinha, S., 'Poverty alleviation: anything goes', *Economic and Political Weekly* XXI, 10 May 1986.

Sinha, S., *Planning for Rural Industrialization*, ITDG Occasional Paper 8, Intermediate Technology Publications, London, 1983.

Smillie, I., *No Condition Permanent: Pump priming Ghana's industrial revolution*, Intermediate Technology Publications, London 1986.

Spence, R. J. S., *Lime and Alternative Cements* Intermediate Technology Publications/NTIS, London, 1974.

Spiropoulos, J., *Small-scale production of lime for building*, GATE, Frankfurt, 1985.

Standards and Specifications for Local Building Materials: The Report of the ARSO/CSC/UNCHS Workshop, Nairobi, 16–24 March 1987, Intermediate Technology Publications, London, 1987.

Stone, L., Shreshta, R. and Gabriel Campbell, J., *The use and misuse of social science research methodology in Nepal*, Tribhuvan University, Kathmandu, n.d.

Streeten, P., 'Development dichotomies', *World Development* 10, Pergamon, Oxford, 1983.

Swaminathan, Dr., *Sustainable nutrition security for Africa: Lessons from India*, World Food Council, Rome, 1986.

Tendler, J., 'Whatever happened to poverty alleviation?', report prepared for the mid-decade review of the Ford Foundation's programmes on livelihood, employment and income generation, March 1987.

Tendler, J., 'Ventures in the informal sector and how they worked out in Brazil', USAID Evaluation Special Study No 12, Washington DC, March 1983.

Tendler, J., 'Turning private voluntary organizations into development agencies: questions for evaluation', AID Programme Evaluation Discussion Paper No 12, USAID, Washington DC, April 1982.

Thingalaya, N. K., *Innovations in banking: the syndicate's experience*, World Bank Domestic Finance Studies 46, Washington DC, 1978.

Timberg, T. A. and Aiyer, C. V., 'Informal credit markets in India',

Economic Development and Cultural Change, October 1984.
Timberg, T. A. and Aiyer, C. V., *Informal credit markets in India*, World Bank Domestic Finance Studies 62, Washington DC, 1980.
Timberg, T. A., 'Small loans for microenterprise, anti-poverty and productivity', unpublished paper, 1986.
Timberg, T. A., 'Comparative Experience with Microenterprise Projects', See Part V.
Tokman, V. E., 'An exploration into the nature of the informal–formal sector relationships', *World Development* 6, Pergamon Press, Oxford, September–October 1978.
Tu XNan, *L'industrie rurale, le nouveau moteur du developpement en Chine*, CERES, November/December 1986.
Vogel, R. C. and Burkett, P., *Mobilizing small-scale savings*, Industry and Finance Series 15, World Bank, Washington DC, 1986.
Wahome, J., *Issues relating to small-scale industrialization in Kenya*, Policy Workshop on SSI, The Hague, June 1987.
Wai, U. Tun, *Economic essays on developing countries*, Sijthoof and Noovdhoff, Netherlands 1980.
Wellons, P., Germidis, B. and Glavanis, B., *Banks and specialized financial intermediaries in development*, OECD Development Centre Studies, Paris 1986.
Whitcombe, R. and Carr, M., *Appropriate Technology Institutions: a review*, ITDG Occasional Papers 7, Intermediate Technology Publications, London, 1982.
Wingate, M. et al., *Small-scale Lime-burning: A practical introduction*, Intermediate Technology Publications, London, 1985.
Yunus, M., 'The poor as an engine of development', *The Washington Quarterly* 10, No 4, Washington DC, Autumn 1987.
Yunus, M., *Credit for self-employment: a fundamental human right* Grameen Bank, Bangladesh, May 1987.

www.ingramcontent.com/pod-product-compliance
Ingram Content Group UK Ltd.
Pitfield, Milton Keynes, MK11 3LW, UK
UKHW041916140426
5217IPUK00013B/176